Society in Question

Seventh Edition

Robert J. Brym
University of Toronto

NELSON / EDUCATION

NELSON EDUCATION

Society in Question, Seventh Edition
by Robert J. Brym

Vice President, Editorial Higher Education:
Anne Williams

Acquisitions Editor:
Maya Castle

Marketing Manager:
Terry Fedorkiw

Developmental Editor:
Toni Chahley

Permissions Coordinator:
Natalie Russell

Content Production Manager:
Jennifer Hare

Copy Editor:
Dawn Hunter

Proofreader:
Linda Szostak

Indexer:
Jin Tan

Production Coordinator:
Ferial Suleman

Design Director:
Ken Phipps

Managing Designer:
Franca Amore

Interior Design Modifications:
Sharon Lucas

Cover Design:
Sharon Lucas

Cover Image:
© AnnaSakin/Demotix/
Demotix/Corbis

Compositor:
MPS Limited

Printer:
RR Donnelley

**Library and Archives Canada
Cataloguing in Publication Data**

Society in question/[edited by]
Robert J. Brym.—7th ed.

Includes bibliographical references
and index.
ISBN 978-0-17-650998-9

1. Sociology—Textbooks.
2. Canada—Social conditions—
Textbooks. I. Brym, Robert J., 1951-

HM586.S654 2013   301
C2012-906177-8

ISBN-13: 978-0-17-650998-9
ISBN-10: 0-17-650998-4

For my students, who keep on encouraging me to do better.

—RJB

Contents

Preface

Society in Question is designed to supplement the main textbook in an introductory sociology course. It therefore aims for balanced coverage of major topics, approaches, and methods in current sociology. However, as the title suggests, the book also tries to convey more than just a sense of what sociologists do for a living. The readings, and the introductions to them, are intended to speak plainly and vividly to contemporary Canadians about how sociology can help them make sense of their lives in a rapidly changing and often confusing world. The book's title is thus a pun: as the nature of social life is called into question by vast and sometimes frightening forces over which we appear to have little control, sociological questioning offers the prospect of helping us understand those forces and make informed choices about how we can best deal with them. Accordingly, the book speaks to key issues of social life today; almost all the articles were written in the past few years.

Although I selected a few articles just because they cover important topics concisely and clearly, more rigorous criteria guided most of my choices. As I reviewed material for this collection, I tried to place myself in the shoes of a contemporary Canadian undergraduate who sensibly takes the time to read only material that says something significant and non-obvious. Most of the articles in this book surprised me when I first read them, and they continue to affect the way I see the world. Therefore, the best indicator of the usefulness of this book will be the number of students who complete it and say that it helped ensure that they can no longer pick up a newspaper without thinking about the broader sociological significance of what they've read. That is just about the highest praise an introductory sociology instructor can receive.

To help students learn how to get the most out of the book, Chapter 1 is accompanied by marginal notations that explain how to take effective notes on the readings.

NEW TO THIS EDITION

The seventh edition of *Society in Question* has been revised in the light of feedback provided by many instructors and students.

The following articles appeared in the previous edition and have been thoroughly updated:

- "Poverty in Canada", by Ann Duffy (Brock University) and Nancy Mandell (York University)
- "Multiculturalism or Vertical Mosaic? Occupational Stratification among Canadian Ethnic Groups", by Hugh Lautard (University of New Brunswick) and Neil Guppy (University of British Columbia)
- "The Canadian Voter in a New Conservative Era", by Lawrence LeDuc (University of Toronto)

The following articles are new to this edition:

- "Beyond Mendel's Ghost", by Michael J. Shanahan, Shawn Bauldry, and Jason Freeman, University of North Carolina–Chapel Hill
- "Social Media: Implications for Social Life", by Sonia Bookman (University of Manitoba)
- "The Inequality Surge", by John Myles (University of Toronto)
- "The State of Early Childhood Education and Child Care in 2009", by Jane Beach; Martha Friendly, Carolyn Ferns, and Nina Brabhu (Childcare Resource and Research Unit); and Barry Forer (University of British Columbia)
- "Are Sports Becoming Less Masculine?", by Steve Dumas (University of Calgary)
- "Climate Change: Causes, Impact, Solutions", by the Intergovernmental Panel on Climate Change
- "The Future of Sociology", by Michael Burawoy (University of California, Berkeley)

STUDENT ANCILLARIES

The Companion Website for *Society in Question*, Seventh Edition, provides students with interactive learning tools, including:

- quizzes
- flashcards
- and more

Visit **www.societyinquestion7e.nelson.com** and access it today.

FOSTERING CONVERSATIONS ABOUT TEACHING SOCIOLOGY IN CANADA

We invite you to join Fostering Conversations about Teaching Sociology in Canada, a virtual community site built by sociology educators for sociology educators. A dynamic, continually evolving blog that houses dozens of self-reflexive pieces about various aspects of teaching—including student engagement, assessment, course preparation, and teaching with technology—Fostering Conversations is an educator's toolkit and a virtual home for sharing teaching ideas, practices, and complexities. Housing contributions by educators from across the country, including universities and colleges, large and small, Fostering Conversations provides a framework for cross-institutional conversations about the craft of teaching in the twenty-first century. Join the conversation today! Visit http://community.cengage.com/Site/fosteringconversations/.

ACKNOWLEDGMENTS

I would like to thank the following reviewers whose helpful feedback helped shape this new edition:

- Linda Cohen, Memorial University of Newfoundland
- Claudio Colaguori, York University
- Tamy Superle, Carleton University
- Eric Tompkins, College of New Caledonia

I would also like to thank the following reviewers, who provided feedback on the sixth edition:

- Graham Cook, Capilano College
- Robert Lanning, Mount Saint Vincent University
- Alice Propper, York University

I am indebted to the Nelson team of Maya Castle, Acquisitions Editor, and Toni Chahley, Developmental Editor, for their sage advice and tireless work in shaping this collection ; Terry Fedorkiw, Marketing Manager; Jennifer Hare, Content Production Manager; Dawn Hunter, copy editor, for her impeccably high standards; and Linda Szostak, proofreader.

ROBERT J. BRYM
University of Toronto

PART 1 THE FIELD OF SOCIOLOGY

I have been writing my autobiography since graduate school. As autobiographies go, it is unconventional. It records no personal events or dates, nor does it sketch interesting characters. My friends, enemies, colleagues, parents, wife, and children are not mentioned in it. It is not written as a personal narrative. Yet the story of my life is embedded in my sociological writings. The pressing issues that trouble me have somehow been transformed into a research agenda.

To the degree that my writings have any value to others, it lies in their contribution, however slight, to conversations and debates in which people who call themselves sociologists have engaged for more than a century. Those sociologists couldn't care less about whether I have found my research and writing useful in answering the political, ethnic, and economic issues that have weighed on me over the years. Nor should they. Sociology is a science—a science that is not as precise as physics, which doesn't have to contend with human caprice, but a science nonetheless. That is, sociologists try to observe their chosen corner of reality in a systematic and controlled manner and to evaluate the validity of their ideas based on whether their observations confirm or disconfirm them. The origins of those ideas are irrelevant, scientifically speaking. That, I think, is what American writer Kurt Vonnegut meant when he wrote that the most beautiful marigold he ever saw was growing in a bucket of cat manure.

Here we have the great irony of much scholarship, sociology included. Scholars try to be dispassionate and objective, yet real-life experiences and individual passions animate much scholarly activity. Albert Einstein believed on philosophical grounds that the universe is a deterministic system operating according to iron laws and that it is the physicist's job to discover them. When confronted by evidence that certain subatomic processes can be described only in terms of probable rather than certain outcomes, he objected: "God does not play dice with the universe." In this case, the evidence did not sway Einstein; his personal bent of mind, even his religious outlook, affected his evaluation of the evidence.

In their laudable efforts to be objective, some scholars lose sight of the fact that personal experiences and individual passions help them define certain problems as urgent and certain solutions to those problems as preferable. However, few thoughtful and honest scholars can fool themselves for long with pious statements about being purely objective in their research. The plain fact is that objectivity and subjectivity each have an important role to play in science, including sociology. Objectivity—the consensus viewpoint—is a reality check. Subjectivity—our own viewpoint—leads us to define which aspect of reality is worth checking in the first place.

In Chapter 1, I ask a question about the subjective, motivational side of sociology: Why study it? I argue that doing so is a matter of life or death. I do not make that claim for dramatic effect. I mean it literally. By helping us understand the social forces underlying the conditions of our death, sociology can help us figure out how to live better. That, I argue, is the promise and the urgency of higher education in general and sociological knowledge in particular.

Some students consider sociology's promise impractical. They may see in principle how sociology can help them navigate the world and contribute to improving it, but they wonder which jobs, if any, benefit from a sociology degree. Scott Davies and David Walters provide useful information on this subject in Chapter 2. They demonstrate that sociology degrees lead to interesting and well-paying jobs in a variety of fields, and they give practical sociological advice to Canadian students on how to expand their job opportunities.

CRITICAL THINKING QUESTIONS

1. What are the roles of subjectivity (our own viewpoint) and objectivity (the consensus viewpoint) in sociological research?
2. What is the value of a sociology degree compared with degrees in other subjects?

ANNOTATED BIBLIOGRAPHY

Robert J. Brym, Lance Roberts, John Lie, and Steven Rytina, *Sociology: Your Compass for a New World*, 4th Canadian ed.

(Toronto: Nelson, 2012) provides a comprehensive, introductory overview of the field of sociology from Canadian and global perspectives.

The Canadian Journal of Sociology featured a debate on the strengths, weaknesses, and challenges of sociology in Canada. The debate began in Vol. 28, No. 3 (2003), continued in Vol. 30, No. 1 (2005), and finished in Vol. 30, No. 4 (2005).

W. Richard Stephens, Jr., *Careers in Sociology*, 2nd ed., available online at www.abacon.com/socsite/careers.html. Eighteen informative case studies of what students did with their sociology degrees.

Chapter 1

Sociology as a Life or Death Issue[1]

ROBERT J. BRYM, University of Toronto

To help students learn how to take notes on their readings effectively, this article is accompanied by marginal comments on note-taking.

DEATH

To inspire you, I will take the unusual course of talking about death. I apologize in advance if this makes you uncomfortable. I know it is customary when addressing first-year university students to remind them that they are young, have accomplished much, and are now in a position to make important decisions that will shape the rest of their lives. I will eventually get around to that. But to arrive at the optimistic and uplifting part, I feel I must take a detour through the valley of the shadow of death.

When I was seven years old, I lived across the street from a park where I engaged in all the usual childhood games with my friends. We played tag, hide-and-seek, baseball, and cops and robbers. We also invented a game that we awkwardly called "See Who Drops Dead the Best." We would line ourselves up on a park bench and choose one boy to shoot the rest of us in turn, using a tree branch as a machine gun. Once shot, we did our best to scream, fall to the ground, writhe, convulse, and expire. The shooter would choose the most convincing victim—the boy who dropped dead the best—to be the shooter in the next round. The game would occupy us for ten minutes or so, after which we'd pick ourselves up and move on to baseball. At the age of seven, death was entertaining.

I didn't live in a war zone, and there were no deaths in my family during my youth, so I really didn't begin to take death personally until I

> **Comment:** The author doesn't tell the reader yet what the article is about but uses a dramatic theme—death—and an unexpected tone—whimsy—to grab the reader's attention. This is a narrative or storytelling approach to beginning an academic article. An alternative and more common approach is to state plainly at the outset what the article is about and how the author intends to make his or her case. If the alternative approach is used, you should summarize the main argument and method of the article as stated in the opening paragraphs.

was 15. Then, one Sunday evening, it quite suddenly dawned on me that someday I would *really* die, losing consciousness forever. The moment this realization hit, I ran to my parents in panic. I rudely switched off the TV and asked them to tell me immediately why we were living if we were going to die anyway. My parents looked at each other, stunned, and then smiled nervously, perhaps thinking their son had taken leave of his senses. They were not especially religious people, and they had only a few years of elementary schooling between them. They had no idea how to address questions about the meaning of life. Eventually my father confessed he didn't know the answer to my question, whereupon I ran to my bedroom, angrily shouting that my parents were fools to have lived half a century without even knowing why they were alive. From that moment and for the next three decades, death became a source of anxiety for me.

DENIAL

And so it is for most adolescents and adults. We all know that we might die at any moment. This knowledge makes most of us anxious. Typically, we react to our anxiety by denying death. To a degree, denying death helps us to calm ourselves.

The denial of death takes many forms. One is religious. Religion offers us immortality, the promise of better times to come, and the security of benevolent spirits who look over us. It provides meaning and purpose in a world that might otherwise seem cruel and senseless (James, 1976 [1902]: 123, 139).

In one of its extreme forms, religion becomes what philosophers call "determinism," the belief that everything happens the way it does because it was destined to happen in just that way. From the determinist's viewpoint, we can't really choose how to live because forces larger than we are control life. Even religions that say we can choose between good and evil are somewhat deterministic because they guarantee eternal life only if we choose to do good, and that requires submitting to the will of God as defined by some authority, not us. Many people worry less about death because they believe that the reward for submitting to the will of God is eternal life in heaven.

A second way in which we calm our anxiety about death involves trying to stay young. Consider the cosmetic surgery craze. Every week, millions of North Americans watch *Nip/Tuck*, *The Swan*, and *Extreme Makeover*—all popular TV series about cosmetic surgery. Every year, millions of North Americans undergo plastic surgery (including

Comment: The main theme of articles are often signifie by subheadings, and they a typically stated at the beginning of each section. Here we have the first main them of the article: knowing that they could die at any mome makes people anxious, and to cope with that anxiety, people typically deny death.

Comment: Typically, one or more examples is offered to illustrate a theme. Here we have an example of how people deny death: by turning to religion, which promises immortality, secu rity, and meaning.

Comment: Definitions of important terms, usually indicated by italics, quotation marks, or boldface, should always be noted. Here, determinism is defin as the belief that everythin happens the way it does because it is destined to happen just that way.

Comment: A second example of how people de death: they try to maintain the *appearance* of being young.

dermabrasion and Botox injections). In 2005 alone, 10.5 million plastic surgeries were performed in North America, up nearly 2500 percent since 1992, when statistics were first collected (American Society of Plastic Surgeons, 2006). And that's not all we do to stay young. We diet. We exercise. We take vitamin supplements. We wear makeup. We dye our hair. We strive for stylishness in our dress. We celebrate youthfulness and vitality in movies, music, and advertising. We even devalue seniors and keep them segregated in nursing homes and hospitals, in part so we won't be constantly reminded of our own mortality.

The search for eternal youth is a form of what philosophers call "voluntarism," the belief that we alone control our destiny. From the voluntarist's point of view, we can overcome forces larger than we are and thereby make whatever we want of our lives. Thus, many people worry less about death because they delude themselves into thinking they can cheat it.

> **Comment:** First-year students frequently ask if they will be expected to know all the statistics in the material they read for tests. Different instructors answer that question differently, so you should check with yours, but most instructors say you should remember only the most important trends rather than the numbers themselves. For example, the important point to take from these highlighted sentences is that cosmetic surgery has become much more popular since the early 1990s.

> **Comment:** Definition: Voluntarism is the belief that we control our destiny. Note that voluntarism is the opposite of determinism.

A TRAP

Ladies and gentlemen, I have good news and bad news for you, and I'm going to deliver the bad news first. The bad news is that the denial of death is a trap. Denying death makes it more difficult to figure out how to live well and thus be happy.

Let's say, for example, that a religion promises you eternal life in exchange for obeying certain rules. One rule says you can marry people only of your own religion. Another says that once you marry, you can't divorce. A third severely limits the steps you can take to limit the number of children you have. A fourth says you have to marry someone of the opposite sex. Many people respect these rules but they happen to make others miserable. That, however, is the price they must pay for the religion's promise of eternal life. In general, by denying people the opportunity to figure out and do what is best for them as individuals, the fatalistic denial of death can make some people deeply unhappy.

The voluntaristic denial of death can also make people unhappy. In the TV series *Nip/Tuck*, plastic surgeons Christian Troy and Sean McNamara begin each consultation with these words: "Tell me what you don't like about yourself." Notice that they don't ask prospective patients what they dislike about their bodies. They ask them what they dislike about their *selves*. They assume that your body faithfully represents your self—that your weight, proportions, colour, scars, and hairiness say something fundamentally important about your character,

> **Comment:** This is the second major theme of the article, again stated at the beginning of a new section: denying death makes it harder to figure out how best to live.

> **Comment:** An example of how the denial of death is a trap: religion can prevent some people from living well and being happy.

about who you are. If, however, you believe your happiness depends on your physical perfection and youthfulness, you are bound to be unhappy because nobody can be perfect and because you will inevitably grow old and die. And in the meantime, pursuing youthfulness in the belief that you are no more than your appearance distracts you from probing deeply and finding out who you really are and what you need from life to make you happy. I conclude that denying death for whatever reason prevents you from figuring out how to live in the way that is best for you.[2]

> **Comment:** A second example of how the denial of death is a trap: pursuing youthfulness distracts people from probing deeply and finding out who they really are and what they need from life to make them happy.

HIGHER EDUCATION

Finally, some good news: you don't have to deny death and thus become distracted from figuring out what you need to do to live a happy life. Instead, you can try to remain aware that you will die and that you could die at any moment. That awareness will inevitably cause you to focus on how best to achieve a meaningful life in your remaining time: the kind of career you need to pursue to make you happiest, the kind of person with whom you need to develop a long-term intimate relationship, the way you can best contribute to the welfare of others, the political principles you should follow, and so forth. As an old saying goes, the gallows in the morning focuses the mind wonderfully (cf. Frankl, 1959).

> **Comment:** The article's third main theme, again stated at the beginning of a new section: refusing to deny death focuses the mind on how best to live.

I have more good news. We have created an institution especially devoted to helping us discover what the good life is for each of us: the system of higher education.

I imagine your parents and teachers have told you to stay in school as long as you can because a degree is a ticket to a good job. They are right, at least in part. A stack of studies shows that each additional year of education will increase your annual income for the rest of your life. Moreover, the economic value of education increases year after year (Appleby, Fougère, and Rouleau, 2004). But the view that colleges and universities are places for job training is a half-truth. Above all, the system of higher education is devoted to the discovery, by rational means, of truth, beauty, and the good life. Said differently, if you treat higher education not just as job training but as a voyage of self-discovery, you will increase your chance of finding out what you value in life, what you can achieve, and how you can achieve it.

> **Comment:** The system of higher education can help people focus on how best to live because it is devoted to just that purpose; it is not merely for job training.

Colleges and universities are divided into different departments, centres, schools, and faculties, each with a different approach to improving the welfare of humanity.[3] The physician heals; the instructor in physical education teaches how to improve strength, stamina, and vigour; and the philosopher demonstrates the value of living an examined life. A good undergraduate education will expose you to many different approaches to improving your welfare and that of humanity as a whole and will give you a chance to discover which of them suits you.

What does the sociological approach offer?

SOCIOLOGY

The sociological approach to improving human welfare is based on the idea that the relations we have with other people create opportunities for us to think and act but also set limits on our thoughts and actions. Accordingly, we can better understand what we are and what we can become by studying the social relations that help shape us.

A classic illustration of the sociological approach to understanding the world and improving human welfare is Émile Durkheim's nineteenth-century study of suicide in France (Durkheim, 1951 [1897]). Most people think that suicide is the most nonsocial and antisocial action imaginable, a result of deep psychological distress, that is typically committed in private and involves a rejection of society and everything it stands for. Yet Durkheim showed that high rates of psychological distress often do not result in a high suicide rate while low rates of psychological distress sometimes do. He also argued that the rate and type of suicide that predominates in a society tells us something fundamentally important about the state of the society as a whole.[4]

According to Durkheim, the probability that your state of mind will lead you to suicide is influenced by the social relations in which you are embedded—in particular, the frequency with which you interact with others and the degree to which you share their beliefs, values, and moral standards. Durkheim referred to the frequency of interaction and the degree of sharing of beliefs, values, and morals in a group as its level of "social solidarity."

Simplifying for brevity's sake, Durkheim analyzed the effects of three levels of social solidarity on suicide rates:

- *Low solidarity:* According to Durkheim, groups and societies characterized by a low level of social solidarity typically have a high suicide rate. Interacting infrequently and sharing few beliefs, values, and moral standards, people in low-solidarity settings lack emotional support and cultural guidelines for behaviour. They are

Comment: The various subjects taught in college and university represent different approaches to improving the welfare of humanity.

Comment: This rhetorical question anticipates the article's fourth main theme: what the sociological approach can offer to people engaged in a voyage of self-discovery.

Comment: Very important. This paragraph defines the sociological approach to improving human welfare: "The relations we have with other people create opportunities for us to think and act but also set limits on our thoughts and actions. Accordingly, we can better understand what we are and what we can become by studying the social relations that help shape us."

Comment: An example—Durkheim's study of suicide—illustrates one of the article's themes, namely, the sociological approach. While most people think that suicide is a nonsocial and antisocial act caused by deep psychological distress, Durkheim showed that this is not necessarily so. Instead, suicide is associated with how frequently people interact with others and share their beliefs, values, and morals. Thus, the likelihood of committing suicide is influenced by specifically *social* forces. Durkheim referred to the frequency of interaction and the degree of sharing of beliefs, values, and morals in a group as its level of social solidarity.

therefore more prone to commit suicide if they experience distress. On a broader canvas, Durkheim viewed rising suicide rates as a symptom of the state of modern society. In general, social ties are weakening, he argued, and people share fewer beliefs, values, and moral standards than they used to.

- *Intermediate solidarity:* It follows that if we want suicide rates to decline, we must figure out ways of increasing the strength of social ties and shared culture in modern society. For example, if Canadians created a system of universally accessible, high-quality daycare with national standards, then more children would be better supervised, enjoy more interaction with peers and adults, and be exposed to similar socializing influences. At the same time, more adults (particularly single mothers) would be able to work in the paid labour force and form new social ties with their workmates. By thus raising the level of social solidarity, we would expect the suicide rate to drop.

- *High solidarity:* Despite a general decline in social solidarity, some groups are characterized by exceptionally high levels of social solidarity. When members of such a group perceive that the group is threatened, they are likely to be willing to sacrifice their lives to protect it. For instance, suicide bombers often see the existence of their group threatened by a foreign power occupying their homeland. They are willing to give up their lives to coerce the occupying power into leaving (Pape, 2005). The increased rate of suicide bombing in the world since the early 1980s is in part a symptom of increasing threats posed to high-solidarity groups by foreign occupying forces. It follows that if we want fewer suicide bombings, one thing we can do is to figure out ways of ensuring that high-solidarity groups feel less threatened.

Much of the best sociological research today follows Durkheim's example. Sociologists frequently strive to identify (1) a type of behaviour that for personal, political, or intellectual reasons they regard as interesting or important; (2) the specifically social forces that influence that behaviour; and (3) the larger institutional, political, or other changes that might effectively improve human welfare with respect to the behaviour of interest. By conducting research that identifies these three elements, sociologists help people to understand what they are and what they can become in particular social and historical contexts (Mills, 1959; Weber, 1964 [1949]).

Comment: Low social solidarity is associated with a high suicide rate because people who lack emotional support and cultural guidelines have little to buffer them against adversity.

Comment: An intermediate level of social solidarity is associated with a low suicide rate because people who enjoy emotional support and cultural guidelines are disinclined to commit suicide if adversity strikes.

Comment: High social solidarity may be associated with a high suicide rate. If members of high-solidarity groups perceive that the group is threatened, they are likely to be willing to sacrifice their lives to protect it.

Comment: This paragraph summarizes the entire section. Such summary paragraphs often appear at the end of a section and are therefore worth highlighting.

LIFE

You have accomplished much and you are now in a position to make important decisions that will shape the rest of your life. At this threshold, I challenge you not to be seduced by popular ways of denying death. I challenge you to remain aware that life is short and that by getting a higher education, you will have the opportunity to figure out how to live in a way that will make you happiest. I personally hope you find sociology enlightening in this regard. But more importantly, you should know that higher education in general ought to encourage you to play the game of "See Who Lives Life the Best." You will be declared a winner if you play the game seriously. Socrates once said to his pupils: "What we're engaged in here isn't a chance conversation but a dialogue about the way we ought to live our lives." Accept nothing less from your professors.

> **Comment:** As soon as you complete an article, you should summarize its main themes, examples, and definitions. Your summary will serve as a useful study guide before tests. It should be roughly 5–10 percent of the length of the article. There is no substitute for taking your own notes. Synthesizing and restating the material in your own words will help you remember it. Reading someone else's notes is far less effective.

NOTES

1. This is an expanded version of a convocation address delivered in May 2005 to graduates of the "Steps to University" program, University of Toronto. Steps to University identifies promising senior high-school students who might otherwise not complete school or attend college or university because of their economic and social situation, and offers them selected university courses to encourage them to pursue postsecondary education. I thank my colleagues, Malcolm Mackinnon and Jack Veugelers, for thoughtful criticisms of an early draft.

2. Some scientists believe we will conquer death before this century is over by developing the ability to upload our minds to robots (Kurzweil, 1999). If that happens, I will have plenty of time to revise my argument accordingly.

3. Paradoxically, "hard" scientists, such as physicists, seem more likely than "soft" scientists, such as sociologists, to acknowledge that the purpose of their field is to contribute to human welfare. Many soft scientists think that their field lacks scientific status, and they believe that by denying the role of values in motivating their work they will appear more objective and therefore scientific. They fail to appreciate that (1) ideas become scientific not when they are motivated by a quest for "value freedom" (or anything else) but

when they are systematically and publicly tested against evidence, and (2) human values are often a source of scientific creativity.

4. Dividing the number of times an event occurs (e.g., the number of suicides in a certain place and period) by the total number of people to whom the event could occur in principle (e.g., the number of people in that place and period), and then calculating how many times it would occur in a population of a standard size (e.g., 100 000) will give you the rate at which an event occurs. Rates let you compare groups of different sizes.

REFERENCES

American Society of Plastic Surgeons. (2006). On the World Wide Web at http://www.plasticsurgery.org/public_education/statistical -trends.cfm (retrieved 14 September 2006).

Appleby, John, Maxime Fougère, and Manon Rouleau. (2004). "Is Post-Secondary Education in Canada a Cost-Effective Proposition?" Applied Research Branch, Strategic Policy, Human Resources Development Canada. On the World Wide Web at http://www11.hrsdc.gc.ca/en /cs/sp/hrsdc/arb/publications/research/2002-000150/page01 .shtml (retrieved 24 May 2005).

Durkheim, Émile. (1951 [1897]). *Suicide: A Study in Sociology*, G. Simpson, ed., J. Spaulding and G. Simpson, trans. New York: Free Press.

Frankl, Viktor E. (1959). *Man's Search for Meaning: An Introduction to Logotherapy*, trans. I. Lasch. Boston: Beacon Press.

James, William. (1976 [1902]). *The Varieties of Religious Experience: A Study in Human Nature*. New York: Collier Books.

Kurzweil, Ray. (1999). *The Age of Spiritual Machines: When Computers Exceed Human Intelligence*. New York: Viking Penguin.

Mills, C. Wright. (1959). *The Sociological Imagination*. New York: Oxford University Press.

Pape, Robert A. (2005). *Dying to Win: The Strategic Logic of Suicide Terrorism*. New York: Random House.

Weber, Max. (1964 [1949]). "'Objectivity' in Social Science and Social Policy." In Edward A. Shils and Henry A. Finch, trans. and eds., *The Methodology of the Social Sciences* (pp. 49–112). New York: Free Press of Glencoe.

Chapter 2

Careers in Sociology

SCOTT DAVIES, McMaster University
and DAVID WALTERS, University of Guelph

FIELDS AND CAREERS

When university students search for a major, who can blame them for seeking career information on various fields? As individuals and families bear heavier debt loads from rising tuition fees, students are understandably curious about their job prospects. The average cost of a B.A. in Canada is still inexpensive relative to both elite American universities, where annual tuition fees can run up to US$30 000, and to deregulated professional programs (e.g., dentistry, medicine, M.B.A., law), the fees of which have recently soared from $8000 to $20 000. Nonetheless, the expense of a B.A. is considerably higher than it was 20 years ago, and students are increasingly mindful of its economic potential.

This chapter presents a sociological analysis of the links between university and employment. It compares the job fortunes of Canadian sociology graduates with those from other liberal arts and sets its findings in the context of emerging labour market trends. For reasons of space, we focus only on economic payoffs and point interested readers to a recent study of sociology's social, political, and intellectual benefits (Spalter-Roth et al., 2006). We urge students to select a field of study that is compatible with their interests and focus on the economic consequences to help guide their choices.

HIGHER EDUCATION TODAY

Today, there is a lot of talk about how the emerging "knowledge economy" requires young people with higher-order cognitive skills acquired through postsecondary schooling. While some sociologists are skeptical about these claims (Livingstone, 1998; Wolf, 2002), Canadian governments are encouraging universities to expand their enrolments at all levels. From a historical vantage point, the sheer growth of university attendance is striking. Enrolments have never been higher and they are projected to grow despite substantial tuition fee hikes.

Faith in the economic value of university education is curious for two reasons. First, many students are choosing fields about which they have little knowledge. For instance, the social sciences attract many students. In fact, they have the highest enrolments in Canadian universities (Statistics Canada, 2005). Such fields as sociology, psychology, economics, business, political science, anthropology, and communications are popular in universities, yet they are not taught much (if at all) in secondary schools. These fields attract many students even though few high-school graduates have a firm sense of what they are about. This situation is quite unlike that of the traditional humanities and natural sciences, such as history, English, biology, and chemistry. Second, when we examine the links between university and job markets, they are remarkably loose. That is, few jobs are directly related to any of the major social sciences and humanities. Check your local newspaper and you won't find many positions for historians, geographers, psychologists, or sociologists. We conclude that the social sciences attract students with little prior knowledge of, and background in, the field and with few role models in the labour market.

The weak connection between the university and job markets is a result of the fact that most university disciplines emerged as research areas, not vehicles for vocational training. They were created to suit the interests of professors, governments, and students, not employers. Their content is shaped by the fascinations of researchers and instructors, not the requests of workplace managers. Their conventions may make sense to academics but not to employers. With the exception of a few professional programs, there are no institutional mechanisms by which economic authorities can influence what is taught in universities. While academic officials may occasionally call for more practical or vocational courses, established universities are governed by powerful norms of academic freedom that grant them considerable autonomy from politicians and employers. As a result, there are few procedures by which employers offer feedback to professors, and few professors are inclined to seek such feedback. To use the language of sociologists who study complex organizations, most university disciplines are "decoupled" from labour markets.

Why do so many students enter the social sciences and humanities given this decoupling? One answer is that a university degree pays off in the labour market. Sociological research shows that university graduates enjoy higher wages and fewer bouts of unemployment than do graduates from high school, trade colleges, and community colleges (Walters, 2004). In fact, *all* studies of which we are aware reveal such advantages. The trick is to understand how these advantages emerge and persist despite the loose connections between most university fields and the vast majority of workplaces.

WHY SOCIOLOGY PAYS

Sociologists offer three broad explanations for why social science fields, such as sociology, are valued in the labour market. The first is that such fields nurture diffuse skills that are useful across a range of service-sector jobs, even though they are directly relevant to only a few occupations. Thus, evidence suggests that liberal arts graduates have high levels of decision-making, interpersonal, and communication skills (Axelrod, Anisef, and Lin, 2001; Rush and Evers, 1985; Allen, 1998; Lowe and Krahn, 1995; Giles and Drewes, 2002; Krahn and Bowlby, 1999). They can think critically and explore new ideas with ease. They can think abstractly and theoretically, and quickly absorb different kinds of information. They can work well with others, manage conflict, and relate abstract ideas to real-life situations. They have the capacity to work effectively and assume authority in large organizations. Such skills allow on-the-job training to be quicker and easier. Many argue that today's labour market has a growing need for the abilities of social science graduates. In contrast, graduates from more applied disciplines, particularly those in trade and community colleges, often lack such breadth of knowledge. Graduates from social science fields, such as sociology, are thus said to enjoy a long-term advantage because their generic skills are portable across many different kinds of jobs. These skills may not be obvious or easily observed. Many students may be unaware that the abilities they develop in sociology courses are useful in any job where written, oral, and critical thinking skills are valued. Yet sociology undoubtedly develops these valued skills in students.

A second reason that general fields like sociology pay off is known as "credentialism" (Brown, 2001). In government and corporate bureaucracies, many applicants compete for few jobs. Employers therefore need legitimate and convenient criteria to shrink the pool of qualified applicants. Educational credentials are often used as a convenient screening device.

Consider the changing value of the high-school diploma over the past half century. As high-school enrolments grew after World War II, most Canadian-born adults were able to obtain a diploma. Many employers began to demand diplomas as a minimum entry requirement. They did so not necessarily because they associated the diploma with any particular skill but because they associated it with dependability (Berg, 1970). Having a diploma signalled a capacity to follow instructions, complete tasks, and be punctual. However, as more young people with high-school diplomas flooded the job market, employers eventually altered their reasoning. As diploma holders became commonplace, employers interpreted the *lack* of a diploma as potentially problematic. They viewed dropping out of high school as an indicator of potential unreliability. Perhaps, they reasoned, dropouts are incapable of fitting in with people, heeding instructions, and completing tasks.

A similar style of thinking has now been applied to higher education. Before the 1970s, a young person with a bachelor's degree was a rarity in the labour market. Employers often assumed that people with B.A.s were especially able. Their assumption was rooted in the long-standing prestige that higher learning had enjoyed and its association with high status and a sense of social superiority. Employers would sometimes hire university graduates in the hope of bringing prestige to their firm. Before the 1980s, those who lacked university degrees were not stigmatized. High-school graduates could still vie for solid middle-class jobs since most job applicants lacked postsecondary credentials.

This situation appears to be changing. As more and more people graduate from university, degree holders become less rare; and with less rarity comes less prestige (Wolf, 2002). University diplomas no longer offer elite status, even when their holders possess exceptional ability. Such "credential inflation" is sparking a new trend: as long as employers continue to link degrees with some measure of ability, they will increasingly associate someone's lack of degree with mediocrity. Since so many people are earning degrees, employers might suspect that something is wrong with people who lack one. While a degree may no longer buy elite status, it appears to be becoming a general marker of trustworthiness and dependability.

Trust is increasingly important in higher education today, as many new suppliers of educational credentials emerge. These suppliers include online universities, for-profit universities, and private training colleges. Many of these new entrants, such as the online University of Phoenix, offer training only in "practical" fields such as business and information technology that are perceived as being in high demand. The entrance requirements of for-profit institutions are typically lower than those of traditional universities since they need to attract as many fee-paying students as possible to survive. Will their apparent job relevance allow them to take over the higher education marketplace? Will their graduates out-compete traditional liberal arts graduates in the job market? Almost certainly not—and for a stark reason: mainstream universities have the key advantage of being more difficult to enter. This difficulty will remain vitally important as long as employers continue to interpret a degree from a relatively selective university as a general marker of trustworthiness. Credentials from online universities, with their lower entry standards, are less likely to be recognized by employers. In a highly uncertain environment, employers are still inclined to trust a degree from a well-known and respected "brand name" university over a new competitor they may have never heard of and therefore suspect of having lower standards.

A third reason for the continuing popularity of such fields of study as sociology is that they offer a passport to valuable professional and graduate degrees. The highest financial payoffs in university accrue to graduates with advanced degrees in medicine, law, dentistry, and business, or to graduates of Ph.D. programs. These programs usually require a previous degree, such as a B.A. or B.Sc. While sociology graduates rarely enter medicine or dentistry given their lack of natural science training (though some medical schools, such as McMaster's, accept humanities and social science graduates), they commonly enter law, M.B.A., public administration, and teaching, all of which offer solid career opportunities and wages (Walters, 2004). Thus, many social science and humanities disciplines continue to thrive by providing a "ticket" for an advanced degree (Collins, 2002). Research shows that humanities and social science graduates are more likely to pursue additional degrees than are other graduates (Statistics Canada, 2001: 27). This tendency seems to be increasingly important as more employers expect workers to return to university and upgrade their skills and credentials. In contrast, a community college diploma is largely a terminal credential and rarely offers eligibility for advanced degrees. Moreover, recent research shows that attending a community college after earning a university B.A. does not usually increase earnings or employability (Walters, 2003).

SOCIOLOGY GRADUATES COMPARED WITH OTHERS

The career opportunities discussed previously are those that sociology shares with other liberal arts programs. We next address how sociology graduates compare with graduates from nearby fields. We use the best available evidence, Statistics Canada's *National Graduate Survey*, which for several decades has traced how Canadian university graduates from all fields perform in the workforce. We report the latest available data on how individuals who graduated from university in 2000 were faring in the labour market in 2002.

Tables 2.1 and 2.2 compare graduates of several liberal arts fields, including sociology. We combined anthropology, religion, and geography into an "Other" category because there were too few respondents in the sample from each of these fields to allow for reliable statistical comparisons. "Liberal arts and sciences" includes students in general studies, fields that are not classified, and those who did not declare a field. The first column in Table 2.1 shows that the largest group of employed graduates come from combined liberal arts and

TABLE 2.1 LIBERAL ARTS GRADUATES BY FIELD OF STUDY AND GENDER (IN PERCENT)

FIELD OF STUDY	PERCENTAGE OF ALL LIBERAL ARTS GRADUATES	PERCENTAGE OF ALL MALE LIBERAL ARTS GRADUATES	PERCENTAGE OF ALL FEMALE LIBERAL ARTS GRADUATES	PERCENTAGE MALE IN FIELD	PERCENTAGE FEMALE IN FIELD	TOTAL
Sociology	8	7	9	29	71	100
English	8	7	9	28	72	100
Liberal arts and sciences	12	12	12	35	65	100
Fine arts and music	7	7	7	35	65	100
Film and performing arts	10	11	9	40	60	100
Media and information studies	7	6	8	29	71	100
Languages	7	4	9	20	80	100
Philosophy	4	6	3	57	43	100
Psychology	11	6	14	18	82	100
Economics	4	8	3	62	38	100
Political science	6	6	6	36	64	100
History	7	11	5	52	48	100
Other (anthropology/ religion/geography)	8	9	8	38	62	100
Total	**99***	**100**	**102***			

*Does not equal 100 because of rounding.

SOURCE: Adapted from Statistics Canada. (2004). *National Graduate Survey (Class of 2000)*. On the World Wide Web at http://www23.statcan.gc.ca/imdb/p2SV.pl?Function=getSurvey&SurvId=20168&SurvVer=3&InstaId=15771&InstaVer=10&SDDS= 5012&lang=en&db=imdb&adm=8&dis=2 (retrieved 10 September 2005).

TABLE 2.2 AVERAGE INCOME OF GRADUATES BY FIELD AND GENDER

FIELD OF STUDY	ALL GRADUATES	MEN	WOMEN
Sociology	31 574	33 367	31 137
English	29 437	28 062*	29 917
Liberal arts and sciences	31 423	31 668	31 263
Fine arts and music	27 477*	25 655*	28 413
Film and performing arts	25 046*	27 191*	23 544*
Media and information studies	33 740	33 658	33 777
Languages	27 730*	27 411	27 810*
Philosophy	28 811	28 593	29 025
Psychology	30 920	37 450	29 397
Economics	33 528	33 510	33 546
Political science	32 171	31 007	32 980
History	30 589	31 561	29 803
Other (anthropology/ religion/geography)	31 592	37 697	28 239*
All	**30 218**	**31 334**	**29 679**

*Indicates a 95 percent or greater chance that the sample figure is different from the actual figure for sociologists in the population.

SOURCE: Adapted from Statistics Canada. (2004). *National Graduate Survey (Class of 2000).* On the World Wide Web at http://www23.statcan.gc.ca/imdb/p2SV.pl?Function=getSurvey&SurvId=20168&SurvVer=3&Instald=15771&InstaVer=10&SDDS=5012&lang=en&db=imdb&adm=8&dis=2 (retrieved 10 September 2005).

science programs (12 percent), while economics and philosophy have the smallest proportion of graduates (4 percent). The second and third columns display this information separately for males and females. Males are least likely to hold a degree in languages (4 percent) and most likely to have a combined liberal arts and science degree (12 percent). Females are most likely to hold a degree in psychology (14 percent) and are least likely to graduate in economics and philosophy (both 3 percent). The last two columns in Table 2.1 show that women outnumber men in every field of study except philosophy, history, and economics. The fields with the largest gender imbalance are psychology (82 percent female) and languages (80 percent female). Males are the majority in economics (62 percent). Sociology graduates make up 8 percent of the liberal arts, representing 7 percent of males and 9 percent of females.

Before going any further, we must emphasize that all social surveys examine a part (the "sample") to make generalizations about a whole (the "population"). There is a certain danger in this practice, for a chance always exists that a sample will differ from the population from which it is drawn. To the degree the sample differs from the population, generalizations based on the sample will be inaccurate.

Thankfully, statisticians have developed ways of figuring out the chance of drawing faulty conclusions from different types of samples. In general, sociologists accept a 5 percent chance of being wrong (a 95 percent chance of being right) in the conclusions they draw from sample surveys. We follow that standard here.

In Table 2.2, for example, we report annual earnings in 2002 of graduates who obtained a bachelor's degree in 2000 and were no longer in school in 2002. We created Table 2.2 because we want to know which graduates earn more or less than sociology graduates. Given that each number in Table 2.2 has a certain margin of error, however, we are limited in the conclusions we can safely draw. Specifically, we can be 95 percent confident that the figures marked with an asterisk are actually below sociology graduates' annual income of $31 574. This means that graduates of programs in fine arts and music, film and performing arts, and languages almost certainly earn less than sociology graduates (see column 1; as columns 2 and 3 show, the below-average fields differ somewhat for men considered alone and women considered alone). We cannot, however, state with 95 percent certainty that annual income for graduates of other fields is either above or below that of sociologists in the population as a whole. Thus, economics graduates lead the pack with annual earnings of $33 528, but all we can safely say about them is that their annual earnings are not significantly more than the $31 574 earned by sociology graduates. In other words, in the Canadian population, sociology and economics graduates seem to enjoy roughly the same annual income two years after graduation.

Columns 2 and 3 reveal that, on the whole, men earn more than women. Two years after graduation, male liberal arts graduates earn $31 668, whereas females earn $31 263, almost 99 percent of the male average. Most fields have rather small gender pay gaps. Only two fields exhibit big gender gaps in favour of men: males with psychology and "other" degrees earn, respectively, about $8000 and $9000 more than their female counterparts. But in 7 of the 13 fields listed in Table 2.2, women report higher annual earnings than men. This finding is consistent with other studies that have found shrinking gender pay gaps among university graduates in recent decades (Walters, 2006).

Overall, the data suggest that the income potential of sociology graduates is roughly the same as that of graduates in most other fields and perhaps above average. Graduates of a few fields in the humanities earn significantly less than sociology graduates do. Graduates from no field earn significantly more than sociology graduates do.

CAREERS FOR SOCIOLOGY GRADUATES

We have argued that sociology, like most other subjects in the social sciences and humanities, is both useful and decoupled from the labour market. Decoupling is evident from the fact that only a minority of sociology graduates in Canada and the United States report that their job is directly related to their schooling (Krahn and Bowlby, 1999; Spalter-Roth et al., 2006). Utility is evident in the fact that sociology graduates readily find good work in a variety of fields. We conclude that while employers place few job ads for sociologists, sociology is a flexible field that allows graduates to work in many occupations and organizations.

A study of McMaster University sociology graduates (Davies and Denton, 1997) from various degree levels found them in a great variety of jobs, including social work, teaching, journalism, business administration, health administration, criminal justice, policing, sales, public relations, private polling, government research, and so on. The *National Graduate Survey* provides data on the percentage of recent sociology B.A.s employed in various occupational categories (see Table 2.3). They illustrate that sociology graduates have opportunities across a broad range of sectors. The largest proportion (35 percent) is in occupations relating to business, finance, and administration. Jobs in the social sciences, education, and government services are the second-largest destination, employing 29 percent of recent graduates. Sales and service jobs are third, accounting for 18 percent of employed graduates; followed by management positions (nearly 7 percent); jobs in primary industry (almost 5 percent); health (about 2 percent); and art, culture, and sport (about 2 percent).

Amid this variety, there are some specific occupations for which sociology prepares its graduates. Most sociology programs have course requirements in research methods and statistics. Such applied research training can be extremely valuable. Many government agencies and companies, such as Statistics Canada, the Centre for Addiction and Mental Health, Proctor and Gamble, Angus Reid, and just about any corporation, federal or provincial ministry, or trade union involved in

TABLE 2.3 SOCIOLOGY GRADUATES BY OCCUPATIONAL CATEGORY (IN PERCENT)

OCCUPATION	PERCENTAGE
Management occupations	6.8
Business, finance, and administrative occupations	35.0
Natural and applied sciences and related occupations	1.2
Health occupations	2.2
Occupations in social sciences, education, government service	29.0
Occupations in art, culture, recreation, and sport	2.2
Sales and service occupations	18.0
Trades, transport, primary industry, and other	4.7

SOURCE: Adapted from Statistics Canada. (2004). *National Graduate Survey (Class of 2000)*. On the World Wide Web at http://www23.statcan.gc.ca/imdb/p2SV.pl?Function=getSurvey&SurvId=20168&SurvVer=3&Instald=15771&InstaVer=10&SDDS=5012&lang=en&db=imdb&adm=8&dis=2 (retrieved 10 September 2005).

large-scale research, seek applicants with a strong aptitude for conducting surveys and analyzing data, and they regularly offer excellent employment opportunities to sociology graduates. In fact, every year Statistics Canada recruits sociology graduates (information can be found at www.statcan.gc.ca/employment-emploi/recruit-recrue/ec/ec-eng.htm). Thus, there is a strong demand for graduates who are capable of administering and analyzing survey data.

In an analysis not reported in detail here, we also found that sociology graduates who specialize in an applied subarea, such as criminology, health, and population studies (demography), had substantially higher earnings than did other sociology graduates. Although the small sample sizes for these subgroups do not permit accurate statistical comparisons with other fields, they suggest both the marketability of applied research areas within sociology and the range of opportunities sociology offers.

Beyond applied and quantitative subfields, many social agencies, hospitals, and market research companies employ graduates with a broad range of research skills that are taught in most sociology undergraduate programs. Many companies want employees with a strong background in qualitative techniques relating to interviewing, organizing, and administering focus groups, who are capable of communicating research findings to audiences unfamiliar with technical terms. This is why the skills provided in research methods and statistics classes nicely complement the communication and critical thinking and writing abilities acquired in theory courses.

ADVICE FOR STRATEGIZING IN NETWORKS AND INTERNAL LABOUR MARKETS

What then is the value of a sociology degree? Sociology resembles other social sciences and humanities: it pays off, but largely indirectly. While offering few unique paths to specific labour markets, sociology fosters generic skills, is a recognized credential in bureaucratic settings, and serves as a passport to graduate and professional school. Because it is loosely connected to job markets, sociology is linked to a variety of occupations.

Such wide-reaching links to job markets force graduates to use job search strategies creatively. For example, you have probably heard the old saying that to get a good job, who you know is as important as what you know. Sociological research suggests that there is much truth in that adage. Creating a wide range of social ties can lead to many job opportunities (Granovetter, 1995). For example, if you secure a middle-management position after you graduate, your newly established contacts may lead to a permanent full-time position. Contacts are particularly useful for securing an interview. Often the people who are offered a job are not the most qualified. Instead, they may be the people with the most interview experience—they knew just what to say, when to say it, and whom to say it to. Forming contacts allows you to gain such experience. After an unsuccessful interview—and for most of us there will be many—always follow up with the interviewer to find out how you can improve your performance.

Networking is important when applying to postgraduate programs, especially master's and doctoral programs. You need to know not only which programs suit your interests but also which faculty members conduct research in your area. Having an undergraduate adviser to work with can often be as important as your grade point average for being accepted into a graduate program. The reputation of the professors writing your letters of reference can be extremely important in being admitted into graduate school and even securing a good job in your research area. Faculty members vary widely in their resourcefulness, their ability to fund graduate students as research assistants, and the quality of their connections in the labour market. Select your mentors wisely!

Diverse networks also allow you to obtain advice from multiple sources and thereby improve the breadth of your information. Whether applying to postgraduate studies or entering the labour market, use a variety of sources to research your options. Aside from personal contacts, seek guidance from career counsellors at your university, secretaries in your department, and, of course, professors. Draw on as many resources as you can. For example, websites (such as www.sociology.ca) offer information on research and employment opportunities for sociology graduates, as well as links to departments that offer master's degrees. Many departmental Web pages provide Internet links to assist students in making academic or career decisions.

Note also that some entry-level jobs lead to better jobs than others. "Internal labour markets" exist in which large organizations hire from within (Krahn and Lowe, 2002). Many government and corporate bureaucracies arrange their positions hierarchically, creating promotional paths that lead upward from entry-level jobs to management. This means that a relatively low-paying job can be worthwhile if it leads to something more, and that seemingly lucrative summer jobs at shopping malls, bars, or factories may yield few long-term benefits. Students may find it difficult to resist such jobs if they pay well, but they are not selling features on a résumé, and they offer little advancement potential. Unless you are absolutely confident of being admitted into a graduate or a professional program, you are much better off applying for summer positions at large organizations, even for clerical, volunteer, or unpaid positions, as long as they allow access to an internal labour market. Some initial grunt work may eventually lead to a position with more creative autonomy and authority. A university-educated, hardworking, ambitious employee who already has experience within a company is an ideal candidate for promotion to one of its well-paying, full-time positions. If you eventually find fewer openings than you initially anticipated, use this experience to acquire a job elsewhere, and you may benefit from the additional interviewing knowledge.

We conclude that although a sociology degree opens up a wide variety of employment opportunities, realizing that potential requires sociology graduates to use job-search strategies creatively. Research suggests that social science graduates, including sociology graduates, initially fare less well than graduates with professional degrees do, but they catch up somewhat over time (Finnie, 2001). This fact illustrates the importance of building networks and entering internal labour markets. Of course, luck helps in the job market, but you will significantly improve your chance of success by studying sociology and adopting sociological strategies for taking advantage of job market opportunities.

REFERENCES

Allen, Robert C. (1998). *The Employability of University Graduates in Humanities, Social Sciences and Education: Recent Statistical Evidence.* Ottawa: Social Sciences and Humanities Research Council of Canada.

Axelrod, Paul, Paul Anisef, and Zeng Lin. (2001). "Against All Odds? The Enduring Value of Liberal Education in Universities, Professions, and the Labour Market." *Canadian Journal of Higher Education, 31* (2), 47–78.

Berg, Ivar. (1970). *Education and Jobs: The Great Training Robbery.* New York: Praeger.

Brown, David K. (2001). "The Social Sources of Education Credentialism." *Sociology of Education* (Extra Issue), 19–34.

Collins, Randall. (2002). "Credential Inflation and the Future of Universities." In Steven Brint, ed., *The Future of the City of Intellect: The Changing American University* (pp. 23–46). Stanford, CA: Stanford University Press.

Davies, Scott and Margaret Denton. (1997). "The Employment of Masters and Ph.D. Graduates from Eleven Sociology Departments." *Society, 21* (1), 9–14.

Finnie, Ross. (2001). "Fields of Plenty, Fields of Lean: The Early Labour Market Outcomes of Canadian University Graduates by Discipline." *Canadian Journal of Higher Education, 31* (1), 141–76.

Giles, P. and T. Drewes. (2002). "Liberal Arts Degrees and the Labour Market." *Perspectives on Labour and Income, 13* (3), 27–33.

Granovetter, Mark. (1995). *Getting a Job: A Study of Contacts and Careers,* 2nd ed. Chicago: University of Chicago Press.

Krahn, Harvey and Jeffrey W. Bowlby. (1999). *Education-Job Skills Match: An Analysis of the 1990 and 1995 National Graduate Surveys.* Applied Research Branch for Strategic Policy. Ottawa: Human Resources Development Canada.

Krahn, Harvey and Graham S. Lowe. (2002). *Work, Industry, and Canadian Society,* 4th ed. Toronto: ITP Nelson.

Livingstone, David W. (1998). *The Education-Jobs Gap: Underemployment or Economic Democracy.* Toronto: Garamond Press.

Lowe, Graham S. and Harvey Krahn. (1995). "Job-Related Education and Training among Young Workers." *Canadian Public Policy, 21* (3), 362–78.

Rush, J.C. and F.T. Evers. (1985). "Making the Match: Canada's University Graduates and Corporate Employers." *Business Quarterly, 50* (Winter), 41–47.

Spalter-Roth, Roberta, William Erskine, Sylvia Polsiak, and Jamie Panzarella. (2006). *A National Survey of Seniors Majoring in Sociology.* American Sociological Association. On the World Wide Web at http://www.asanet.org/images/research/docs/pdf /What%20Can%20You%20Do%20with%20BA%20in%20Soc.pdf (retrieved 12 December 2006).

Statistics Canada. (2001). "The School-to-Work Transition of Post-Secondary Graduates in Canada: Research Findings Based on the National Graduates Surveys." *Applied Research Bulletin* (Special Edition). On the World Wide Web at http://publications. gc.ca/collections/Collection/MP32-27-2001-3E.pdf (retrieved 30 July 2012).

Statistics Canada. (2005). "University Enrollment." *The Daily* 11 October. On the World Wide Web at http://www.statcan.ca/Daily /English/051011/d051011b.htm (retrieved 12 December 2005).

Walters, David. (2003). "Recycling: The Economic Implications of Obtaining Additional Postsecondary Credentials at Lower or Equivalent Levels." *Canadian Review of Sociology and Anthropology, 40* (4), 463–80.

Walters, David. (2004). "A Comparison of the Labour Market Outcomes of Postsecondary Graduates of Various Levels and Fields over a Four-Cohort Period." *Canadian Journal of Sociology, 29* (1), 1–27.

Walters, David. (2006). "An Examination of the School-to-Work Transitions of Male and Female College and University Graduates of Applied and Liberal Arts Programs in Canada." *Higher Education Policy, 19*, 225–50.

Wolf, Alison. (2002). *Does Education Matter? Myths About Education and Economic Growth.* New York: Penguin.

PART 2 | FOUNDATIONS OF SOCIETY

Imagine standing at the end of a road 30 kilometres long. Allow each metre of the road to represent 100 000 years. The entire road will then signify the amount of time that has passed since life first appeared on the planet: about three billion years. From this long view, human beings are recent arrivals, first assuming their present form only about 100 000 years ago, or just a metre down the road.

Recorded human history spans a much shorter distance. The development of agriculture, the single most important event in human history, began approximately 10 000 years ago (only 10 centimetres down the road). The beginning of modern industry, arguably the second most important event in human history, dates from just about 240 years ago (a mere 2.4 millimetres down the road).

The evolution of agriculture and modern industry hint at what makes humans different from other animals: our advanced ability to create complex symbols (**abstraction**), make and use tools that improve our ability to take what we want from nature (**production**), and develop a complex social life (**cooperation**). These characteristics enabled humans to survive and multiply despite a harsh natural environment and relatively poor physical endowments.

Symbolic communication between people, or **social interaction**, enables us to engage in social learning, or **socialization**. By means of socialization, people acquire the languages, laws, sciences, values, customs, practices, and beliefs—in short, the **culture**—of the groups to which they belong. When social interaction assumes a regular or patterned form, the relations among people form a **social structure**. Social structures may be, for example, hierarchical or egalitarian, tightly integrated or loosely organized; and different social-structural forms influence human thought and action in different ways. The patterned behaviour of people embedded in a social structure is called a **role**. For instance, in some types of hierarchy, some people perform the role of slave, others that of master.

Social structures and cultures are paradoxical features of social life. On the one hand, they are constructed anew and often modified, at least a little, by each person. On the other hand, because social structures and cultures exist before any particular individual does, they help define and limit what the individual can think and what he or she can do. Hence, the answer of many sociologists to the philosophers' debate about whether people are free or determined: they are both.

GLOSSARY

Abstraction is the human ability to create symbols in order to classify experience and generalize from it.

Cooperation is the human ability to give and receive aid from other humans. Social structures are typically created to facilitate cooperation.

Culture consists of the symbols that people use to communicate and organize their social life.

Production is a distinctively human mode of interacting with nature that involves inventing tools and using them to make and improve the means of survival.

Roles are the behaviour patterns of people embedded in a social structure.

Social interaction is symbolic communication between people.

Socialization is the social process by which culture is learned.

Social structures are the patterns of social relations in which people are embedded and that provide opportunities for, and constrain, action.

CRITICAL THINKING QUESTION

1. If we accept that social structures influence human thought and action, are people responsible for what they think and do? Should criminals, for example, be held responsible for their crimes? Should society be held responsible for producing criminals? Or is there a middle ground between these two extreme views? If so, how and where do you draw the line between individual and social responsibility?

ANNOTATED BIBLIOGRAPHY

Patrick Nolan and Gerhard Lenski, *Human Societies: An Introduction to Macrosociology*, 11th ed. (Boulder, CO: Paradigm Publishers, 2008). Imaginatively traces the evolution of human societies, focusing on the relationship between technological innovation and social stratification.

Three main models inform the socialization literature. The **developmental model** likens people to acorns that have growth potential and develop in stages set by their inherent characteristics. The **normative model** construes people as empty bowls into which society and culture pour a defined assortment of beliefs, symbols, values, and roles. The **interactive model** thinks of people as the imaginative, two-legged creatures that you and I deal with every day. From the interactive point of view, socialization is a creative process that takes place in the company of others. To be sure, inherent biological and psychological traits set broad potentials and limits on what people can become. The broader society and culture define the general outlines of people's beliefs, symbols, values, and roles. However, people are continually socialized in face-to-face settings where they interact with others. In those settings, they imaginatively interpret, accept, and reject the opportunities and demands of socialization in ways that suit them.

Although people are ultimately agents of their own destiny, as the interactive model of socialization emphasizes, the developmental and normative models are not pure fantasy. The articles in this section highlight the way social and biological forces (and the interaction between them) increase the probability that people will act in certain ways.

Chapter 3 emphasizes the value of the normative theory. It describes Philip Zimbardo's famous experiment, which shows how quickly and completely young adults can abandon two decades of socialization when placed in an artificial social setting that demands a transformation of their behaviour.

In Chapter 4, Michael Shanahan, Shawn Bauldry, and Jason Freeman emphasize the value of the developmental model—or at least a new variant of it that is a lot more complex than the old "acorn" model. They explain how people's genetic makeup can modify the effect of social forces on their behaviour. They also note that the social environment can alter associations between genes and behaviours. Their article establishes that the interaction between sociology and biology is an exciting new area of research that promises to add much to our understanding of socialization processes.

GLOSSARY

The **developmental model of socialization** likens people to acorns that have growth potential and develop in stages set by their inherent characteristics.

The **interactive model of socialization** regards socialization as a creative process that takes place in groups.

The **normative model of socialization** likens people to empty bowls into which society and culture pour a defined assortment of beliefs, symbols, values, and roles.

CRITICAL THINKING QUESTIONS

1. What are the strengths and limitations of the three main social-psychological theories of socialization?

2. How does the old developmental theory (the "acorn" model) differ from the new developmental theory described by Shanahan, Bauldry, and Freeman?

3. Do parallels exist between the Zimbardo experiment and the mistreatment of Iraqi prisoners by American forces at Abu Ghraib prison in Iraq? For a simulation of the Zimbardo experiment on the Web and links to the parallels with Abu Ghraib, visit www.prisonexp.org.

ANNOTATED BIBLIOGRAPHY

Patricia Adler and Peter Adler, *Peer Power: Preadolescent Culture and Identity* (New Brunswick, NJ: Rutgers University Press, 1998). A definitive statement of the interactive model of socialization and its application to socialization from preschool through Grade 5. The authors find developmental stages and sociocultural pressures but argue that children are agents of the socialization process, adapting circumstances to their needs as much as they are compelled to adapt to their circumstances. For example, children are not born with gender identities, nor do they simply learn them; they must "do" gender before it becomes theirs.

R.C. Lewontin, *Biology as Ideology: The Doctrine of DNA* (Toronto: Anansi, 1991). This brief book is a brilliant critique of the "acorn" model of socialization by a famous Harvard geneticist. Lewontin explains variation in individuals' traits within species as a function of the interaction of genes, environment, and random variation in cell growth and division.

Chapter 3

Pathology of Imprisonment

PHILIP E. ZIMBARDO, Stanford University

In an attempt to understand just what it means psychologically to be a prisoner or prison guard, Craig Haney, Curt Banks, Dave Jaffe, and I created our own prison. We carefully screened over 70 volunteers who answered an ad in a Palo Alto city newspaper and ended up with about two dozen young men who were selected to be part of this study. They were mature, emotionally stable, normal, intelligent college students from middle-class homes throughout the United States and Canada. They appeared to represent the cream of the crop of this generation. None had any criminal record, and initially all were relatively homogeneous on many dimensions.

Half were arbitrarily designated as prisoners by a flip of a coin, the others as guards. These were the roles they were to play in our simulated prison. The guards were made aware of the potential seriousness and danger of the situation and their own vulnerability. They made up their own formal rules for maintaining law, order, and respect, and were generally free to improvise new ones during their eight-hour, three-man shifts. The prisoners were unexpectedly picked up at their homes by a city policeman in a squad car, searched, handcuffed, finger-printed, booked at the Palo Alto station house, and taken blindfolded to our jail. There they were stripped, deloused, put into a uniform, given a number, and put into a cell with two other prisoners, where they expected to live for the next two weeks. The pay was good ... and their motivation was to make money.

We observed and recorded on videotape the events that occurred in the prison, and we interviewed and tested the prisoners and guards at various points throughout the study. Some of the videotapes of the actual encounters between the prisoners and guards were seen on the NBC News feature "Chronolog" on November 26, 1971.

Source: Philip G. Zimbardo, Inc.

At the end of only six days, we had to close down our mock prison because what we saw was frightening. It was no longer apparent to most of the subjects (or to us) where reality ended and their roles began. The majority had indeed become prisoners or guards, no longer able to clearly differentiate between role playing and self. There were dramatic changes in virtually every aspect of their behavior, thinking, and feeling. In less than a week, the experience of imprisonment undid (temporarily) a lifetime of learning; human values were suspended, self-concepts were challenged, and the ugliest, most base, pathological side of human nature surfaced. We were horrified because we saw some boys (guards) treat others as if they were despicable animals, taking pleasure in cruelty, while other boys (prisoners) became servile, dehumanized robots who thought only of escape, of their own individual survival, and of their mounting hatred for the guards.

We had to release three prisoners in the first four days because they had such acute situational traumatic reactions as hysterical crying, confusion in thinking, and severe depression. Others begged to be paroled, and all but three were willing to forfeit all the money they had earned if they could be paroled. By then (the fifth day), they had been so programmed to think of themselves as prisoners that when their request for parole was denied, they returned docilely to their cells. Now, had they been thinking as college students acting in an oppressive experiment, they would have quit once they no longer wanted the [money] we used as our only incentive. However, the reality was not quitting an experiment but "being paroled by the parole board from the Stanford County Jail." By the last days, the earlier solidarity among the prisoners (systematically broken by the guards) dissolved into "each man for himself." Finally, when one of their fellows was put in solitary confinement (a small closet) for refusing to eat, the prisoners were given a choice by one of the guards: give up their blankets and the incorrigible prisoner would be let out, or keep their blankets and he would be kept in all night. They voted to keep their blankets and to abandon their brother.

About a third of the guards became tyrannical in their arbitrary use of power, in enjoying their control over other people. They were corrupted by the power of their roles and became quite inventive in their techniques of breaking the spirit of the prisoners and making them feel they were worthless. Some of the guards merely did their jobs as tough but fair correctional officers, and several were good guards from the prisoners' point of view because they did them small favors and were friendly. However, no good guard ever interfered with a command by any of the bad guards; they never intervened on the side of the prisoners, they never told the others to ease off because it was only an experiment, and they never even came to me as prison superinten-dent or experimenter in charge to complain. In part, they were good because the others were bad; they needed the others to help establish their own egos in a positive light. In a sense, the good guards perpetu-ated the prison more than the other guards because their own need to be liked prevented them from disobeying or violating the implicit guards' code. At the same time, the act of befriending the prisoners created a social reality that made the prisoners less likely to rebel.

By the end of the week, the experiment had become a reality.... The consultant for our prison, Carlo Prescot, an ex-convict with six-teen years of imprisonment in California's jails, would get so depressed and furious each time he visited our prison, because of its psychological similarity to his experiences, that he would have to leave. A Catholic priest, who was a former prison chaplain in Washington, DC, talked to our prisoners after four days and said they were just like the other first-timers he had seen.

But in the end, I called off the experiment, not because of the horror I saw out there in the prison yard, but because of the horror of realizing that I could have easily traded places with the most brutal guard or become the weakest prisoner full of hatred at being so power-less that I could not eat, sleep, or go to the toilet without permission of the authorities....

Individual behavior is largely under the control of social forces and environmental contingencies rather than personality traits, char-acter, will power, or other empirically unvalidated constructs. Thus, we create an illusion of freedom by attributing more internal control to ourselves, to the individual, than actually exists. We thus under-estimate the power and pervasiveness of situational controls over behavior because (a) they are often non-obvious and subtle, (b) we can often avoid entering situations in which we might be so controlled, and (c) we label as "weak" or "deviant" people in those situations who do behave differently from how we believe we would.

Each of us carries around in our heads a favorable self-image in which we are essentially just, fair, humane, and understanding. For example, we could not imagine inflicting pain on others without much provocation or hurting people who had done nothing to us, who in fact were even liked by us. However, there is a growing body of social psy-chological research that underscores the conclusion derived from this prison study. Many people, perhaps the majority, can be made to do almost anything when put into psychologically compelling situations—regardless of their morals, ethics, values, attitudes, beliefs, or personal convictions. My colleague, Stanley Milgram, has shown that more than 60 percent of the population will deliver what they think is a series of painful electric shocks to another person even after the victim cries for mercy, begs them to stop, and then apparently passes out. The subjects complained that they did not want to inflict more pain but blindly obeyed the command of the authority figure (the experimenter) who said that they must go on. In my own research on violence, I have seen mild-mannered coeds repeatedly give shocks (which they thought were causing pain) to another girl, a stranger whom they had rated very favorably, simply by being made to feel anonymous and put in a situation in which they were expected to engage in this activity.

Observers of these and similar experimental situations never predict their outcomes and estimate that it is unlikely that they themselves would behave similarly. They can be so confident only when they are outside the situation. However, because the majority of people in these studies do act in non-rational, non-obvious ways, it follows that the majority of observers would also succumb to the social psychological forces in the situation.

With regard to prisons, we can state that the mere act of assigning labels to people and putting them into a situation in which those labels acquire validity and meaning is sufficient to elicit pathological behavior. This pathology is not predictable from any available diagnostic indicators we have in the social sciences, and it is extreme enough to modify in very significant ways fundamental attitudes and behavior. The prison situation, as presently arranged, is guaranteed to generate severe enough pathological reactions in both guards and prisoners as to debase their humanity, lower their feelings of self-worth, and make it difficult for them to be part of a society outside their prison.

Chapter 4

Beyond Mendel's Ghost

MICHAEL J. SHANAHAN, SHAWN BAULDRY, and JASON FREEMAN, University of North Carolina–Chapel Hill

At a major conference on genetics in 2003, a team of researchers reported that the Maori, the indigenous people of New Zealand, are far more likely than Caucasians to carry a variant of the MAOA gene that has been associated with aggressive behavior. The scientists argued that the difference made sense and reflected the fact that more aggressive individuals survived the migratory journey by which the Maori originally populated Aotearoa, the islands that would later become New Zealand.

Unfortunately, it took little imagination for editorialists to deform this line of reasoning, arguing that such genetic differences would explain the Maori's higher rates of crime. Substantial segments of the New Zealander public agreed, and the "warrior gene" was born.

The media is filled with coverage of findings like this, linking genetic variation to behavioral traits such as violence, generosity, personal success, and even political beliefs. Unfortunately, these studies are often publicized by the media—and sometimes by study authors themselves—in a way that glosses over the nuances of what we know about genetics as well as sociology.

During the 20th century, sociology's relationship to genetics was frequently combative. In the 1980s and 1990s, inflammatory arguments propounded by the likes of Charles Murray and Richard Herrnstein about a genetically-based American underclass put sociologists in the position of arguing against the relevance of genetics for explaining social behavior. But, as the 21st century commences, sociologists are now engaging in the genetically-informed study of behavior and including molecular genetic information in their data collection efforts.

Source: Adapted from "Beyond Mendel's Ghost" by Michael J. Shanahan, Shawn Bauldry, and Jason Freeman, *Contexts 9(4)*, pp. 34–39, © 2010 by the American Sociological Association. Reprinted by Permission of SAGE Publications.

Why the sea change? Contrary to simplistic news coverage, genetic factors do not determine behaviors in any straightforward way. Rather, they combine with—and even change in response to—"environmental factors," which include everything from the mother's womb to nutrition and prescription drugs to the subject of sociology proper, social context. A person may have genetic risks for alcoholism, but whether that person becomes an alcoholic depends on a wide range of environmental experiences—including social factors—occurring over the life course. People are not Mendel's famous pea plant flowers, the coloration of which was almost completely determined by genes. And if genes and environments combine in complex ways to predict behavior, who better to help map out these social complexities than sociologists, who have been developing this expertise for over a century?

As sensationalist stories about "warrior genes" jazz up the front page, an understanding of how genetics and sociology interact is increasingly necessary to make sense of research that claims to find a relationship between microscopic genes and macro-level social outcomes. While sociologists and geneticists are just beginning to flesh out this relationship between genes and social actors, a glimpse at the early results can go a long way towards helping us interpret the ongoing stream of studies trumpeting the genetic basis of our social lives.

GENES

Scientists have long drawn on studies of rats and mice to show that genetic and social factors combine in complex ways to predict behaviors. Decades of research in psychology showed that "creating" an aggressive mouse takes generations of selective breeding coupled with a consistently stressful environment. Neither the breeding nor the stressors by themselves reliably led to a mouse prone to attack. At the same time, studies of familial lineages suggested that specific genes are associated with specific behaviors, including aggression. So, for example, scientists observed that a risk variant (or "allele") of the MAOA gene—which metabolizes neurotransmitters like dopamine—was much more common than would be expected across several generations of a Dutch family marked by high levels of violence.

With advances in genotyping (the measurement of genes), these lines of research merged and focused on human behavior, allowing for the study of *gene-environment interactions* (sometimes referred to as "GxE") how the effects of genes on behavior are conditioned by environmental features, or vice versa. For example, in a highly cited and replicated study in *Science*, Avshalom Caspi and his colleagues show that an MAOA allele coupled with childhood maltreatment before the age of five significantly increases the likelihood of an antisocial psychiatric disorder in young adulthood. The gene *alone*, however, had little effect.

Studies like Caspi's quickly proliferated and sociologists joined in the "GxE rush" to identify combinations of genes and environments that reliably predicted specific behaviors of long-standing interest to their discipline—physical and mental health, the stress process, indicators of status attainment, interpersonal relationships, health-related behaviors, violence, sexual behavior, and so on. It seemed to be just a matter of finding the magic genetic bullet and its appropriate environmental trigger.

But such research faces challenges. Like much of sociology, gene-environment research is usually non-experimental: people are not randomly assigned to genes (like MAOA alleles) and to environments (like maltreatment), with their behaviors recorded by observers wearing white coats and safety glasses. So it's rarely clear whether a specific environmental feature's relationship to a specific gene is actually causal. Features of the environment like child maltreatment are highly correlated with other negative social experiences (e.g., parental drug use) and it is also known that genes "hunt in packs," meaning that behaviors likely reflect networks of genes that work together. For that matter, behaviors are often highly correlated. Even if MAOA and maltreatment are the real culprits, do they actually predict antisocial behaviors or something else, like substance abuse?

Also, a great deal of gene-environment research has proceeded with little reference to conceptual models. Ideally, empirical analyses are guided by prior research about how the brain works—how specific genes are related to brain structure and function and, therefore, to how people perceive and react to their experiences. A causal account can then be formulated to link chains of biological, psychological, and social processes that reliably lead to specific behaviors.

Despite these challenges, sociology has an important role to play in helping to conceptualize and measure environmental factors. Indeed, developments in genetics have only served to underscore the importance of social context and the need for a sociological presence in gene-environment research. A major theme of this new research is that the image of DNA as an unchanging set of instructions is downright inaccurate. Although it is true that the base pairs that make up a person's DNA (remember A, G, C, and T from high school biology?) never change, social experiences alter their *expression*, or how the base pairs are interpreted and translated into their "products" (typically proteins). These differences in gene expression can help us to understand *how* social contexts alter associations between genes and behaviors.

One class of expression mechanisms is *epigenetic processes*, which change how the long and spindly DNA molecule is compacted. Many scholars believe that they are a principle mechanism by which social context "turns genes on and off." Studies with mice and rats show that epigenetic changes account, to some degree, for why stress is related to depression, complex settings to intellectual development, and lack of maternal warmth to anxiety—all topics of interest to sociologists. Given close similarities between these animals and humans, scientists have little doubt such findings will inform human behavioral science.

Apparently more common are *transcriptional processes*, which alter the rate at which genes make proteins and other goodies. Recent research in humans shows that transcription accounts for why chronic stress and loneliness each lead to a heightened inflammatory response, which is in turn related to a wide range of disease states (such as depression, asthma, and cardiovascular disease). For example, even among people with high socioeconomic status (SES) in adulthood, low SES during childhood is associated with cardiovascular disease. Gregory Miller and his colleagues recently showed that low SES in childhood increases the likelihood of a heightened stress response in adulthood by way of transcription. Thus, an adverse environment early in life increases the likelihood of heightened reactions to stressors throughout later life, regardless of one's achievements and status in society, culminating in stress-related illnesses.

Although gene expression studies of social context and human behavior are still novel, they have already vividly shown that DNA is highly reactive to status, stress, and one's connectedness to other people, topics of long-standing interest in sociology. And, in a nutshell, there has never been more empirical evidence pointing to the importance of social factors in regulating genetic action. The rift between sociology and molecular genetics is, at this point in history, very narrow indeed.

ACTORS

Perhaps the greatest benefits to sociology from paying attention to genetics are major clues about how people experience and react to their environments. As noted, most gene-environment research is premised, hopefully explicitly, on neuroscience (and increasingly the immune system, which is tightly linked to the brain): genes are related to differences in the brain, which in turn are related to how people pay attention and regulate their behaviors, learn, are motivated, and experience emotional states. And in fact, modern neuroscience is progressing by leaps and bounds in understanding these intricacies. Given the differences among individuals, what aspects of social settings matter?

Our own research has focused on one genetic variant, TaqIA, and educational continuation. The research builds on a large body of findings—many studies based on experimental designs—showing that TaqIA is associated with dopamine and how efficiently people learn from mistakes. In brief: it may be that people with TaqIA risk do not perceive adverse experiences as negatively as other people, and so they tend not to learn from their mistakes as efficiently. Because of these differences, they also tend to be more impulsive and perhaps more aggressive, prone to addictions, and distractable.

Our research began with a simple question: what happens to such people in modern settings—families, workplaces, and schools? To date, we have focused exclusively on one outcome: educational attainment. Assuming that students with TaqIA risk do not learn efficiently from their mistakes, we should see differences in how far they and students without TaqIA risk continue in their schooling. In fact, the results, which are preliminary but intriguing, suggest that TaqIA has an association with whether boys graduate from high school and continue to college. We have also found that there are several combinations of social capital that can compensate for TaqIA risk. For example, TaqIA has little effect on educational continuation among male students who report having a teacher who is a mentor. Having educated parents who are highly involved in a quality high school also makes a big difference.

One of the implications of this research is that impulsive and attentional difficulties may be decisively detrimental in classrooms, a theme that has received very little attention in sociological research on education to date. That is, molecular genetics has provided a clue as to the features of social settings that might matter and that might help students, peers, and teachers find academic success in spite of some kids' diminished capacity to learn from mistakes.

Is one implication of this research that students be genotyped for TaqIA status (thereby creating new opportunities for prejudice and discrimination)? No. Although TaqIA suggests a series of behaviors that may detract from educational processes, many children with this risk *will not* exhibit them and many children without it *will* exhibit them.

As we noted, there is a strong consensus that single genes do not cause complex behaviors in any straightforward way. To name but a few biological complications: genes often work in tandem, forming networks that are presently not well understood; within these networks, single genes may be "turned on or off" based on what other genes are doing, social experiences, and other biological processes; and RNA transcription processes—how RNA "writes out" the DNA's code to make other molecules—is far more complex than was once thought. Moreover, our research shows that the connections between TaqIA and education are highly dependent on social circumstances (forms of social capital).

The big point is that the behaviors suggested by TaqIA should now be studied with great care and, should these behaviors explain the TaqIA-education association, then the focus should be on them. Impulsivity and related behaviors, irrespective of TaqIA status, may be detrimental to educational attainment. The even bigger point is, however, that our example shows how a realistic view of the actor—one that specifies differences in how people perceive, interpret, and react to their social setting—holds the promise of enriching the study of social processes.

There is a final consideration for why sociology should engage with genetics. It's part promise of intellectual enrichment and part *realpolitik:* universities, governmental agencies, and many intellectual societies and their journals are now thoroughly interdisciplinary in their outlook. In this new intellectual environment, sociology is beginning to bring its unique expertise to a wider community of behavioral scientists who are collaboratively studying the central issues of human health and well-being. Such efforts have been and will continue to be major opportunities for intellectual cross-fertilization. The alternative would be to insist on "sociological purity" and, in the process, run the very real risk of intellectual irrelevance.

WARRIORS

We began by talking about the controversy over a "warrior gene" among New Zealand's Maori, in which we could see (alongside the promises just discussed) the dangerous side of research linking genetics and behavior. Two such dangers—genetic reductionism and genetic ascription—go hand-in-hand. Genetic reductionism refers to attempts to explain a phenomenon based solely on genetic factors. Genetic ascription extends these explanatory accounts, attributing a characteristic behavior to a group that is defined by genetic factors. The "warrior gene" case illustrates the "perfect storm" of these problems.

Yet, a distinction needs to be made between what the scientists claimed and how these claims were construed. The scientists reported differences in the percentages of MAOA alleles in subpopulations. This is a very common type of observation for a geneticist to make since many alleles differ in how they are distributed across subpopulations, a phenomenon called *population stratification*. The scientists also developed an argument to explain why these differences might make sense. Although their argument is obviously speculative, post hoc arguments of this sort—especially emphasizing migratory patterns—are also common lines of reasoning for geneticists who study population stratification.

Importantly, however, their arguments are far removed from how public discourse "processed" them: that differences in the distribution of MAOA alleles explain why the Maori commit more crimes than Caucasians. Again, genes are not related to complex behaviors in any simple way. So the vast majority of geneticists (and sociologists) are simply incredulous when confronted with reports about the "gene for X" where X refers to a complex social behavior. A gene like MAOA may indeed be related to aggressive behavior (or, for example, TaqIA to impulsivity), but these associations are highly contingent on a multitude of biological and social considerations. And of course the leap from a tendency toward aggressive impulses and committing a crime is complicated by a multitude of social factors encompassing, among other things, families, neighborhoods, and enforcement patterns. Although there is little scientific disagreement about these contingencies, such a level of nuance is difficult to convey to the public.

The warrior gene controversy is a case study in why many sociologists are (and should be) wary of genetic studies of socially-imbued behaviors: genetic reductionism and ascription, particularly in the rough-and-tumble world of public discourse, could lead to new forms of discrimination.

RESPONSIBILITIES

Reacting to the warrior gene controversy, bioethicists Dana Wensley and Michael King drew a useful distinction (and one that applies to all science). On the one hand, scientists are trained extensively in their "internal responsibilities"—making sure that the many steps of the scientific procedure are followed carefully. But many biological scientists may not be sufficiently aware of ideological baggage that they bring to their research because they are members of societies with histories of racism, sexism, and a host of unscientific presumptions about how groups differ. Sociology provides much-needed perspective on the social factors that influence the production of scientific knowledge. Indeed, this point has already been capably illustrated by ethnographic studies of, for example, how scientists in the lab study genetic markers for race and how teachers in medical schools teach about racial disparities in health.

On the other hand, according to Wensley and King, scientists also have "external responsibilities": with journalists, they share a responsibility for what groups in society do with their findings. As Wensley and King note, "Beyond the traditional obligation to provide reliable knowledge, science has an obligation to provide 'socially robust' knowledge, which can only be achieved through scientists being sensitive to the wide range of social implications of their research." These external responsibilities have been the subject of sociological research as well. How is genetic research reported in the mass media? And how do people interpret such reports? Much of this work is inspired by the research of Celeste Condit, who was trained as a rhetorician and studies how the public construes media reports about genetics and behavior and formulates understandings. This body of research suggests that media reports of genetics and behavior tend to be technically accurate but the tone of such reports often highlights the power of genes and overstates scientific understanding of how genes are related to complex outcomes. These issues of representation and construal will require further study if science is to provide "socially robust" knowledge.

Sociology thus has many roles to play with respect to both the internal and external responsibilities that Wensley and King identify. The internal responsibility is to make sure that genetic studies of behavior adequately appreciate the role of social context. Genes are highly responsive to social experiences and their associations with behavior are highly conditioned by social factors. In contributing to this line of research, sociology will likely benefit from refined views of the actor and cross-fertilization from other, closely related fields of study. The external responsibility is to make sure that society continues to appreciate the central place of social factors in shaping behaviors. Rules, scripts, norms, small group processes, and organizational and institutional structures all influence human behavior in complex ways that have little to do with genetics. This is of course the *raison d'être* of sociology. And cutting across these internal and external responsibilities, questions inspired by a sociology of knowledge perspective must also be addressed: what social forces influence how genetic research into behavior is regulated, produced, interpreted, disseminated, and used?

In what must be one of the great intellectual ironies of the behavioral sciences, it turns out that the genetic study of behavior will be markedly incomplete without reference to social forces.

RECOMMENDED RESOURCES

Peter Bearman, Sara Shostak, and Molly Martin (eds). "Exploring Genetics and Social Structure," *American Journal of Sociology* (2008), 114 (supplement). A collection of essays illustrating the diverse ways that sociology and genetics can be integrated.

Jeremy Freese and Sara Shostak. "Genetics and Social Inquiry," *Annual Review of Sociology* (2009), 35: 107–128. A broad examination of how social scientists are incorporating molecular genetics into their research and studying genetic research as a social phenomenon.

Kenneth S. Kendler, Sara Jaffee, and Dan Romer (eds). *The Dynamic Genome and Mental Health: The Role of Genes and Environments in Development* (Oxford University Press, 2010). A volume of cutting-edge papers that explore how genetic and environmental factors jointly give rise to psychopathology.

Jo C. Phelan, Bruce G. Link, and Naumi M. Feldman. "The Genomic Revolution and Beliefs about Essential Racial Differences: A Back-door to Eugenics?" *Annual Meeting of the American Sociological Association,* 2010. An empirical study that examines how people construe the meaning of race from media reports of genetic differences.

Michael J. Shanahan and Scott Hofer. "Molecular Genetics, Aging, and Well-Being: Sensitive Period, Accumulation, and Pathway Models." In Robert H. Binstock and Linda K. George (eds), *Handbook of Aging and the Social Sciences,* 7th edition (Elsevier, 2010). A discussion of recent epigenetic and transcription studies and their implications for life course models of health.

PART 2B

SOCIAL STRUCTURE

Social structures are the patterns of social relations that bind people together and give shape to their lives. Consider hierarchy, one feature of social structure. Hierarchy refers to the degree to which power is unequally distributed in a social group. The more unequal the distribution of power, the greater the degree of hierarchy. In a family, for instance, the degree of hierarchy and the position of a child in the hierarchy profoundly influence the quality of his or her life. In a highly hierarchical family, the child may grow up to resent authority or cringe before it—or both. In a family without hierarchy, the child may be spoiled and remain selfish. As these examples illustrate, who you are is partly the result of the social structures through which you pass.

Despite its importance in shaping who we are, we seldom notice social structure in our everyday lives. In fact, we often deny its significance. That is because our culture places such strong emphasis on individual freedom and responsibility. Accordingly, we learn three rules about human behaviour from an early age:

- People are perfectly free to act as they want.
- People can therefore choose right over wrong.
- If people choose wrong, we should judge them as moral inferiors.

Such thinking may be good for our egos, but it has little in common with sociology and is one of prejudice's most stubborn roots.

Émile Durkheim's *On Suicide* is a forceful, classical exposition of the way one aspect of social structure—**social solidarity**—helps to shape us. A group's level of social solidarity is higher to the degree its members share the same values and interact frequently and intimately. In the section reprinted here as Chapter 5, Durkheim argues that social solidarity anchors people to the social world. It follows, he argues, that the lower the level of social solidarity in a group, the more a group member will be inclined to take his or her own life if he or she is in deep distress. Durkheim tests his argument by examining the level of social solidarity that characterizes the major religious groups in Europe. He demonstrates that the propensity of group members to take their own lives does indeed vary inversely with social solidarity. On the strength of Durkheim's argument, we are obliged to conclude that social structure powerfully affects even an uncommon, antisocial action that is committed in private.

Durkheim worried that social solidarity was in decline in the faceless bureaucracies, anonymous cities, and giant factories of the modern world. His concern resurfaces with every major technological innovation. Thus, some analysts argue that the Internet destroys community ties by decreasing the frequency of face-to-face interaction. Yet, as Barry Wellman reports in Chapter 6, his study of one of the world's first "wired" communities near Toronto shows that the Internet does not loosen the bonds of community. Instead, it increases the volume of communication, thereby complementing "real life" and helping to establish new communities and strengthen existing ones. New technologies like the Internet change social structures, but rarely do they destroy them. Chapter 7, by Sonia Bookman, develops this important theme. She outlines the implications of social media, such as Facebook, for four areas of social life: identity, sociability, social activism, and surveillance. Reading her article should convince you that social media, while hardly socially destructive innovations, are certainly socially transformative, although not always in benign ways.

GLOSSARY

Social solidarity is higher in a group to the degree its members share the same values and interact frequently and intimately.

CRITICAL THINKING QUESTIONS

1. "Suicide varies inversely with the degree of integration of the social groups of which the individual forms a part." Explain this statement and give examples to support your answer.
2. How do cellphones decrease and increase social interaction?
3. What are the negative implications of social media, such as Facebook, for social life?

ANNOTATED BIBLIOGRAPHY

Robert Brym, "Regional Social Structure and Agrarian Radicalism in Canada: Alberta, Saskatchewan and New Brunswick." *Canadian Review of Sociology and Anthropology* (15, 3: 1978), pp. 339–51. Analyzes how the different social structures of Canadian provinces shaped political protest before World War II.

Arlie Russell Hochschild, "Emotion Work, Feeling Rules, and Social Structure." *American Journal of Sociology* (85: 1979), pp. 551–75. Shows how social structures shape the emotional life of people in different work settings.

Chapter 5

Egotistical Suicide

ÉMILE DURKHEIM, Université De Bordeaux

Anyone who glances at the map of suicides in Europe will notice at once that in purely Catholic countries, such as Spain, Portugal, and Italy, the rate of suicide is low, while it reaches its maximum in Protestant countries, such as Prussia, Saxony, and Denmark. This first impression is confirmed by the following averages, calculated by Morselli:

AVERAGE NUMBER OF SUICIDES PER MILLION INHABITANTS	
Protestant states	190
Mixed (Protestant and Catholic) states	96
Catholic states	58
Greek orthodox states	40

Now, if there is one essential difference between Catholicism and Protestantism, it is that the latter allows a great deal more freedom of inquiry than the former does. Of course, Catholicism, by the very fact that it is an idealistic religion, gives a much larger place to thought and reflection than did Graeco-Roman polytheism or Judaic monotheism. It is no longer satisfied with mechanical observances, but aspires to reign over the understanding and the conscience. It therefore addresses itself to these and, even when it demands blind submission from reason, it speaks to it in the language of reason. Yet it is also true that the Catholic receives his faith ready-made, without inquiry. He cannot even submit it to historical verification, because he is barred from reading the original texts on which it is founded. A whole hierarchical system of authorities is organized with wonderful ingenuity so as to make tradition unchanging. The Protestant is more the author of his own belief. The Bible is put into his hands and no interpretation imposed on him. The very structure of the reformed faith gives expression to this religious individualism. Nowhere except in England is the Protestant clergy organized in a hierarchy. The priest, like the ordinary believer, depends only on himself and on his conscience. He is a more learned guide than most believers, but he has no particular authority to impose dogma. But what most clearly demonstrates that this freedom of inquiry proclaimed by the founders of the Reformation has not remained at the level of some Platonic assertion is the growing number of sects of every kind, in such vigorous contrast with the indivisible unity of the Catholic Church.

We are now reaching our first conclusion, which is that the tendency toward suicide among Protestants must be related to the spirit of free inquiry that informs that religion.

Consequently, if Protestantism gives a greater place to individual thought than Catholicism, this is because it involves fewer common beliefs and practices. A religious society does not exist without a collective *credo*, and it is more or less strong and united according to whether this *credo* is more widely held. Such a society does not draw men together through an exchange and reciprocity of services, a temporal link that involves and even assumes differences, for a religious society is not able to form such a bond. It socializes them only by attaching all to a single body of doctrine and to the extent to which this body of doctrine is wider and more solidly constructed. The more ways there are to act and think that are marked by their religious character and consequently removed from free inquiry, the more the idea of God will be present in every aspect of life and make individual wills converge toward a single, identical end. Conversely, the greater the area of inquiry that a religious group abandons to the judgment of individuals, the more it will be absent from their lives, and the less cohesion and vitality it will possess. We therefore arrive at the conclusion that Protestantism's numerical superiority in suicide derives from the fact that it is a less firmly integrated Church than the Catholic one.

At the same time, we have an explanation for the situation of Judaism. The long-standing hostility of Christianity toward the Jews has created unusually strong feelings of solidarity among them. The need to struggle against general animosity, and even the impossibility of communicating freely with the rest of the population, obliged them to clasp one another tightly. As a result, each Jewish community became a little society in itself, compact and cohesive, which had a very strong feeling of its own identity and unity. Everyone within it thought and lived in the same way; individual divergences were made more or less impossible because of the communality of existence and the unceasing, tight surveillance exercised by all over each. Thus the Jewish Church found itself to be more strongly concentrated than any other, being driven back into itself by the intolerance directed against it. So, by analogy with what we have just observed on the subject of Protestantism, the disinclination of Jews to commit suicide is attributable to the same cause, despite circumstances of every kind that should, on the contrary, incline them toward it. No doubt, in a sense, they owe this privilege to the hostility that surrounds them. But while it may have this effect, it is not because it imposes a higher morality on them; rather, that it obliges them to live side by side. They are protected to this extent because the religious society to which they belong is solidly bound together. Moreover, the ostracism to which they are subject is only one of the causes that produce this result; the very nature of Jewish beliefs must also contribute to it to a great extent. Indeed, like all inferior religions, Judaism consists essentially in a body of practices that minutely control every detail of life and leave only a little room for individual judgment.

So it is not the particular nature of religious beliefs that explains the beneficial influence of religion. If religion does protect man from the desire to kill himself, it is not because it preaches to him respect for his person in itself, but because it is a community. What makes up this community is the existence of a certain number of traditional and, consequently, obligatory beliefs and practices that are common to all the faithful. The more numerous and strong these collective states are, the more the religious community is strongly integrated; and the greater, too, is its protective value. Detail of rituals and dogmas is secondary. The essential is that these rituals and dogmas should be of a kind that nourishes a sufficiently intense collective life. It is because the Protestant Church does not have the same degree of consistency as the others that it does not exercise the same moderating influence on suicide.

So, we arrive at this general conclusion: suicide rates vary inversely with the degree of integration of the social groups to which the individual belongs.

Chapter 6

Connecting Communities On and Offline

BARRY WELLMAN, Director, NetLa
University of Toron

The Internet is no longer a separate world for the techno-savvy. Tens of millions of people around the world now go online daily. Rather than isolating users in a virtual world, the Internet extends communities in the real world. People use it to connect in individualized and flexible social networks rather than in fixed and grounded groups.

The 2004 documentary film *Almost Real* tells true-life Internet stories. For some characters, the Internet provides an escape from human interaction. A recluse living alone on an abandoned North Sea oil rig runs a data storage haven supposedly free of government interference. An antisocial eight-year-old boy hides from his schoolmates through home schooling and the Web. Meanwhile, the Internet brings other people together. A man and woman in a bondage and domination relationship communicate daily over webcams thousands of miles apart. And teenagers socialize by incessantly playing a cooperative online game.

These stories are fascinating but misleading because they describe people whose social lives are wholly online. Few people dedicate most of their waking lives to the Internet. The Internet usually supplants solitary activities, like watching television, rather than other forms of social life. Most uses of the Internet are not "almost real," but are actual, quite normal interactions. The Internet has become an ordinary part of life.

Consider my own use. I have received several e-mail messages in the past hour. Friends confirm dinner for tonight. Even though it is the weekend, a student sends a question and expects a quick answer. So does a graduate student from Europe, with an urgent request for a letter of recommendation. Cousin Larry shares some political thoughts from Los Angeles. I arrange to meet friends at a local pub later in the week. My teenage niece avoids e-mail as "for adults," so I send her an instant

Source: "Connecting Communities: On and Offline" by Barry Wellman, *Contexts 3(4)*, pp. 22–28, © 2004 American Sociological Association. Reprinted by Permission of SAGE Publications.

message. And one of my most frequent correspondents writes twice: Ms. Miriam Abacha from Nigeria, wanting yet again to share her millions with me.

In addition to communication, the Internet has become an important source of information. To check facts for this article, I use Google to search the Web. It is too rainy to go out and buy a newspaper, so I skim my personalized Yahoo! News instead. My friend Joe is driving to my house for the first time and gets his directions online from MapQuest.

The Internet has burrowed into my life, but it is not separate from the rest of it. I integrate offline and online activities. I e-mail, chat, web search, and instant message—but, I also walk, drive, bike, bus, fly, phone, and send an occasional greeting card. I am not unique. Both the exotic aura of the Internet in the 1990s and the fear that it would undermine "community" have faded. The reality is that using the Internet both expands community and changes it in subtle ways.

DIGITAL DIVIDES

Between 1997 and 2001, the number of Americans using computers increased by 27 percent—from 137 million to 174 million—while the online population rose by 152 percent. Nielsen Net Ratings reported in March 2004 that three-quarters of Americans over the age of two had accessed the Internet. Many used the Internet both at home and at work, and about half went online daily. Instant messaging (IM) has spread from teenagers to adults in growing popularity, with more than one-third of all American adults now IM-ing.

A decade ago, the Internet was mainly North American, and largely the domain of young, educated, urban, white men. It has since become widely used. About one-third of users live in North America, one-third in Europe and Japan, and one-third elsewhere. India and China host many users, although the percentages of their population who are online remain small. China now has the second largest number of Internet users, growing from half a million in 1997 to 80 million in January 2004. Although the proliferation of computers is no longer headline news, 41 million PCs were shipped to retailers and customers worldwide in the first quarter of 2004.

As more people go online, the digital divide recedes. Yet, even as the overall percentage of people online rises, differences in usage rates persist: between affluent and poor, young and old, men and women, more and less educated, urban and rural, and English and non-English readers. Moreover, there are substantial international differences, even among developed countries. For instance, the digital divide between high-income households and low-income households ranges from a gap of more than 60 percentage points in the United Kingdom to less than 20 percentage points in Denmark. In the United States, 79 percent of relatively affluent people (family income of $75 000 or more) were Internet users in September 2001, when just 25 percent of poor people (family income of less than $15 000) were online. And while the gender gap is shrinking in many developed countries, it is increasing in Italy and Germany as men get connected at a higher rate than women do. Moreover, the digital divide cuts several ways. For instance, even among affluent Americans, there was a 31 percentage point gap in Internet access between those with a university education (82 percent) and those with less than a high school education (51 percent).

Digital divides are particularly wide in developing countries, where users tend to be wealthy, students, employees of large corporations, or people with easy access to cybercafés. The risk of a "digital penalty" grows as Internet use among organizations and individuals becomes routine. Those without access to the Internet will increasingly miss out on information and communication about jobs, social and political news, and community events.

The many who are using the Internet and the many more who will eventually use it face the question of how the experience might affect their lives. Fast messages, quick shopping, and instant reference works aside, widespread concerns focus on the deeper social and psychological implications of a brave new computer-mediated world.

HOPES, FEARS, AND POSSIBILITIES

Just a few years ago, hope for the Internet was utopian. Entrepreneurs saw it as a way to get rich, policymakers thought it could remake society, and business people hoped that online sales would make stock prices soar. Pundits preached the gospel of the new Internet millennium. For example, in 1995, John Perry Barlow, co-leader of the Electronic Frontier Foundation, said, "We are in the midst of the most transforming technological event since the capture of fire. I used to think that it was just the biggest thing since Gutenberg, but now I think you have to go back farther."

The media generally saw the Internet as a weird, wonderful, and sometimes scary thing. The cover of the December 1999 issue of *Wired* depicted a lithesome cyber-angel leaping off a cliff into the glorious unknown. Major newspapers unveiled special Internet sections, and new computer magazines became fat with ads, advice, and influence. The meltdown of the dot-com boom in March 2000 snuffed out many dreams of a radiant Internet future. The pages of *Wired* magazine shrank by 25 percent from September 1996 to September 2001 and another 22 percent by September 2003. Revenue and subscription rates also plummeted. The editors ruefully noted in February 2004 that their magazine "used to be as thick as a phone book."

The advent of the Internet also provoked fears of personal danger and the loss of community. News media warned of men posing as women online, cyberstalking, identity theft, and dangerous cyber-addiction. As recently as March 2004, computer scientist John Messerly warned that "computer and video games ... ruin the social and scholastic lives of many students."

Much of the hype and fear about the Internet has been both *presentist*—thinking that the world started anew with its advent—and *parochial*—thinking that only things that happened on the Internet were relevant to understanding it. Yet, sociologists have long known that technology by itself does not determine anything. Rather, people take technology and use it (or discard it) in ways its developers never dreamed. For example, the early telephone industry marketed its technology simply as a tool for practical business and spurned the notion that it could be a device for sociability. Indeed, telephones, airplanes, and automobiles enabled far-flung communities to flourish well before the coming of the Internet.

Technologies themselves neither make nor break communities. Rather, they create possibilities, opportunities, challenges, and constraints for what people and organizations can do. For example, automobiles and expressways make it possible for people to live in sprawling suburbs, but they do not determine that people will do so. Compare the sprawl of American cities with the more compact suburbs of neighbouring Canada. The Internet's low cost, widespread use, asynchronicity (people do not have to be connected simultaneously), global connectivity, and attachments (pictures, music, text) make it possible to communicate quickly and cheaply across continents and oceans. For example, emigrants use e-mail to chat with family and friends back home and visit websites to learn home news. *Yahoo! India Matrimonial* links brides and grooms in India, Europe, and North America. In countries with official censorship, emigrants use e-mail to gather news from back home and post it on websites for information hungry readers. Thus, the Internet allows mobile people to maintain community ties to distant places and also supports face-to-face ties closer to home.

COMMUNITY ONLINE AND OFFLINE

Online communication—e-mail, instant messaging, and chat rooms—does not replace more traditional offline forms of contact—face-to-face and telephone. Instead, it complements them, increasing the overall volume of contact. Where some had feared that involvement in the Internet would detract from "real life" ties with friends and relatives, intensive users of e-mail contact others in person or by phone at least as frequently as those who rarely or never use the Internet. People who frequently use the Internet to contact others also tend to be in frequent contact with people in other ways (even after taking into account differences of age, gender, and education). Extroverts especially benefit from its use, simply adding another means of communication to their contact repertoire. For example, a 2001 National Geographic survey reports that North Americans who use e-mail to discuss important matters do so an average of 41 times per month, in addition to having an average of 84 face-to-face discussions and 58 phone discussions. Those who do not use e-mail to discuss important matters have about the same number of monthly face-to-face discussions, 83, but only 36 phone discussions. Thus, those who use e-mail report 183 significant discussions per month, 54 percent more than for those who do not use e-mail. The result: the more e-mail, the more overall communication.

This is not surprising, because the Internet is not a separate world. When we talk to people about what they do on the Internet, we find out that the great majority of the people they e-mail are people they know already. They are keeping in touch between visits, often by exchanging jokes, sharing gossip, or arranging to get together. If they e-mail someone they have not already met in person, they are frequently arranging a face-to-face meeting. Telephone calls also get intermixed with e-mails, because phone chats better convey nuances, provide more intrinsic enjoyment, and better accommodate complex discussions. Andrea Baker's book *Double-Click* reports that few cyberdates stay online; they either proceed to in-person meetings or fade away. People also bring to their online interactions such offline baggage as their gender, age, family situation, lifestyle, ethnicity, jobs, wealth, and education.

E-mail is not inherently better or worse than other modes of communication. It is just different. E-mails are less intrusive than visits or phone calls and often come with useful attachments, be they baby pictures or maps to someone's home. The spread of high-speed ("broadband") Internet access makes it easier for people to integrate the Internet into the rest of their lives without long waits. By April 2004, 39 percent of U.S. Internet users had broadband at home and 55 percent either at work or home. Broadband means that people can always leave their Internet connection on so that they can spontaneously send e-mails and search websites. Broadband connections also make it easier to surf the Web and download large image, music, and video files.

The longer people have been on the Internet, the more they use it. Most Americans—and many in the developed world—have online experience. According to the Pew Internet and American Life study, by February 2004 the average American had been using the Internet for six years. Internet use is becoming even more widespread as home users get access to broadband networks and as access proliferates from desk-bound computers to small portable devices, such as "third-generation" mobile phones and personal digital assistants (Palm, Pocket PC). Yet, these small-screen, small-keyboard, lower-speed instruments are used differently than computers are: to contact a small number of close friends or relatives or to coordinate in-person meetings. Far from homogenizing people's communications, Internet technology is used in different ways by different people.

THE INTERNET GLOBALLY AND LOCALLY

A decade ago, analysts believed that as the rest of the world caught up to the United States in Internet use, they would use it in similar ways. Experience shows that this is not always so. For example, in Scandinavia and Japan, people frequently use advanced mobile phones to exchange e-mail and short text messages. Their Internet use is much less desktop-bound than that of Americans. Teens and young adults are especially heavy users of e-mail on their Internet-connected mobile telephones. Time will tell whether young people continue their heavy mobile use as they get older. Manuel Castells (2000) and his associates have shown that people in Catalonia, Spain, use the Internet more for information and services than for communication. They extensively search the Web to answer questions and book tickets, but they are much less likely to exchange e-mails. This may be because many Catalans live near each other and prefer to meet in cafés at night. Mobile phones sit beside them, ready to incorporate other close friends and relatives into conversations via short text messages. Many developing countries exhibit a different mode of use. Even if people can afford to connect to the Internet from their homes, they often do not have reliable electrical, telephone, or broadband service. In such situations, they often use public access points, such as Internet cafés or schools. They are connecting to the Internet while their neighbours sit next to them in person.

Such complexities illuminate the role the Internet can play specifically in local communities. The issue is whether the Internet has fostered a "global village," to use Marshall McLuhan's phrase, and thereby weakened local community. Some intensive and engrossing online communities do exist, such as the "BlueSky" group of young male friends who appear to live online, as described by Lori Kendall in her book *Hanging Out in the Virtual Pub*. Yet, they are a small minority. Despite the Internet's ability to connect continents at a single bound, it does not appear to be destroying local community.

For example, in the late 1990s Keith Hampton and I studied "Netville" near Toronto, a suburban housing tract of middle-priced single-family homes. The teachers, social workers, police officers, and technicians who lived there were typical people buying homes to raise young families. The community was exceptional in one important way: as part of an experiment by the telephone company, many residents were given free, high-speed Internet access and became members of a neighbourhood e-mail discussion group.

When we compared those who were given this Internet access with those who did not receive it, we found that those on the Internet knew the names of three times as many neighbours as those without Internet access. The "wired" residents had been invited into the homes of an average of 4 neighbours, compared with 2.5 for the unwired, and they regularly talked with twice as many neighbours. The Internet gave wired residents opportunities to identify others in the neighbourhood whom they might want to know better. E-mail and the discussion group made it easier for them to meet fellow residents who were not their immediate neighbours: the wired residents' local friends were more widely dispersed throughout Netville than those of the unwired. The e-mail discussion group was frequently used to discuss common concerns. These included household matters, such as plumbing and yard work, advice on setting up home computer networks, finding a local doctor, and skills for hire, such as those of a tax accountant or carpenter. As one resident commented on the discussion group: "I have walked around the neighbourhood a lot lately and I have noticed a few things. I have noticed neighbours talking to each other like they have been friends for a long time. I have noticed a closeness that you don't see in many communities."

Not only did these wired residents talk to and meet one another more, they did most of Netville's civic organizing online, for example, by warning neighbours about suspicious cars in the development and inviting neighbours to social events, such as barbecues and block parties. One typical message read: "For anybody interested there is a Sunday night bowling league looking for new people to join. It's lots of fun with prizes, playoffs and more. For both ladies and gents. If interested e-mail me back or give me a call."

These community activities built bonds for political action. When irate Netville residents protested at City Hall against the developer's plans to build more houses, it was the wired Internet members who organized the protest and showed up to make their voices heard. Others grumbled, just like new residents of housing developments have often grumbled, but the Internet supplied the social bonds and tools for organizing, for telling residents what the issues were, who the key players were, and when the protest would be.

The Netville experience suggests that when people are offered an easier way of networking with the Internet, the scope and amount of neighbourly contact can increase. Evidence from other studies also shows that the Internet supports nearby relationships. For example, the National Geographic Society asked visitors to its website about their communication with friends and relatives living within a distance of 50 kilometres. Daily Internet users contacted nearby friends and relatives 73 percent more often per year than they contacted those living further away.

At the same time, the Internet helped Netville's wired residents to maintain good ties with, and get help from, friends and relatives who lived in their former neighbourhoods. The evidence shows that Internet users are becoming "glocalized," heavily involved in both local and long-distance relationships. They make neighbourly contacts—on and offline—and they connect with far-flung friends and relatives—mostly online.

"NETWORKED INDIVIDUALISM"

As the Internet has been incorporated into everyday life, it has fostered subtle changes in community. In the old days, before the 1990s, places were largely connected—by telephone, cars, planes, and railroads.

Now with the Internet (and mobile phones), people are connected. Where before each household had a telephone number, now each person has a unique e-mail address. Many have several, in order to keep different parts of their lives separate online. This change from place-based community to person-based community had started before the Internet, but the developing personalization, portability, and ubiquitous connectivity of the Internet are facilitating the change. By April 2004, 17 percent of American users could access the Internet wirelessly from their laptop computers and the percentage is growing rapidly. As wireless portability develops from desktops to laptops and handheld devices, an individual's whereabouts become less important for contact with friends and relatives.

The Internet and other new communication technologies are facilitating a basic change in the nature of community—from physically fixed and bounded groups to social networks, which I call "networked individualism." These technologies are helping people to personalize their own communities. Instead of being rooted in homes, cafés, and workplaces, people are becoming connected as individuals, available for contact anywhere and at anytime. Instead of being bound up in a neighbourhood community where all know all, each person is becoming an individualized switchboard, linking a unique set of ties and networks. In a society where people rarely know friends of friends, there is more uncertainty about who will be supportive under what circumstances, more need to navigate among partial social networks, and more opportunity to access a variety of resources. The Internet provides communication and information resources to keep in closer touch with loved ones—from new friends to family members left behind in international migrations.

REFERENCES

Castells, Manuel. (2000). *The Rise of the Network Society*. Oxford, UK: Blackwell.

Jones, Steve, and Philip Howard, eds. (2003). *Society Online: The Internet in Context*. Thousand Oaks, CA: Sage Publications.

Rheingold, Howard. (2000). *The Virtual Community: Homesteading on the Electronic Frontier*. Cambridge, MA: MIT Press.

Wellman, Barry, and Caroline Haythornthwaite, eds. (2000). *The Internet in Everyday Life*. Oxford, UK: Blackwell.

http://www.pewinternet.org. The Pew Internet in American Life studies have carried out a large number of surveys on Internet use in American life.

http://virtualsociety.sbs.ox.ac.uk. This is a British scholarly network doing a variety of mostly qualitative analyses of Internet and society.

http://www.webuse.umd.edu. This site is an interactive statistical database that makes it relatively easy to analyze a variety of surveys about the Internet and American life.

http://www.worldinternetproject.net. This site contains the reports of survey researchers in many nations on the nature of the Internet and society.

Chapter 7

Social Media: Implication for Social Life

SONIA BOOKMAN, University of Manitoba

INTRODUCTION

Launched in 2004, Facebook has become an important feature of contemporary social life. With more than 800 million active users, it is the leading social networking site globally (Facebook, 2011; Levinson, 2009). Reflecting its growing popularity, a 2010 hit film told the story of how Facebook was founded. Its founder, Mark Zuckerberg, was named "Person of the Year" by *Time* magazine.

For many of us, Facebook is part of our everyday lives. We use it to create and craft profiles, add friends, post photos, and invite people to social events. On our birthdays, we eagerly anticipate the hundreds of birthday greetings that will be displayed on our Facebook wall (Eckler, 2011). We join Facebook pages and groups to meet others with similar interests and support social causes.

Facebook is a form of social media. Social media are playing an increasingly significant role in shaping the way we communicate, collaborate, and connect. This chapter explores some of the social implications of social media, bearing in mind that their influence is not yet fully understood since social media and their widespread adoption are relatively recent developments. The chapter begins with a definition and brief overview of social media. It then considers some of the key social consequences of social media for social life, focusing on how they are implicated in social relations, social activism, and surveillance.

SOCIAL MEDIA

Social media are a category of new media that facilitate online exchanges and interaction. They encompass a diverse range of web-based and mobile services that allow people to exchange text messages, music, photos, and videos, and participate in online communities (Dewing, 2010a).

There are five main types of social media (Dewing, 2010a; Kaplan and Haenlein, 2010). *Social networking sites* are services that people use to create personal profiles, establish a list of people they are connected to, and share information. Facebook is the most prominent of these (Dewing, 2010b). *Virtual worlds* include virtual game environments, such as World of Warcraft and Second Life. Users create three-dimensional avatars (personalized graphical representations) that interact in various settings. Second Life simulates real life. Avatars own and furnish apartments, shop in malls with "Linden Dollars," and go clubbing in virtual bars. Nearly 800 000 people log on to Second Life at least once a month (Cremore, 2011), and it is growing in popularity. *Blogs* (short for "web log") and *microblogs* consist of online journals or short status updates that allow people to communicate and comment. These include the fast-growing Twitter service, which is used to send out 140-character tweets to a network of "followers." *Collective projects* include websites where people participate in the joint creation and ongoing modification of content. A well-known example is the online encyclopedia Wikipedia. Finally, *online content communities* consist of services that allow people to share media, such as photos or videos. They include YouTube and Flickr.

Social media are distinguished from traditional mass media by four key traits (Lievrouw, 2011). First, they are characterized by *hybridity* since they enable the integration and recombination of various new and old technologies. For example, Facebook is primarily a networking site, but it combines with other media technologies such as videos, as users post links to YouTube. Second, social media are *networked* and *nonlinear*. Instead of broadcasting a message from a central producer to a mass audience, as in film or broadcast television, social media are many-to-many in their connectivity. For example, Twitter allows tweets to be sent by "Tweetheart" celebrities, such as Ashton Kutcher, to millions of "followers" at once. Individuals and groups (such as TwitterMoms) in a network can also respond, comment, or view the whole conversation online (Levinson, 2009). Third, social media are *interactive*. Instead of providing people with a finished product, the content of social media is user generated and continually modified in collaborative fashion. Think of how much content on Facebook is actually contributed by users, who upload upward of 250 million photos a day (Facebook, 2011). Finally, social media are *almost everywhere all the time*, wherever an Internet or a mobile phone connection is available.

With a growing number of mobile devices, from the BlackBerry and the iPhone to wireless tablets, we can be "always on" and linked in to various networks.

Some 83 percent of Canadians enjoy Internet access and we have adopted social media quickly and widely (Ipsos Reid, 2011). According to a 2009 survey, 80 percent of Canadian Internet users engage in social media, making Canadians the top social media users in the world (Dewing, 2010b). A 2011 survey found that over half of Canadian Internet users access social networking sites, and of those, 90 percent had a Facebook account (Ipsos Reid, 2011).

While more and more Canadians are using social media, rates of use vary among different groups. For example, only 65 percent of rural dwellers are likely to be online, and they engage in fewer web-based activities than city residents do, partly owing to a lack of high-speed service (Dewing, 2010b). In addition, social media are used more extensively by young people. According to 2009 figures, of people under 35 who were online, 86 percent had a social network profile, compared with 44 percent of those over 55 (Dewing, 2010b). However, this gap is shrinking. As a 2011 survey showed, 94 percent of new social networking profiles were opened by Canadians over 35 (Ipsos Reid, 2011).

MEDIATING SOCIAL RELATIONS

What are the implications of social media for our identities, the way we think about who we are? How do they shape the way we socialize and connect with others? Much of the initial research on the social impact of social media was contradictory. It trumpeted either social media's ability to help create liberating new identities and communities or its capacity to isolate people from one another by reducing face-to-face interaction (Woolgar, 2002: 9). Since then, however, research has produced more nuanced accounts of the way we express identities and socialize through social media (Flew and Smith, 2011).

IDENTITY

Let's first consider the question of identity. Writing in the mid-1990s, Sherry Turkle (1995) argued that virtual worlds would enable people to construct and express their identities in new and potentially liberating ways. Examining how people engaged with virtual worlds, such as MUDs (multi-user dungeons) and MOOs (multi-user object-oriented domains), she proposed that these text-based precursors to Second Life operated as "identity workshops." Unlimited by an embodied presence, people could experiment with their identities in these spaces: "the obese can become slender, the beautiful plain, the 'nerdy' sophisticated" (Turkle, 1995: 12). In Second Life, participants design a customized avatar by selecting body type, hair colour, clothing, tattoos, and more, shaping the way they will look to others. This allows people to play with their self-presentation. For Turkle, online identity play suggests a fluidity of identity, consistent with postmodern arguments that identity is not singular and constant but variable and multiplex—an ongoing construction project, as it were (Bell, 2001: 115). Social media of all types afford ample opportunity to construct our selves as we shape and adjust our personal profiles, modify the look of our avatars, and manage our presentation of self.

However, many writers have noted the limits to online identity play. Virtual worlds are not separate from real life; we bring our embodied selves and "baggage" to the way we present our selves in online worlds. Although it is possible in principle to swap genders in virtual worlds, such as Second Life, various accounts suggest that this is not common practice (Bell, 2001). Furthermore, possibilities for identity play vary, depending on the type of social media we are using to express our selves (Baym, 2006). Facebook profiles usually correspond fairly closely with our real life identities and are contextualized in offline social contexts by displaying photos or links to local events. That is because the people we interact with on Facebook include online and many offline friends. Still, our profiles on social networking sites are carefully crafted as we construct, edit, and perform idealized versions of our selves, selecting images, "likes," and activities to shape impressions about who we are (Utz, 2010).

Recently, Turkle (2011) has reconsidered her earlier enthusiasm about online identities and possibilities for self-expression. With the growth in mobile social media technologies, she argues that we are now expected to be available at all times—to respond to Facebook messages and tweets even when on holiday or having dinner with friends. Significant amounts of time and anxiety-ridden energy go into maintaining and managing our online profiles and relationships. It is increasingly difficult to just turn off and relax. What kind of interests and life should I say I have on Facebook? Who should I be friends with online? Constant online performances not only represent but also reshape us: "Over time, such performances of identity may feel like identity itself" (Turkle, 2011: 12). Social media technologies are so much a part of us, we don't feel like ourselves without them; we are tethered. The question that continues to concern Turkle is how our identities are being reshaped by the new realities of life online.

SOCIABILITY

Let's now consider how social media are implicated in the formation of online groups and virtual communities. In one of the most influential early accounts of online communities, Rheingold (1993) argued that the Internet was a new frontier for forging social connections, unbound by local time or location. He was enthusiastic about the potential for virtual communities to reinvigorate community building and social engagement. Based on shared interests, such virtual communities are nurtured over time, through participation in discussion and information sharing. Rheingold's version of community evokes the nostalgic image of a traditional, tight-knit circle of friends that we might find in a neighbourhood pub (Bell, 2001).

Established in 1998, the GimpGirl Community illustrates this potential. It is an online group whose members and organizers are women living with disabilities. Using a range of social media from list-servs and MOOs to Second Life, Facebook, and Twitter, the group was initiated to create a "safe, open space" where like-minded individuals could discuss issues of common concern, share information, and participate in community building (Cole et al., 2011: 1161). Members socialize and share personal writings and art. They provide emotional support and offer links to resources for women with disabilities. While disagreements occur and debates arise over group definition, these are moderated by staff members who endeavour to ensure a welcoming environment. Persisting over many years, this group forms an important part of many members' social lives and plays a significant role in the articulation of identity—what it means to be a woman with disabilities.

Not all online groups conform to this ideal of virtual community. There is a great deal of variation among online groups, just as there is offline (Baym, 2006). Some online groupings are less robust or intimately connected. For example, Twitter feeds are networks of loosely associated individuals who share an interest in a particular topic or celebrity. These groups are more temporary than Rheingold's virtual communities. People can opt out as easily as they join in, and they flit between Twitter feeds. Other groups, such as those that emerge in online gaming worlds, are more enduring and involve more intense interaction. For example, World of Warcraft encourages the development of teams in the form of clans or guilds. Members take on specific roles via their avatars and coordinate actions with others to pursue a common goal. While playing in character, members socialize online in groups that last from hours to years (Schroeder, 2011).

David Bell prefers to use the German word *bund* (covenant) to think about these kinds of online social groupings. A bund is "an elective grouping, bonded by affective and emotional solidarity, sharing a strong sense of belonging" (Bell, 2001: 107). For Bell, this concept is somewhat more open than Rheingold's version of "virtual community." It better reflects the interest-based, elective, and diverse kinds of online sociability facilitated by Facebook groups, blogging communities, and virtual gaming worlds.

While social media provide new possibilities for socializing online, it is important to remember that virtual communities do not exist in a vacuum. They are embedded in our everyday real worlds and offline social lives (see Wellman, Chapter 6). The groups that we establish online are often extensions of offline sociability and they enhance it. With social media, many of us now enjoy a mash-up of online and offline social lives that we move between with ease (Turkle, 2011).

SOCIAL ACTIVISM

Increasingly, we use social media to debate social issues, engage in social activism, and mobilize social movements. Social media have become a means of facilitating social change. Many books are dedicated to this aspect of social media, with such titles as *Cyberactivism* (McCaughey and Ayers, 2003) and *@ Is for Activism* (Hands, 2011).

Scholars have identified two main ways in which social media facilitate social activism. First, people use social media for awareness or advocacy purposes. Second, they use social media to organize and mobilize others for political action (Harlow, 2011; Vegh, 2003). Of course, the potential of social media to enhance the effectiveness of activism depends on access to technology and know-how; it is limited by the "digital divide," which separates urban, better-educated, and higher-income people from others (Brodock, 2010).

With regard to awareness and advocacy, social media allow people to share information and draw attention to causes and issues of concern in a way that bypasses conventional media gatekeepers. Using blogs, Twitter, and independent news sites, activists create content and disseminate their own news stories. By posting reports, videos, and local news, people engage in participatory journalism (Lievrouw, 2011: 120). The creation of such independent, alternative media has played a central role in the widely studied global justice movement. In 1999, the movement held demonstrations in Seattle to coincide with the meeting of the World Trade Organization. It was here that activists set up the first Independent Media Centre (IMC). The IMC site offered streaming video and audio reports, providing in-depth coverage of the event as a counterpoint to accounts in the mainstream media (Lievrouw, 2011). Since then, a network of 175 IMCs has been established to follow movement activity and circulate news content submitted by users. Along the same lines, activists involved with the Occupy Wall Street movement developed an online *Occupied Wall Street Journal* to disseminate information. They used YouTube videos to expose incidents of violence against participants. In addition, members of the movement are establishing a social network that allows them to convene, share information, and build solidarity (Community Team, 2011).

The networked dimension of social media facilitates the organization and mobilization of social activists. Social networking sites enable people to cultivate large networks of online and offline "friends." Facebook messages travel rapidly and from many to many, unrestricted by time and space. Each Facebook user has approximately 130 "friends," so if one user posts a message requesting support for a cause, it can travel to many people quickly. This feature of social networking sites allows social movements to enlist the support and participation of interested individuals at the click of a mouse.

Such networks can be mobilized to engage in at least two kinds of collective action (Harlow, 2011). The first includes mediated online action, such as signing online petitions or conducting email campaigns. Some writers suggest that the simplicity of such online activism leads to "slacktivism," giving people the false impression that they are socially engaged by clicking "like" on a Facebook page established for a cause (Scholz, 2010). Instead of relying solely on online involvement, analysts of digital activism suggest that combining online and offline activity is important to sustaining social movements (Kavada, 2010). Indeed, many social activists use social media networks to coordinate offline protests, demonstrations, and other events. This has certainly been the case for the global justice movement, which has enlisted an array of social media to organize street protests and demonstrations around the world in a short time (Lievrouw, 2011). Social media such as Twitter also played a significant role in recent civil uprisings in Egypt and elsewhere in the Middle East and North Africa. Because of their ubiquity and mobility, technologies like Twitter quickly facilitate the mobilization of a critical mass. Much hype was generated in the mainstream media about the so-called "Twitter revolutions" based on the notion that these were new kinds of uprisings "coordinated online in real time" with social media technologies (Hands, 2011: 1). However, others caution against claims that Twitter was at the root of social activism and change (Hands, 2011).

Recent studies highlight how people use social media to initiate online activism that subsequently moves offline. For example, Harlow (2011) documents how social media, such as Facebook and Twitter, were used to generate a pro-justice and anti-violence movement in Guatemala. Following the shooting of a prominent lawyer, young Guatemalans, frustrated with high levels of violence in the country, started Facebook fan pages and groups to inform the public and call for justice. The pages brought together thousands of like-minded Facebook users, who made comments, followed threads, and built solidarity. This online "virtual" movement prompted offline "real" world action, spilling over to the streets in the form of mass demonstrations and public protests (Harlow, 2011).

SURVEILLANCE

The same social media technologies that enable social activism are used as a means of surveillance and social control by authorities. Surveillance involves "focused systematic and routine attention to personal details for the purposes of influence, management, protection, or direction" (David Lyon, quoted in Flew and Smith, 2011: 231). Some surveillance is planned, some unintended. Targeted surveillance is facilitated by sophisticated monitoring systems that intercept communications, including text messages and tweets. These systems can also track location with mobile phone positioning technologies, scan messages for certain words, and recognize voices. Companies sell surveillance technology to law enforcement agencies around the world. Although usually employed with strict privacy protections, the authors of a recent article show how surveillance technologies have also been used to repress civil uprisings (Silver and Elgin, 2011). They give the example of Bahrain, where authorities gathered information about rights activists by monitoring their text messages and other online communications, resulting in their persecution and imprisonment.

More broadly, social media allow people, companies, and organizations to watch, profile, and monitor us. We produce a mountain of data about ourselves through social media. We take photos on our mobile phones and post them on Facebook. These photos are tagged with detailed information, such as the date, location, and names of those pictured. We share ideas in blogs and update our whereabouts on Twitter. On Facebook alone, users shared more than six billion photos, wall messages, and status updates every *week* during 2010 (Flew and Smith, 2011). This digital content is not easily deleted, and employers use it to screen candidates for jobs and monitor employee behaviour. Police use information posted by the public on sites like YouTube as evidence in crime investigations. For example, after the 2011 Stanley Cup riots in Vancouver, police gathered evidence from social media sites and set up a 2011 Riot website to track down people responsible for looting and property damage. The website asked the public to submit photos or video footage taken at the scene and identify individuals from the thousands of photos the public had already provided (Vancouver Police Department, 2011). In addition, corporations keep track of our online consumption choices and use the data we create using social media to tailor marketing strategies to particular demographic niches. For instance, PlanetOut. com is a popular online portal serving the lesbian, gay, bisexual, and transgendered communities. It functions as a meeting place, shopping mall, and newsroom for millions of members. It is presented to members as a virtual community, but it is also used by corporate marketers to solicit data used in targeted marketing (Campbell, 2005).

Sensing that we are constantly watched, we watch ourselves; we monitor our online behaviour, conforming to certain norms and the expectations of those who might see us (Turkle, 2011). Resigned to a lack of privacy, some teens remind each other not to post certain pictures and to be careful about the information they post, concerned that school officials or the police might look up their profiles. Furthermore, they realize that in a world of cut, edit, and paste, the information they generate is public and permanent. Nonetheless, it seems that most young people ignore the dangers of surveillance as they enjoy engaging in social media.

REFERENCES

Baym, Nancy. (2006). "Interpersonal Life Online." In Leah Lievrouw and Sonia Livingstone, eds., *The Handbook of New Media: Social Shaping and Social Consequences of ICTs,* updated student ed. (pp. 35–54). London: Sage.

Bell, David. (2001). *An Introduction to Cybercultures.* London: Routledge.

Brodock, Katharine. (2010). "Economic and Social Factors: The Digital (Activism) Divide." In Mary Joyce, ed., *Digital Activism Decoded: The New Mechanics of Change* (pp. 71–84). New York: International Debate Education Association.

Campbell, John. (2005). "Outing PlanetOut: Surveillance, Gay Marketing and Internet Affinity Portals." *New Media Society,* 7 (5), 663–83.

Cole, Jennifer, Jason Nolan, Yukari Seko, Katherine Mancuso, and Alejandra Ospina. (2011). "GimpGirl Grows Up: Women with Disabilities Rethinking, Redefining, and Reclaiming Community." *New Media Society, 13* (7), 1161–79.

Community Team. (2011). "Would You Join a Facebook-Style Occupy Social network?" *CBC News,* 28 December. On the World Wide Web at http://www.cbc.ca/news/yourcommunity/2011/12/would-you-join-a-facebook-style-occupy-social-network.html (retrieved 1 August 2012).

Cremore, Lowell. (2011). "First Quarter 2011 Results for Second Life: Steady Sailing." *The Metaverse Journal* 12 May. On the World Wide Web at http://www.metaversejournal.com/2011/05/12/first-quarter-2011-results-for-second-life-steady-sailing/ (retrieved 1 August 2012).

Dewing, Michael. (2010a). *Social Media: 1. An Introduction.* Background Paper No. 2010-03-E. Ottawa: Library of Parliament.

Dewing, Michael. (2010b). *Social Media: 2. Who Uses Them?* Background Paper No. 2010-05-E. Ottawa: Library of Parliament.

Eckler, Rebecca. (2011). "This Is My Best Birthday Ever." *Maclean's Magazine* 26 September, 75.

Facebook. (2011). "Statistics." On the World Wide Web at http://www.facebook.com/press/info.php?statistics (retrieved 1 August 2012).

Flew, Terry and Smith, Richard. (2011). *New Media: An Introduction,* Cdn ed. Toronto: Oxford University Press.

Hands, Joss. (2011). *@ Is for Activism: Dissent, Resistance and Rebellion in a Digital Culture.* London: Pluto Press.

Harlow, Summer. (2011). "Social Media and Social Movements: Facebook and an Online Guatemalan Justice Movement that Moved Offline." *New Media & Society* (August 5, online), 1–19.

Ipsos Reid. (2011). *The Ipsos Canadian Inter@ctive Reid Report 2011 Fact Guide.* On the World Wide Web at http://www.ipsos-na.com/knowledge-ideas/media-content-technology/research-briefings/Default.aspx?q=the-canadian-internet-fact-guide (retrieved 1 August 2012).

Kaplan, Andreas and Michael Haenlein. (2010). "Users of the World, Unite! The Challenges and Opportunities of Social Media." *Business Horizons, 53,* 59–68.

Kavada, Anastasia. (2010). "Activism Transforms Digital: The Social Movement Perspective." In Mary Joyce, ed., *Digital Activism Decoded: The New Mechanics of Change* (pp. 101–18). New York: International Debate Education Association.

Levinson, Paul. (2009). *New New Media.* Boston: Allyn & Bacon.

Lievrouw, Leah. (2011). *Alternative and Activist New Media.* Cambridge, UK: Polity Press.

McCaughey, Martha and Michael Ayers. (2003). *Cyberactivism: Online Activism in Theory and Practice.* London: Routledge.

Rheingold, Howard. (1993). *The Virtual Community: Finding Connection in a Computerized World.* London: Secker & Warburg.

Scholz, Trebor. (2010). "Infrastructure: Its Transformations and Effect on Digital Activism." In Mary Joyce, ed., *Digital Activism Decoded: The New Mechanics of Change* (pp. 17–32). New York: International Debate Education Association.

Schroeder, Ralph. (2011). *Being There Together: Social Interaction in Virtual Environments.* Oxford, UK: Oxford University Press.

Silver, Vernon and Ben Elgin. (2011). "Torture in Bahrain Becomes Routine With Help From Nokia Siemens." *Bloomberg* 23 August. On the World Wide Web at http://www.bloomberg.com/news/2011-08-22/torture-in-bahrain-becomes-routine-with-help-from-nokia-siemens-networking.html (26 December 2011).

Turkle, Sherry. (1995). *Life on the Screen: Identity in the Age of the Internet.* New York: Simon & Schuster.

Turkle, Sherry. (2011). *Alone Together: Why We Expect More from Technology and Less from Each Other.* New York: Basic Books.

Utz, Sonja. (2010). "Show Me Your Friends and I Will Tell You What Type of Person You Are: How One's Profile, Number of Friends, and Type of Friends Influence Impression Formation on Social Network Sites." *Journal of Computer-Mediated Communication, 15,* 314–35.

Vancouver Police Department. (2011). "Riot 2011." On the World Wide Web at https://vancouver.ca/police/riot2011/index.html (retrieved 1 August 2012).

Vegh, Sandor. (2003). "Classifying Forms of Online Activism: The Case of Cyberprotests Against the World Bank." In Martha McCaughey and Michael Ayers, eds., *Cyberactivism: Online Activism in Theory and Practice* (pp. 71–96). London: Routledge.

Woolgar, Steve. (2002). "Five Rules of Virtuality." In Steve Woolgar, ed., *Virtual Society? Technology, Cyberbole, Reality* (pp. 1–22). Oxford, UK: Oxford University Press.

PART 2C

CULTURE

Chapter 8 - Movies and Society, by Shyon Baumann, University of Toronto

Chapter 9 - Do Video Games Kill?, by Karen Sternheimer, University of Southern California

Earlier, I defined *culture* as the languages, laws, sciences, values, customs, practices, and beliefs of the groups to which people belong. Chapters 8 and 9 explain how two elements of popular culture—movies and video games—affect social behaviour.

In Chapter 8, Shyon Baumann first shows how economic and cultural forces shape movie content and production. He then finds that movies influence some individuals' behaviour; a certain number of children and adolescents who watch violent films apparently tend to become more verbally and physically aggressive, at least in the short term.

However, in Chapter 9, Karen Sternheimer explains that the number of children and adolescents who are encouraged to act violently by media violence is small. Moreover, social circumstances having nothing to do with media violence typically prompt this small group of children to engage in violent action. These background circumstances include poverty, schoolyard bullying, ineffective parenting, dysfunctional communities and neighbourhoods, and the availability of guns. Sternheimer concludes that the independent effect of media violence on real-world violence is actually minimal.

CRITICAL THINKING QUESTIONS

1. Apply insights from Baumann's analysis of movies to another element of popular culture, such as music. How does society shape music? How does music shape society?
2. Based on the findings of Bauman and Sternheimer, what policy recommendations would you make for lowering youth violence?

ANNOTATED BIBLIOGRAPHY

Richard Gruneau and David Whitson, *Hockey Night in Canada: Sport, Identities and Cultural Politics* (Toronto: Garamond, 1993). The authors place Canada's national sport under the microscope in this engaging account. They show how the global marketplace for commercial spectacle has altered the game and, along with it, Canadians' sense of themselves.

John R. Hall, Laura Grindstaff, and Ming-Cheng Lo, eds., *Handbook of Cultural Sociology* (New York: Taylor & Francis, 2010). Sixty-five essays by leadings experts in the field comprehensively analyze the relationship of culture to social structure and everyday life.

Chapter 8

Movies and Society

SHYON BAUMANN, University of Toronto

THE SOCIOLOGY OF FILM

Quick—name a movie star. Is there anyone who cannot name one— or 20? Is there anyone who does not know where Hollywood is, or who has not seen an image of the Hollywood sign, spelling out the place name in giant white letters on a hillside? The movies occupy a central place in our popular culture, just as they do in many other cultures around the world. Millions of Canadians see movies in theatres every year, and millions more see movies on television and DVD.

As an integral part of our popular culture, movies merit close socio-logical examination. The primary question of interest for sociologists of film is, What is the relationship between movies and society? Two sec-ondary questions are built into the primary question. First, how do social factors influence the kinds of movies that are made? In other words, how do the social and organizational conditions under which movies are made affect their content? The second question reverses the causal arrow. It asks how movies influence society, particularly the attitudes and behav-iours of audience members. As we will see, there is good evidence for arguing that just as society influences movies, movies influence society.

TWO PERSPECTIVES ON HOW SOCIETY INFLUENCES FILM

ORGANIZATIONAL ANALYSIS

Do films represent the creative thoughts and actions of filmmakers? Of course they do. For example, the six *Star Wars* films bear the mark of the primary creative force behind them, writer and producer George Lucas. The distinctive characters and plotlines are his inven-tions. But a sociological perspective can show how movies reflect more than individual creativity. A review of the film industry's organizational history demonstrates how the way in which filmmaking has been organized played a role in shaping the kinds of films that were made (Peterson, 1994). The organizational foundations of filmmaking were, in turn, influenced by wider social factors.

Depending on which sources you consult, a camera that could take moving pictures was either a French or an American invention, though inventors in both countries probably contributed equally to the final product. Regardless of who gets the credit, moving pictures were invented in the final decade of the nineteenth century without any awareness that they would form the basis of a major cultural industry and art form for decades to come. In fact, moving pictures were first used to document everyday events for scientific and informational purposes. Not long after they were invented, however, cultural entrepreneurs realized their entertainment potential.

To capitalize on audience interest, many owners of shops and lunch counters converted their stores and restaurants into makeshift cinemas. Initially, movies were just a few minutes long, but the new technology so dazzled audiences, they would pay just to see footage of a train approaching or a horse galloping. By the second decade of the twentieth century, however, movies had already begun to develop in length and content and to adopt the narrative style with which we are familiar today. As movies evolved, so did the industrial organization of film production and distribution. Movie theatres seating hundreds and even thousands of people were built. A small group of companies emerged as forerunners in film production, with production facilities in Los Angeles to take advantage of the consistently favourable weather for filming.

Before long, this small group of companies was responsible for the vast majority of films being made in the United States, which also meant that they were responsible for the vast majority of films being seen in the United States and in many other countries, including Canada. Before television became widespread in the late 1940s and early 1950s, movies were the primary form of mass entertainment. A large proportion of the population attended the movies weekly, and it was not uncommon for people to go to the movies several times a week (Brown, 1995). Movies were big business, and they continue to be big business today, even though people see fewer movies than they used to.

Despite the economic success of the film industry, movies were heavily criticized at the time for being formulaic. That is, critics found movies to be bland, predictable, and altogether too similar (White, 1936). Part of their criticism of the movies was directed at the way movies were made.

Because they were the default entertainment option for many people, films were virtually guaranteed a minimum audience size. The incentive for the film companies, then, was to produce a large number of films to meet the high demand. This supply and demand dynamic encouraged a production process for films that resembled that for most other mass-produced goods. For the sake of efficiency, film companies made films in assembly-line fashion. Moreover, the centralization of production by a handful of companies meant that there were relatively few opportunities to create diversity in the kinds of films that were made. Adding to uniformity was the system of "block booking" that studios forced on theatre owners (Hanssen, 2000). Theatre owners leased movies from studios, but rather than being allowed to choose which movies they leased, they were required to lease whole "blocks" of films, ranging from three or four to about 20 at a time. Of these blocks of films, only one or two would be "A" movies, and the rest would be cheaply made "B" movies. To book "A" movies, theatre owners had to book the more numerous "B" movies as well. For the most part, this method "encouraged the production and consumption of as vast an avalanche of triviality as has ever been inflicted on a public," where the workers involved in producing "B" movies "seemed to consider the assignment a chore below their personal dignity, to be performed perfunctorily, carelessly and ineptly" (Mayer, 1948).

As a whole, the films produced in Hollywood during the era of the "studio system" bear the stamp of the method through which they were created. A "Fordist" assembly-line production model fashioned films that were largely standardized. Unlike cars, however, there were some standout films that exhibited the artistic impulses of particular directors, producers, and screenwriters. Orson Welles, the director of such films as *Citizen Kane* and *The Magnificent Ambersons*, fought hard for his artistic independence from studio executives and was able to make lasting works of art as a result. Walt Disney founded his own studio to pursue the art of animation and was able to create *Snow White and the Seven Dwarfs* and *Fantasia* among many other treasured films. Although these great films are still appreciated today, they are exceptions to the general character of films produced by the studio system.

The studio system came to an end in the 1950s. For a variety of reasons, including the introduction of television, suburbanization, and a rising birth rate, film audience numbers fell dramatically. In the absence of guaranteed audiences, the assembly-line production method of the studio system was no longer effective. Over the next few decades, new modes of production emerged to suit the changing economic circumstances of the film industry.

The current model for film production is the "blockbuster" model. Production companies make a smaller number of films, and within that smaller pool, they select a few to receive most of the funding for production and promotion. In effect, they put most of their eggs in a few baskets. This production logic has, again, an economic foundation. Great uncertainty surrounds every film; producers do not know if an audience will turn up at the theatres. By investing large sums in the production and promotion of certain films, studios increase the likelihood that audiences will flock to them. An example is *The Dark Knight*, which was made for about US$185 million and grossed US$970 million worldwide. Despite these efforts, big-budget films often fail. For example, one failure was *Evan Almighty*, starring Steve Carell and Morgan Freeman. It cost approximately US$200 million to produce and market, but generated worldwide revenue of just over US$170 million. For this reason, the studios hedge their bets and produce smaller budget films on the off chance that they will strike a chord with audiences. While many of these films also lose money, others are surprisingly successful. The original *Texas Chainsaw Massacre*, for example, was made for around US$140 000 and grossed more than US$30 million in 1974. More recently, the remake of that movie was produced for about US$9 million in 2003 and grossed more than US$80 million in the United States and tens of millions of dollars more in overseas markets (www.imdb.com). The blockbuster production model is profitable for studios because the popular films generate more than enough profit to cover the losses incurred by unpopular films.

As with the studio system, the blockbuster system involves a correspondence between the production model and the nature of the films that are made. The blockbuster system encourages the making of narrative and visual spectacles designed to generate fascination, mass interest, and big profits. Such films as *Titanic*, *Spiderman*, and *The Lord of the Rings* trilogy rely on stunning visual effects and archetypal storylines of good versus evil to appeal to as wide an audience as possible, not just domestically but around the globe. Such films require enormous capital investment, so film studios want to franchise them. After all, spinoff toys, video games, and sequels can add much to the bottom line. Films that can be franchised are more likely to be produced and to be given large budgets.

Films that do not receive as much funding for production and promotion tend to be given more freedom to experiment with narrative elements and lesser-known actors. Sometimes, these lower-budget productions pay off hugely and become hits, as in the case of *My Big Fat Greek Wedding* and *Slumdog Millionaire*.

In sum, an organizational perspective offers an important corrective to the conventional view that cultural productions, such as movies, represent only the work of individual creators. Individual creators surely have an influence on the final product, but if we want to understand the character of movies, it is crucial to take into account the organizational conditions under which they are made.

CULTURAL REFLECTION

A second perspective for understanding how social factors influence the content of films points to the elements of culture reflected in them. In this view, films mirror society for two main reasons. First, filmmaking occurs within a social context and is constrained by that context. Second, films are designed to be popular with audiences and so are made to reflect the interests and concerns of audience members.

As with other artistic media, movies are preoccupied with universal themes, such as love and intimacy, family life, growing up, and examining what constitutes true happiness. Because these issues are an integral part of our culture, they enjoy a central place in movies.

Films also mirror society at the level of everyday life. Thus, movies today differ in many ways from the movies of, say, the 1920s. That is partly because the technology of filmmaking has evolved. Today, sound, editing, lighting, camera work, and special effects create movies that look entirely different from the films of the past. Today's movies also look different from movies made in the past because (with the exception of movies set in the future or in the past) they must realistically depict the lives of characters in contemporary social settings, and these settings, including the objects people encounter in everyday life, change over time.

Just as the facts of our everyday existence evolve over time, so do important social problems, concerns, and interests. Consider the villains that populate movies. During the Cold War (1947–91), many people in North America felt threatened by communism, particularly communist infiltration of Western democracies and nuclear annihilation at the hands of communists. Films from that period often featured communists, especially Soviets, as archetypal bad guys. Since the fall of communism in the Soviet Union and Eastern Europe, the threat no longer looms large in the public consciousness. Communist villains are neither plausible nor interesting to today's audiences. As a result, they generally no longer appear in films. The public is now preoccupied with the threat of terrorism, and that is reflected in an increase in the depiction of terrorist villains in recent films, such as *The Sum of All Fears*, *Spy Game*, *The Siege*, and *Collateral Damage*, among many others.

The Cold War is just one of many evolving social concerns and interests that are reflected in the movies. Following the rise of feminism in the 1960s, people became more interested in exploring the roles of women in society, and films reflected that interest. The same can be said of such issues as environmental protection, corporate crime, government corruption, genetic engineering, and HIV/AIDS.

Film scholars argue that social concerns influence films at a deeper, metaphorical level, too. Accordingly, even films not explicitly dealing with the Cold War can be interpreted as expressions of the anxiety associated with it. Science fiction films in which aliens seek to expand their dominion by colonizing Earth were especially popular in the 1950s, when Cold War anxieties were at their peak. The aliens embodied many of the qualities that were attributed to communists; they were godless, emotionless invaders intent on destroying Western democracy, traditions, and prosperity (Hendershot, 1999).

Similarly, horror films often depict creatures that afflict humans through implantation or infection. They often end up inside people or they take the form of people. One interpretation of this recurring theme is that it reflects anxiety over health and illness, particularly the viruses, bacteria, and cancers that invade and destroy their human hosts (Guerrero, 1990). *Alien* and its three sequels, for example, involve a vicious monster that reproduces itself by inhabiting a human host who is killed when the creature is eventually "born." At a certain level, a film in which people are saved from the dangers of bodily invasion and destruction reassures the audience that it can be saved from the dangers of real-world illness.

HOW FILMS SHAPE SOCIETY

Having considered two ways in which society influences the movies, let us now examine how movies influence society. For almost as long as movies have been made, people have feared that they corrupt us. Initially, concern arose from the fact that moving images proved to be a captivating and fascinating innovation in a way that is hard to imagine for people like us who grew up with the movies. Observers predicted disastrous consequences, including the thoughtless imitation of dangerous activities, the learning of criminal techniques, and the rapid deterioration of moral standards.

By the late 1920s, such concern initiated the Payne Fund Studies, which attempted to assess whether going to the movies influenced children negatively. The studies have been thoroughly criticized for their flawed methods and suspect findings. Nevertheless, they indicate the high level of early concern over the possibility—and, in some people's minds, the certainty—that movies were corrupting youth.

More than 80 years later, that fear has not abated. New articles about the dangers of the movies appear in the popular press without any pretence of social scientific rigour. We often read that the movies are responsible for promiscuity, materialism, violence, depression, loss of religion, sexism, ageism, racism, and much else. These are serious allegations, but before we conclude that movies actually have these effects, we need strong evidence.

Movies may influence people on both the societal and the individual level. Societal-level influences include those that change the nature of our culture, particularly our norms and values. Consider materialism—the view that wealth buys happiness. Some people note that movies typically depict wealthy lifestyles as a source of happiness. The lavish and hedonistic lives of movie stars reinforce the message. How many North Americans envied Jennifer Lopez when Ben Affleck proposed to her with a pink diamond engagement ring worth more than $1 million? People are more inclined to accept the notion that wealth buys happiness when they are surrounded by such images.

The problem with arguments about societal-level influences is that they are difficult to support or refute with data. There are two reasons for this. First, our culture is affected by many social forces of which the movies are only one. We have no way of separating the effect of movies from all other effects. In the case of materialism, for example, we cannot know if changing values result from changing levels of wealth, changing levels of wealth inequality, messages contained in mass media other than movies, or many other factors. Movies may play a large role, a small role, or no role at all. Given what we know about the complexity of cultural change in general, however, it seems highly unlikely that the movies play a large role in shaping society's values. It is more likely that they reflect existing values.

The second reason for doubting arguments about the societal-level influence of films is that such arguments assume films are understood by members of society in the same way and affect them similarly. We know, however, that some people never or infrequently see films and that different people take away different messages from the same film. For example, do people become more tolerant of promiscuity when they see it portrayed in movies or more repulsed? Without knowing what messages audience members are getting from films, it is impossible to make an argument about how films influence society.

Arguments about certain kinds of *individual-level* effects stand on firmer empirical ground. These arguments hold that movies shape the attitudes and behaviours of individuals in specific ways. For example, one vein of research on the effects of movies investigates whether exposure to movies in which the characters smoke increases the likelihood that young people who see these movies will take up smoking. The most recent studies on this topic asked a large number of adolescents about the movies they had seen in recent years and whether they had ever tried smoking (Sargent et al., 2005; Sargent et al., 2007). It found that increased exposure to movies in which characters smoked was correlated with the likelihood that an adolescent would try smoking, even after taking into account many other factors usually associated with starting smoking. Thus, while movies are by no means the only relevant factor, they seem to have an influence on smoking initiation among some adolescents. Research done in this fashion, however, only gains general acceptance by scholars as reliable after many replications. Time will tell if these initial results hold up.

A much larger body of research conducted over the past 40 years has been done on the topic of violence, again focusing on the potential effects on children. This research attempts to understand whether and in what ways individuals are affected by onscreen violence. Studies take the form of laboratory experiments (in which some children are shown violent content and compared with a control group of children who are shown nonviolent content), field experiments (in which the same kinds of comparisons are made in natural social settings), cross-sectional studies (in which surveys allow researchers to examine correlations between exposure to onscreen violence and real-world violence in different segments of the population), and longitudinal studies (in which researchers track samples of people for months or years and look for correlations between exposure to onscreen violence and violent behaviour).

Several recent reviews of the research literature find strong evidence that in the short term, children and adolescents who watch violent films become physically and verbally aggressive. The evidence for long-term effects is significant but requires further research before firm conclusions can be drawn (Anderson and Bushman, 2002; Browne and Hamilton-Giachritis, 2005; Office of the Surgeon General, 2001).

Research shows that violent movies increase the likelihood that some audience members will behave more aggressively. Significantly, however, not all individuals are affected in the same way or to the same extent by violent movies. Moreover, violent behaviour has many causes, of which media violence is only one and by no means the most important. It is important to note that critics have expressed much concern about the graphic nature of violence, as in horror movies where people are butchered. However, onscreen violence tends to have more of an effect on audience members if it is presented without a reasonable moral context. Violence is sometimes presented as a legitimate way to resolve conflict, as an action that goes unpunished, and without a depiction of the devastating emotional consequences that it has on people's lives. It is more the lack of contextualization of violence than its graphic quality that makes onscreen violence problematic (Potter, 1999).

Frequently lost in the conversation about how movies influence society is consideration of their positive effects. Yet movies benefit us by entertaining us and by addressing important issues that deserve public awareness and understanding. *On the Beach* (1959) sparked debate about the nuclear arms race, *Guess Who's Coming to Dinner* (1967) provoked dialogue about interracial relationships, *Philadelphia* (1993) generated widespread discussion about discrimination against people with AIDS, *The Insider* (1999) raised awareness of the influence of the tobacco industry on the mass media, and *Syriana* (2005) raised questions about the oil industry's manipulation of politicians in the United States and the Middle East. As these examples suggest, the influence of movies on society can be informative and progressive.

REFERENCES

Anderson, Craig A. and Brad J. Bushman. (2002). "The Effects of Media Violence on Society." *Science* 29 March 29: 2377–78.

Brown, Gene. (1995). *Movie Time: A Chronology of Hollywood and the Movie Industry from Its Beginnings to the Present.* New York: Macmillan.

Browne, Kevin D. and Katherine Hamilton-Giachritis. (2005). "The Influence of Violent Media on Children and Adolescents: A Public-Health Approach." *The Lancet, 19* (February), 702–10.

Guerrero, Edward. (1990). "AIDS as Monster in Science Fiction and Horror Cinema." *Journal of Popular Film and Television, 18* (3), 86–93.

Hanssen, F. Andrew. (2000). "The Block Booking of Films Reexamined." *Journal of Law and Economics, 43* (2), 395–426.

Hendershot, Cyndy. (1999). *Paranoia, the Bomb, and 1950s Science-Fiction Films.* Bowling Green, OH: Bowling Green State University Press.

Mayer, Arthur L. (1948). "An Exhibitor Begs for 'B's.'" *Hollywood Quarterly, 3* (2), 172–77.

Office of the Surgeon General. (2001). *Youth Violence: A Report of the Surgeon General.* Washington, DC: Dept. of Health and Human Services, U.S. Public Health Service.

Peterson, Richard. (1994). "Cultural Studies Through the Production Perspective: Progress and Prospects." In Diana Crane, ed., *The Sociology of Culture: Emerging Theoretical Perspectives* (pp. 163–89). Cambridge, MA: Blackwell Publishers.

Potter, W. James. (1999). *On Media Violence.* Thousand Oaks, CA: Sage Publications.

Sargent, James D., M.L. Beach, et al. (2005). "Exposure to Movie Smoking: Its Relation to Smoking Initiation among US Adolescents." *Pediatrics, 116* (5), 1183–91.

Sargent, James D., M. Stoolmiller, et al. (2007). "Exposure to Smoking Depictions in Movies: Its Association with Established Adolescent Smoking." *Archives of Pediatric Adolescent Medicine, 161,* 849–56.

White, William Allen. (1936). "Chewing-Gum Relaxation." In William J. Perlman, ed., *The Movies on Trial* (pp. 3–12). New York: The Macmillan Company.

Chapter 9

Do Video Games Kill?

KAREN STERNHEIMER,
University of Southern California

When white, middle-class teens kill, the media and politicians are quick to blame video games. Are they right?

As soon as it was released in 1993, a video game called *Doom* became a target for critics. Not the first, but certainly one of the most popular first-person shooter games, *Doom* galvanized fears that such games would teach kids to kill. In the years after its release, *Doom* helped video gaming grow into a multibillion-dollar industry, surpassing Hollywood box-office revenues and further fanning public anxieties.

Then came the school shootings in Paducah, Kentucky; Springfield, Oregon; and Littleton, Colorado. In all three cases, press accounts emphasized that the shooters loved *Doom*, making it appear that the critics' predictions about video games were coming true.

But in the ten years following *Doom's* release, homicide arrest rates fell by 77 percent among juveniles. School shootings remain extremely rare; even during the 1990s, when fears of school violence were high, students had less than a 7 in 10 million chance of being killed at school. During that time, video games became a major part of many young people's lives, few of whom will ever become violent, let alone kill. So, why is the video game explanation so popular?

CONTEMPORARY FOLK DEVILS

In 2000, the FBI issued a report on school rampage shootings, finding that their rarity prohibits the construction of a useful profile of a "typical" shooter. In the absence of a simple explanation, the public symbolically linked these rare and complex events to the shooters' alleged interest in video games, finding in them a catchall explanation for what seemed

Source: "Do Video Games Kill?" by Karen Sternheimer, *Contexts 6(1)*, pp. 13–17, © 2007 American Sociological Association. Reprinted by Permission of SAGE Publications.

unexplainable—the white, middle-class school shooter. However, the concern about video games is out of proportion to their actual threat.

Politicians and other moral crusaders frequently create "folk devils," individuals or groups defined as evil and immoral. Folk devils allow us to channel our blame and fear, offering a clear course of action to remedy what many believe to be a growing problem. Video games, those who play them, and those who create them have become contemporary folk devils because they seem to pose a threat to children.

Such games have come to represent a variety of social anxieties: about youth violence, new computer technology, and the apparent decline in the ability of adults to control what young people do and know. Panics about youth and popular culture have emerged with the appearance of many new technologies. Over the past century, politicians have complained that cars, radio, movies, rock music, and even comic books caused youth immorality and crime, calling for control and sometimes censorship.

Acting on concerns like these, politicians often engage in battles characterized as between good and evil. The unlikely team of Senators Joseph Lieberman, Sam Brownback, Hillary Rodham Clinton, and Rick Santorum introduced a bill in March 2005 that called for $90 million to fund studies on media effects. Lieberman commented, "America is a media-rich society, but despite the flood of information, we still lack perhaps the most important piece of information—what effect are media having on our children?" Regardless of whether any legislation passes, the senators position themselves as protecting children and benefit from the moral panic they help to create.

CONSTRUCTING CULPABILITY

Politicians are not the only ones who blame video games. Since 1997, 199 newspaper articles have focused on video games as a central explanation for the Paducah, Springfield, and Littleton shootings. This helped to create a groundswell of fear that schools were no longer safe and that rampage shootings could happen wherever there were video games. The shootings legitimated existing concerns about the new medium and about young people in general. Headlines, such as "Virtual Realities Spur School Massacres" (*Denver Post*, July 27, 1999), "Days of Doom" (*Pittsburgh Post-Gazette*, May 14, 1999), "Bloodlust Video Games Put Kids in the Crosshairs" (*Denver Post*, May 30, 1999), and "All Those Who Deny Any Linkage between Violence in Entertainment and Violence in Real Life, Think Again" (*New York Times*, April 26, 1999), insist that video games are the culprit.

These headlines all appeared immediately after the Littleton shooting, which had the highest death toll and inspired most (176) of the news stories alleging a video game connection. Across the country, the press attributed much of the blame to video games specifically, and to Hollywood more generally. The *Pittsburgh Post-Gazette* article "Days of Doom" noted that "eighteen people have now died at the hands of avid *Doom* players." The *New York Times* article noted above began, "By producing increasingly violent media, the entertainment industry has for decades engaged in a lucrative dance with the devil," evoking imagery of a fight against evil. It went on to construct video games as a central link: "The two boys apparently responsible for the massacre in Littleton, Colo., last week were, among many other things, accomplished players of the ultraviolent video game *Doom*. And Michael Carneal, the 14-year-old boy who opened fire on a prayer group in a Paducah, Kentucky, school foyer in 1997, was also known to be a video-game expert."

Just as many stories insisted that video games deserved at least partial blame, editorial pages around the country made the connection as well:

President Bill Clinton is right. He said this shooting was no isolated incident, that Kinkel and other teens accused of killing teachers and fellow students reflect a changing culture of violence on television and in movies and video games. (*Cleveland Plain Dealer*, May 30, 1998)

The campaign to make Hollywood more responsible ... should proceed full speed ahead. (*Boston Herald*, April 9, 2000)

Make no mistake, Hollywood is contributing to a culture that feeds on and breeds violence. ... When entertainment companies craft the most shocking video games and movies they can, peddle their virulent wares to an impressionable audience with abandon, then shrug off responsibility for our culture of violence, they deserve censure. (*St. Louis Post-Dispatch*, April 12, 2000)

The video game connection took precedence in all these news reports. Some stories mentioned other explanations, such as the shooters' social rejection, feelings of alienation at school, and depression, but these were treated mostly as minor factors compared with video games. Reporters gave these other reasons far less attention than violent video games, and frequently discussed them at the end of the articles.

The news reports typically introduce experts early in the stories who support the video game explanation. David Grossman, a former army lieutenant described as a professor of "killology," has claimed that video games are "murder simulators" and serve as an equivalent to military training. Among the 199 newspaper articles published, 17 of them mentioned or quoted Grossman. Additionally, an attorney who has filed several lawsuits against video game producers wrote an article for the *Denver Post* insisting that the games are to blame. By contrast, only seven articles identified sociologists as experts. Writers routinely presented alternative explanations as rebuttals but rarely explored them in depth.

REPORTING ON RESEARCH

By focusing so heavily on video games, news reports downplay the broader social contexts. While a handful of articles note the roles that guns, poverty, families, and the organization of schools may play in youth violence in general, when reporters mention research to explain the shooters' behavior, the vast majority of studies cited concern media effects, suggesting that video games are a central cause.

Since the early days of radio and movies, investigators have searched for possible effects—typically negative—that different media may have on audiences, especially children. Such research became more intense following the rise in violent crime in the United States between the 1960s and early 1990s, focusing primarily on television. Several hundred studies asked whether exposure to media violence predicts involvement in actual violence.

Although often accepted as true—one scholar has gone so far as to call the findings about the effects of media violence on behavior a "law"—this body of research has been highly controversial. One such study fostered claims that television had led to more than 10 000 murders in the United States and Canada during the twentieth century. This and many other media-effects studies rely on correlation analysis, often finding small but sometimes statistically significant links between exposure to media violence and aggressive behavior.

But, such studies do not demonstrate that media violence causes aggressive behavior, only that the two phenomena exist together. Excluding a host of other factors (such as the growing unrest during the civil rights and antiwar movements, and the disappearance of jobs in central cities) may make it seem that a direct link exists between the introduction of television and homicides. In all likelihood any connection is incidental.

It is equally likely that more aggressive people seek out violent entertainment. Aggression includes a broad range of emotions and behaviors, and is not always synonymous with violence. Measures of aggression in media-effects research have varied widely, from observing play between children and inanimate objects to counting the number of speeding tickets a person received. Psychologist Jonathan Freedman (2002) reviewed every media-violence study published in English and concluded that "the majority of studies produced evidence that is inconsistent or even contradicts" the claim that exposure to media violence causes real violence.

Recently, video games have become a focus of research. Reviews of this growing literature have also been mixed. A 2001 meta-analysis in *Psychological Science* concluded that video games "will increase aggressive behavior," while a similar review published that same year in a different journal found that "it is not possible to determine whether video game violence affects aggressive behavior." A 2005 review found evidence that playing video games improves spatial skills and reaction times, but not that the games increase aggression.

The authors of the *Psychological Science* article advocate the strong-effects hypothesis. Two of their studies were widely reported on in 2000, the year after the Columbine High School shootings, with scant critical analysis. But their research was based on college undergraduates, not troubled teens, and it measured aggression in part by subjects' speed in reading "aggressive" words on a computer screen or blasting opponents with sound after playing a violent video game. These measures do not approximate the conditions the school shooters experienced, nor do they offer much insight as to why they, and not the millions of other players, decided to acquire actual weapons and shoot real people.

Occasionally reporters include challenges like this in stories containing media-effects claims, but news coverage usually refers to this body of research as clear, consistent, and conclusive. "The evidence, say those who study violence in culture, is unassailable: Hundreds of studies in recent decades have revealed a direct correlation between exposure to media violence—now including video games—and increased aggression," said the *New York Times* (April 26, 1999). The *Boston Herald* quoted a clinical psychologist who said, "Studies have already shown that watching television shows with aggressive or violent content makes children more aggressive" (July 30, 2000). The psychologist noted that video game research is newer, but predicted that "in a few years, studies will show that video games increase a child's aggression even more than violent TV shows." News reports do not always use academic sources to assess the conclusiveness of media effects research. A *Pittsburgh Post-Gazette* story included a quote by an attorney, who claimed, "Research on this has been well-established" (May 14, 1999).

It is no accident that media-effects research and individual explanations dominate press attempts to explain the behavior of the school shooters. Although many politicians are happy to take up the cause against video games, popular culture itself suggests an apolitical explanation of violence and discourages a broader examination of structural factors. Focusing on extremely rare and perhaps unpredictable outbursts of violence by young people discourages the public from looking closely at more typical forms of violence against young people, which is usually perpetrated by adults.

The biggest problem with media-effects research is that it attempts to decontextualize violence. Poverty, neighborhood instability, unemployment, and even family violence fall by the wayside in most of these studies. Ironically, even mental illness tends to be overlooked in this psychologically oriented research. Young people are seen as passive media consumers, uniquely and uniformly vulnerable to media messages.

MISSING MEDIA STUDIES

News reports of the shootings that focus on video games ignore other research on the meanings that audiences make from media culture. This may be because its qualitative findings are difficult to turn into simple quotations or sound bites. Yet, in seeking better understanding of the role of video games in the lives of the shooters and young people more generally, media scholars could have added much to the public debate.

For instance, one study found that British working-class boys boast about how many horror films they have seen as they construct their sense of masculinity by appearing too tough to be scared. Another study examined how younger boys talk about movies and television as a way to manage their anxieties and insecurities regarding their emerging sense of masculinity. Such studies illustrate why violent video games may appeal to many young males.

Media scholars have also examined how and why adults construct concerns about young people and popular culture. One such study concluded that some adults use their condemnation of media as a way to produce cultural distinctions that position them above those who enjoy popular culture. Other researchers have found that people who believe their political knowledge is superior to that of others are more likely to presume that media violence would strongly influence others. They have also found that respondents who enjoy television violence are less likely to believe it has a negative effect.

Just as it is too simplistic to assert that video game violence makes players more prone to violence, news coverage alone, however dramatic or repetitive, cannot create consensus among the public that video games cause youth violence. Finger-wagging politicians and other moralizers often alienate as many members of the public as they convert. In an ironic twist, they might even feed the antiauthoritarian appeal that may draw players of all ages to the games.

The lack of consensus does not indicate the absence of a moral panic, but reveals contradictory feelings toward the target group. The intense focus on video games as potential creators of violent killers reflects the hostility that some feel toward popular culture and young people themselves. After adult rampage shootings in the workplace (which happen more often than school shootings), reporters seldom mention whether the shooters played video games. Nor is an entire generation portrayed as potential killers.

AMBIVALENCE ABOUT JUVENILE JUSTICE

The concern in the late 1990s about video games coincided with a growing ambivalence about the juvenile justice system and young offenders. Fears about juvenile "super-predators," fanned by former Florida Representative Bill McCollom's 1996 warning that we should "brace ourselves" against the coming storm of young killers, made the school shootings appear inevitable. McCollom and other politicians characterized young people as a "new breed," uniquely dangerous and amoral.

These fears were produced partially by the rise in crime during the late 1980s and early 1990s, but also by the so-called echo boom that produced a large generation of teens during the late 1990s. Demographic theories of crime led policymakers to fear that the rise in the number of teen males would bring a parallel rise in crime. In response, virtually every state changed its juvenile justice laws during the decade. They increased penalties, imposed mandatory minimum sentences, blended jurisdiction with criminal courts, and made it easier to transfer juvenile cases to adult criminal courts.

So, before the first shot was fired in Paducah, politicians warned the public to be on the lookout for killer kids. Rather than being seen as tragic anomalies, these high-profile incidents appeared to support scholarly warnings that all kids posed an increasing threat. Even though juvenile (and adult) crime was in sharp decline by the late nineties, the intense media coverage contributed to the appearance of a new trend.

Blaming video games meant that the shooters were set aside from other violent youth, frequently poor males of color, at whom our get-tough legislation has been targeted. According to the National Center for Juvenile Justice, African-American youth are involved in the juvenile justice system more than twice as often as whites. The video game explanation constructs the white, middle-class shooters as victims of the power of video games, rather than fully culpable criminals. When boys from "good" neighborhoods are violent, they seem to be harbingers of a "new breed" of youth, created by video games rather than by their social circumstances. White, middle-class killers retain their status as children easily influenced by a game, victims of an allegedly dangerous product. African-American boys, apparently, are simply dangerous.

While the news media certainly asked what role the shooters' parents may have played, the press tended to tread lightly on them, particularly the Kinkels of Springfield, Oregon, who were their son's first murder victims. Their middle-class, suburban, or rural environments were given little scrutiny. The white school shooters did more than take the lives of their classmates; their whiteness and middle-class status threatened the idea of the innocence and safety of suburban America.

In an attempt to hold more than just the shooters responsible, the victims' families filed lawsuits against film producers, Internet sites, and video game makers. Around the same time, Congress made it more difficult to sue gun manufacturers for damages. To date, no court has found entertainment producers liable for causing young people to commit acts of violence. In response to a lawsuit following the Paducah shootings, a Kentucky circuit judge ruled that "we are loath to hold that ideas and images can constitute the tools for a criminal act," and that product liability law did not apply because the product did not injure its consumer. The lawsuit was dismissed, as were subsequent suits filed after the other high-profile shootings.

GAME OVER?

Questions about the power of media and the future of the juvenile justice system persist. In March 2005, the U.S. Supreme Court ruled that juvenile executions were unconstitutional. This ruling represents an about-face in the 25-year trend toward toughening penalties for young offenders. While many human rights and children's advocates praised this decision, it was sharply criticized by those who believe that the juvenile justice system is already too lenient. Likewise, critics continue to target video games, as their graphics and plot capabilities grow more complex and at times more disturbing. Meanwhile, youth crime rates continue to decline. If we want to understand why young people, particularly in middle-class or otherwise stable environments, become homicidal, we need to look beyond the games they play. While all forms of media merit critical analysis, so do the supposedly "good" neighborhoods and families that occasionally produce young killers.

REFERENCES

Burns, Ronald and Charles Crawford. (1999). "School Shootings, the Media, and Public Fear: Ingredients for a Moral Panic." *Crime, Law, and Social Change, 32*, 147–68.

Freedman, Jonathan L. (2002). *Media Violence and Its Effect on Aggression: Assessing the Scientific Evidence*. Toronto: University of Toronto Press.

Goode, Erich and Nachman Ben-Yehuda. (1994). *Moral Panics*: *The Social Construction of Deviance*. Oxford, UK: Blackwell.

Springhall, John. (1998). *Youth, Popular Culture and Moral Panics: Penny Gaffs to Gangsta-Rap, 1830–1996*. New York: St. Martin's.

Zimring, Franklin E. (1998). *American Youth Violence*. New York: Oxford University Press.

PART 3

SOCIAL INEQUALITY

Social inequality is a core—some would say the central—sociological problem. It has provoked and confounded analysts since the founding of the discipline. For example, the simplification of the capitalist class system forecast by Marx never took place. Instead of polarizing around a large class of impoverished workers and a tiny class of wealthy capitalists, the stratification system became more complex. Small business owners did not disappear. In recent years, they have actually become more numerous as a proportion of the economically active population. What C. Wright Mills called an "occupational salad" of **white-collar workers**—professionals, educated office holders, clerks, and so on—became the largest component of the stratification system. Manual or **blue-collar workers** experienced a rising standard of living (at least until the mid-1970s) while their numbers as a proportion of the total labour force shrank. In recent decades, inequality has increased to varying degrees in different countries, but the revolution that Marx expected never happened.

Poverty persists. Nearly one in 10 Canadians was in the low-income category in 2009. Moreover, poverty has been feminized. A substantial majority of low-income adults are women. True, most adult women now work for a wage in the paid labour force, a development unforeseen by Marx, Weber, Durkheim, and other classical sociologists. However, women tend to be segregated as **pink-collar workers**—doing jobs that pay relatively low wages and are analogous to women's traditional family roles as servers, teachers, and nurturers. Even today, it is uncommon for women to have authority over men in the workplace, and the distribution of authority between the sexes influences even intimate relations between women and men. Sharp inequality persists between heterosexuals and members of various sexual minorities, too.

Another unanticipated development in the realm of social stratification concerns the tenacity of ethnic and racial inequality, which the founders of sociology expected to disappear under capitalism. They believed that large factories and bureaucracies would homogenize people, forcing them to work together, treating them all the same, and making cultural differences between them less pronounced. In reality, although ethnic and racial stratification has declined in Canada and many other places, different ethnic and racial groups still tend to occupy definite niches in the social hierarchy.

These are some of the key problems in stratification research and some of the chief issues examined in the chapters that follow.

GLOSSARY

Blue-collar workers do manual work in manufacturing, construction and the like.

Pink-collar workers include teachers, secretaries, nurses, and the like. Their work is analogous to women's traditional family roles.

White-collar workers include professionals, educated office holders, clerks, and other nonmanual workers.

CRITICAL THINKING QUESTIONS

1. Is social inequality inevitable or necessary? Why or why not?
2. Why does the level of inequality among classes, among ethnic groups, and between women and men vary over time and place?

ANNOTATED BIBLIOGRAPHY

Karl Marx and Friedrich Engels, "Chapter 1: Bourgeois and Proletarians," *Manifesto of the Communist Party.* Available online at www.marxists .org/archive/marx/works/1848/communist-manifesto/ch01 .htm#007. The classic statement on the inevitability of classlessness.

John Porter, "Distinguished Canadians: John Porter." Available online at www.cbc.ca/archives/discover/programs/d/distinguished -canadians/john-porter.html. A rare interview from 1972 with the first sociologist to conduct an in-depth analysis of class and ethnic inequality in Canada.

A survey of Canada's ultra-affluent—people with a net worth of $10 million or more—shows that they can easily afford more than two luxury cars each on average. They typically collect art (90 percent), antiques (72 percent), and fine wines (69 percent). The ultra-affluent are apparently pragmatic. Thus, while they contribute generously to philanthropic causes, their number one reason for doing so is that it provides personal tax and estate benefits. Their number two reason for giving to charities is that it makes good sense in terms of providing opportunities for developing business relationships. Just like you and me, the ultra-affluent worry. After all, the rate of inflation for luxury items, including high-end German automobiles, art, antiques, and fine wines, is two or three times the inflation rate for the goods and services consumed by the general population. Moreover, they are deeply concerned that their children will develop "affluenza," a rare disease whose symptoms include a lack of ambition brought on by a life of extraordinary privilege. (Okay, maybe they don't worry just like you and me.)

Meanwhile, since the early 1970s, the average real income (or "purchasing power") of Canadians has risen little, substantially modifying the post–World War II trend to higher real incomes. Also since the early 1970s, income inequality has increased. The richest 20 percent of Canadians earn a larger share of total national income than they did 40 years ago, the middle 60 percent earn less, and the poorest 20 percent earn about the same.

However, substantial increases in income inequality did not occur in Canada until the late 1990s. As John Myles shows in Chapter 10, three factors are responsible for the surge. First (and of least importance), the federal government taxed and redistributed money to the neediest Canadians with less vigour. Second, earnings inequality (the amount of money earned in the market) increased. Third (and most important), a rising proportion of families consisted of single mothers, and the federal government did little to assist such families. The only exception to this pattern was Quebec, where the provincial government instituted low-cost universal daycare and other innovations.

Poverty remains a serious and persistent problem in Canada, as Ann Duffy and Nancy Mandell show in Chapter 11. Statistics Canada sets **low-income cut-offs (LICOs)**. They are the income levels below which people are considered to live in "straitened circumstances." Below the LICOs, people must spend more than 54.7 percent of their gross income on essentials (food, clothing, and shelter). Using that standard, the percentage of Canadians below the LICOs fell between the end of World War II and the early 1970s. It remained fairly steady at about one-eighth of the population up to the early 1990s, rose to about one-sixth of the population by the end of the 1990s, and fell to just under a tenth of the population in 2009. Most low-income people work for a living, but more of them are lone women and their small children than used to be the case. As Duffy and Mandell document, the social and personal costs of poverty remain staggering.

GLOSSARY

The **low-income cut-off (LICO)** is the income level below which people are considered to live in "straitened circumstances." Below the LICO, people must spend more than 54.7 percent of their gross income on essentials (food, clothing, and shelter).

CRITICAL THINKING QUESTIONS

1. Why are Canadian women and children at greater risk of being poor than men are? What social factors are responsible for this?
2. While income inequality is higher in the United States than in Canada, it is lower in Western Europe than in Canada. How do you account for these differences?

ANNOTATED BIBLIOGRAPHY

Edward Grabb and Neil Guppy, eds., *Social Inequality in Canada: Patterns, Problems, Policies,* 5th ed. (Scarborough, ON: Prentice-Hall Canada, 2008). A definitive collection of up-to-date research on social stratification in Canada.

Chapter 10

The Inequality Surge

JOHN MYLES, University of Toronto

Up to the late 1990s, a certain smugness was evident in studies of Canadian income inequality. While an upward trend in inequality was evident in the United States and Britain by the 1980s, any signs of rising income inequality in Canada appeared to be offset by the welfare state. Taxes and transfers were doing their job. Canadians might not be as kind and gentle as the Swedes but we were certainly kinder and gentler than those nasty Americans or the increasingly unlovely Brits.

However, it turned out that Canada was not different from the United States and Britain, just a little behind. In the latter half of the 1990s, income inequality in Canada surged upward after four decades of relative stability. This surge in inequality is especially disturbing because it occurred during a period of economic expansion when, if anything, we should expect inequality to decline. A reasonable expectation given its cyclical nature was that by 2003 or so our Gini index of inequality would have fallen back to 1989 levels, just under 0.28. Instead, it was close to 0.32.

When inequality or poverty measures change significantly, there are always three likely suspects to account for the shift: changes in labour markets (e.g. rising earnings inequality), changes in families (e.g. more lone parents) and changes in public policies (cuts to the "welfare state").

Given the timing of the inequality surge, it is tempting to point the finger at the welfare state. The latter half of the 1990s was the period when Unemployment Insurance (UI) became Employment Insurance (EI) and access to benefits became more restrictive. Social assistance benefits were overhauled in a number of provinces, especially Alberta, British Columbia and Ontario. And federal and provincial surtaxes on high-income earners were abandoned.

Source: "The Inequality Surge" by John Myles. From *Inroads: The Canadian Journal of Opinion, 26,* pp. 66–73. © 2010. Reprinted with permission from the publisher.

As it turns out, however, these efforts at welfare state "retrenchment" constitute a small part of the story. Two recent studies of the effect of taxes and transfers on this trend tell much the same story,[1] and the answer is not as simple as one might suspect.

The *redistributive* impact of taxes and transfers on income inequality has actually risen, not fallen, over the past two decades. So despite the retrenchment efforts of the 1990s, the welfare state has not been withering away. However, it has not been keeping pace with the changes in labour markets and families that are driving the surge. During the 1980s, the increase in the redistributive effect of taxes and transfers more than offset the increase in inequality due to changes in labour markets and families. By contrast, between 1989 and 2004, the increase in the redistributive effect offset less than a quarter of the increase due to changes in labour markets and families.

The main conclusion from these studies is that politics and policy change matter a little but not very much. The other two suspects, changes in labour markets and especially changes in families, matter much more. However, that leaves open the question: what *might* have happened had the Canadian welfare state taken a more aggressive stance toward the underlying trends in labour markets and family formation? Fortunately, the experience of the province of Quebec provides some clues. As Pierre Fortin documents in this issue, policy and politics do matter.[2] Quebec's more aggressive approach to family well-being has mattered a lot.

Changes in labour markets are important but for most families/households, changes in family formation and the family life course are the big drivers of the surge in inequality. Aggressive policy change was required to keep pace with these developments. Outside Quebec, that didn't happen.

So what did happen?

Figure 10.1 illustrates the main story: the surge in *market* family income inequality that extended from roughly 1980 to 2000. *Market* family income refers to all income that family members (and unattached persons) bring home from work or receive in the form of dividends, rents and the like. It does not include income transfers from government or take account of taxes paid.

The stunning fact here is that for three decades market incomes in the middle and the bottom of the income scale have been essentially stagnant while incomes at the top have been rising. Canada has been producing more wealth, but the bottom half has not been getting its share. In the early postwar decades in the United States, a rising tide was lifting all boats. While Canada does not have data for those

FIGURE 10.1 MARKET INCOME, CANADA, BY SELECTED PERCENTILES, 1976–2006

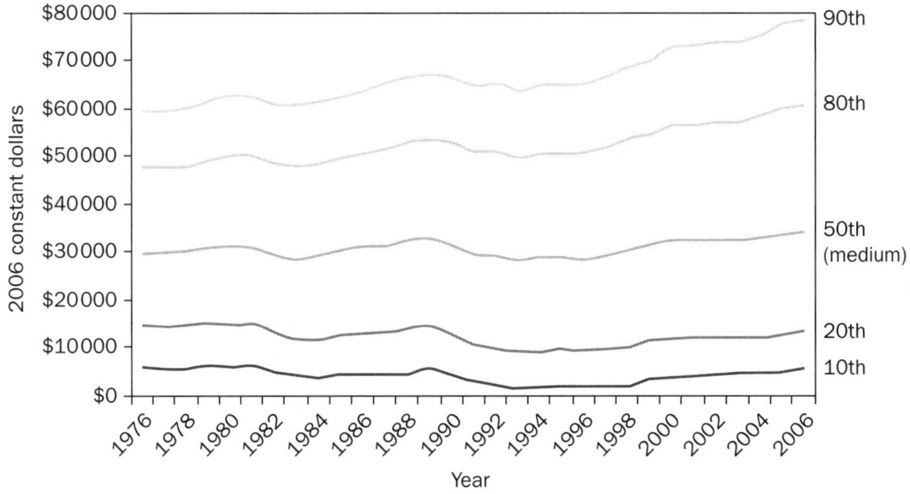

SOURCE: Reprinted by permission of *Inroads Journal*.

decades, it is likely that trends were similar north of the border. So what accounts for this historic shift?

Changes in labour markets matter. Surging compensation among the top 1 percent was a key factor.[3] Declining unionization rates played an important role, as did the declining earnings of recent immigrants.[4] Rising inequality in male and female earnings was also important. But the main conclusion of a recent fine study by Yuqian Lu, René Morissette and Tammy Schirle is that changes in *families* matter more.[5] This is a nontrivial result, since family formation and family behaviour are not easily amenable to policy intervention.

Divorce rates have risen and marriage rates have fallen. There are many more lone parents raising children as a result and fewer adults are benefiting from the economies of scale associated with shared living arrangements or the "insurance" provided by an employed spouse during spells of unemployment. The result is a "quantity" problem. Some households have lots of labour to sell (two or more earners) while more families have comparatively little (single earner-households with and without children).

Changes in families can have offsetting effects. Rising education and employment rates among women have had strong equalizing impacts among families. But the relative importance of these changes depends on who marries whom. Educational "homogamy" (the tendency of like to marry like) has risen substantially since the 1970s. Between 1971 and 2001, the proportion of educationally homogamous marriages among young Canadian adults (34 and under) rose from 42 percent to 55 percent of all marriages. This was a period when the employment and earnings gap between the more and less educated was also rising. This can be thought of as a "quality" problem: the divide between households with lots of high-quality (educated) labour to sell and those with fewer labour market skills has grown.

To illustrate, consider Figure 10.2. In 1980, the highest-paid wives were married to men earning between $30,000 and $40,000 per year. Women married to men earning less than $30,000 earned substantially less—and so did women married to men earning more than $40,000. By 2000, in contrast, all this had changed. Women married to men with low earnings (less than $10,000) saw their own relative earnings fall by about 35 percent, while women married to men with high earnings saw their earnings rise by about 21 percent. In 1980, the relationship between husbands' and wives' earnings looked somewhat like an inverted U: women married to men in the lower middle of the earnings distribution were earning the most. By 2000, the relationship was such that the highest-paid women were married to the highest-paid men, and the lowest-paid women to the lowest-paid men. And over the entire period, rising returns to education favoured families in the top half of the scale.

That well-educated women and men tend to marry each other and subsequently have high earnings and low rates of unemployment

FIGURE 10.2 AVERAGE EMPLOYMENT EARNINGS FOR MARRIED MOTHERS, BY HUSBAND'S EARNINGS INTERVALS, 1980, 1990, AND 2000

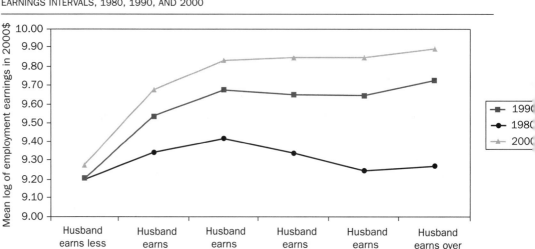

SOURCE: Reprinted by permission of *Inroads Journal*.

is unlikely to change as a result of public policy. A "Lavalife Canada" program aimed at introducing university grads to high-school drop-outs is not on anyone's policy agenda for the near future.

There has also been a steady increase in lone-parent families—from about 6 percent of all families in 1980 to 11 percent in 2005—and a rising number of families without kids. Lu, Morrissette and Schirle estimate that, together, these changes accounted for about 20 percent of the rise in inequality since 1980.

There were some good news stories over the period. Between 1980 and 2000, employment earnings among lone mothers rose by 39 percent as a result of rising employment rates. This led some observers to conclude that "tough love" policies in some provincial social assistance schemes, notably B.C., Alberta and Ontario, had been effective. Colleagues and I showed, however, that most of these gains were the result of changes in the demographic composition of lone mothers: by 2000 lone mothers were simply older, better educated and hence more likely to be employed than in 1980.[6]

The outstanding exception was Quebec. Quebec lone mothers had the largest employment gains in the 1990s (9.4 percentage points) and by 2000 their employment levels were four percentage points *higher* than in the rest of Canada. Demographic changes in Quebec accounted for only 28 percent of the growth in lone mothers' employment in the 1990s, results that are consistent with conclusions concerning the effects of liberalized child care provisions in that province.[7]

The interesting puzzle here is that while the surge in income inequality measured *after* taxes and transfers did not appear until the latter half of the 1990s, the growth in *market* income inequality had been underway for at least a decade and a half by then. In their new study of the impact of taxes and transfers on income inequality, Marc Frenette, David Green and Kevin Milligan show that growth in market income inequality was roughly similar in the 1980s and the 1990s.[8] The ratio of those at the 90th percentile to those at the 10th percentile grew by 12.8 percent between 1980 and 1990 and by a further 11.4 percent between 1990 and 2000. As they demonstrate, this was because income redistribution was rising between 1980 and 1995, offsetting changes in the labour market and families.[9] These changes did not result in less inequality; rather, the welfare state was running hard to keep inequality levels stable.

Importantly, rising income redistribution through the 1980s and the first half of the 1990s was largely driven by changes at the provincial level, a result of rising transfers under social assistance and surtaxes on top-earning families. As a result, the level of income redistribution peaked in 1995 but then declined because of cuts to social assistance, changes in UI and the elimination of surtaxes on high-income families.

However, the important conclusion is that inequality would have risen even in the *absence* of these cuts.[10] The big story of the 1990s was not so much one of retrenchment—the tax-transfer system in 2000 was still much more redistributive than that of the 1980s—but rather of the failure of the tax-transfer system to expand and to keep pace with underlying trends toward increasing inequality in labour markets and families. In short, at the national level, the welfare state was "running out of gas." And most of the action was at the provincial, not the federal, level. As Frenette, Green and Milligan conclude, "The steady after-tax income inequality of the 1980s arose because the tax and transfer system increased its redistributiveness over that decade. In the 1990s, the tax and transfer systems ceased becoming more redistributive, allowing the changes in pre-tax inequality to pass through to increases in after-tax inequality."[11]

WE STILL NEED ROBIN HOOD

So what should we make of all this? Big changes in labour markets and especially families have been driving the inequality surge. As a result, welfare states have had to run fast simply to keep the income distribution standing still. The impact of labour market and family changes, moreover, have been especially severe for young adults (those under 35). Their work careers have been starting later and their earnings relative to older adults have been falling since the 1980s. As a result, we have made relatively little progress in reducing child poverty. While the social and economic life course has changed, the biological life course has not. Because of biology, young adults (under 35) are still the parents of the majority of our young children—60 percent of those under six—and no social policy can change this.

If we look at the world from the vantage point of the young adults who are entering the labour market today and who will be supporting our pensions and health care system for the next 30 years, things look a little gloomy for the bottom half.

The world our thirtysomethings of today are entering is very different from the one encountered by the young cohorts of even a quarter century ago. A new high-inequality equilibrium in the distribution of family earnings has emerged and appears to be a relatively permanent feature of our postindustrial world. The cohorts turning 30 this year and those now completing their schooling will make up the core of our prime-age workforce well into the 21st century.

Changing the labour market would help the most. Most people get most of their income from employment for most of their lives. Full employment and decent wages for the employed, not generous welfare states, were the primary objective of social democrats and reformers like John Maynard Keynes and William Beveridge who sought to shape postwar societies in the 1940s. Countries could afford generous welfare states under conditions of high employment and high wages at the bottom of the scale, but not otherwise.

But labour markets change only over the long term. Canada has lots of low-wage jobs by international standards, and that has ever been so. Cross-national differences in wage structures of the current magnitude are the product of longstanding historical differences in wage-bargaining institutions and labour market regulation. Institution building and reform are by definition long-term projects.

Early childhood education programs intended to compensate for the weak cultural capital of many low-income parents have come into favour in many policy circles. Economists like human capital investments of this sort, and so do I. Improving people's capabilities, as Amartya Sen argues, should always be at the top of our agenda. But the distribution of human capital among those now entering the labour market is unlikely to change very much over their working lives. Early childhood education looks like it could help a lot—but not until the kids who benefit enter the labour market some 25 years in the future.

I value the search for alternatives and complements to the tax-and-transfer welfare state—Robin Hood. And the Quebec experience demonstrates that it's not just about Robin Hood. While improved transfers were a factor in Quebec's better performance, Quebec's child care program is also an "employment" program, enabling single moms and women married to low-wage men to enter the labour market and raise the living standards of their families. Nevertheless, my conclusion is that we are probably going to need more rather than less Robin Hood for some time to come.

NOTES

1. Andrew Heisz, "Income Inequality and Redistribution in Canada: 1976 to 2004," Statistics Canada, Analytic Studies Branch Paper Series, No. 298, May 2007; Marc Frenette, David Green and Kevin Milligan,

"Looking for Smoking Guns: The Impact of Taxes and Transfers on Canadian Income Inequality," *Canadian Public Policy,* in press.

2. Pierre Fortin, "Quebec is Fairer: There is Less Poverty and Less Inequality in Quebec," *Inroads*, Winter/Spring 2010, pp. 58–65.

3. Emmanuel Saez and Michael R. Veall, "The Evolution of High Incomes in Northern America: Lessons from Canadian Evidence," *American Economic Review*, Vol. 95, No. 3 (June 2005), pp. 831–849.

4. John DiNardo, Nicole Fortin and Thomas Lemieux, "Labor Market Institutions and the Distribution of Wages, 1973–1992: A Semiparametric Approach," *Econometrica*, Vol. 64, No.5 (1996), pp. 1001–44.

5. Yuqian Lu, René Morissette and Tammy Schirle, "The Growth of Family Earnings Inequality in Canada, 1980–2005," Presentation to Canadian Economic Association annual meetings, 2009.

6. John Myles, Feng Hou, Garnett Picot and Karen Myers, "Why Did Employment and Earnings Rise among Lone Mothers in Canada during the 1980s and 1990s?", *Canadian Public Policy*, Vol. 23, No. 2 (2007), pp. 1–26.

7. Michael Baker, Jonathan Gruber and Kevin Milligan, *Universal Childcare, Maternal Labor Supply, and Family Well-Being*, National Bureau of Economic Research Working Paper No. W11832, 2005; Pierre Lefebvre and Philip Merrigan, *Low-fee ($5/day /child) Regulated Childcare Policy and the Labor Supply of Mothers with Young Children: A Natural Experiment from Canada*, Centre Interuniversitaire sure le Risque, les Politiques Économiques et l'Emploi (CIRPEE), Cahiers de recherche 0508, 2005.

8. Frenette, Green and Milligan, "Looking for Smoking Guns," p. 10.

9. See also Heisz, "Income Inequality and Redistribution in Canada."

10. Frenette, Green and Milligan, "Looking for Smoking Guns," p. 13.

11. Ibid., pp. 30–31.

SUGGESTION FOR FURTHER READING

The Canadian experience over the last quarter century is a national variant of distributional trends in *all* Western societies. For further reading on these developments, see Gosta Esping-Andersen, *The Incomplete Revolution: Adapting to Women's New Roles* (Cambridge, UK: Polity Press, 2009).

Chapter 11

Poverty in Canada

ANN DUFFY, Brock University

and NANCY MANDELL, York University

POVERTY TODAY

The first decade of the twenty-first century has witnessed almost unprecedented economic upheaval and insecurity. Not since the Great Depression of the 1930s has economic turbulence figured so prominently in people's lives. Today, many Canadians are experiencing layoffs, unemployment, or underemployment. While the national unemployment rate was 7.3 percent in September 2012, the unemployment rate among 15- to 24-year-olds stood at 14.8 percent, and some people are concerned that a large part of an entire generation has been locked out of meaningful employment. At the same time, concerns about government-funded pensions and the company and private pension funds that were ravaged by the 2008–09 recession mean that many seniors face an insecure economic future. For more and more Canadians, poverty edges closer, and the line presumed to separate the secure from the marginalized blurs.

Although an estimated 3.2 million Canadians or 9.6 percent of the population live on low income, poverty remains one of the great unresolved and underreported social issues confronting Canadians (Statistics Canada, 2011a). Canada is among the wealthiest countries in the world, but many of its citizens, especially children, people with disabilities, and single mothers, are unable to escape the debilitating effects of impoverishment. Despite periods of strong economic growth, some sectors of the population have been left behind. Today, it appears that their economic marginalization is likely to become even more harrowing.

Evidence of poverty is everywhere. In nearly every town and city, the persistent appeals from food banks speak to the hunger in our midst. In March 2011, 851 014 Canadians used a food bank at least once, and fully one-third of food banks reported difficulty meeting the demand for their services (Food Banks Canada [FBC], 2012; Swift, Balmer, and Dineen, 2010). Since 2008, food bank use has increased 26 percent and is at the second-highest level on record. Across Canada, there are considerable variations in reliance on food banks. Between 2008 and 2011, Ontario and Quebec, with their large urban populations, experienced increases of more than 20 percent while British Columbia, Saskatchewan, and New Brunswick registered around 15 percent increases. Considered at their inception in the 1980s as a short-term form of assistance for the extremely poor, food banks have become permanent fixtures of our communities. Harsh economic times underscore their growing significance (FBC, 2012).

Food bank clients include university and college students, seniors, families, workers, and welfare recipients. In 2011, reflecting the dramatic expansion of precarious and part-time employment, almost one in five people using food banks had recent or current paid employment but their wages were too low to cover their living expenses (Albo, 2010; FBC, 2012). More than one-third of food bank clients were children or youth. Half of food bank users rely on social assistance, underscoring the inability of welfare payments to meet numerous families' basic requirements (FBC, 2012).

Equally grim reminders of poverty can be found during any walk through the inner core of Canada's major cities. There, huddled on hot air gratings or squatting in bus shelters, are some of the estimated 200 000 to 300 000 Canadians who are homeless for at least part of the year (Haan, 2011: 43). According to Human Resources and Skills Development Canada (HRSDC, 2008), an estimated 1020 shelters provided 26 872 beds on a regular basis in 2008. These statistics only hint at the dimensions of the problem. According to the Metro Vancouver Homeless Count for 2011, 2623 people were homeless in the city on March 16 of that year. While many spent the night in shelters, safe houses, transition houses, and detox or recovery facilities, 731 were unsheltered—living on the street and in parks (Greater Vancouver Regional Steering Committee on Homelessness, 2011). In Metro Toronto on April 15, 2009, an estimated 5086 people were homeless; 400 of them slept outdoors. In 2010, more than 22 000 people turned to Toronto shelters (Toronto Shelter, Support, and Housing Administration, 2011).

Embedded in these statistics are the tens of thousands of individuals who have been pushed to the extreme margins of our society by mental illness, injury, addiction, and other misfortune.

According to a recent study, one-third of Toronto's homeless had experienced a severe head trauma before ending up on the streets (Alphonso, 2008: A11). Similarly, a 2008 survey conducted by the Salvation Army of 469 Canadians living in a shelter found that nearly half had physical or mental health issues or were dealing with drug- or alcohol-related addictions (Salvation Army, 2009). Not surprisingly, research suggests that life on the streets may have deadly consequences. A study in England found that homeless people die 30 years younger than the national average ("Homeless People," 2011).

Even these grim realities only scrape the surface. Researchers are calling attention to the large numbers of rural youth who number among the invisible homeless. Enjoying few social supports and suffering high rates of unemployment, these rural youth may find themselves with little recourse other than sleeping "rough," "couch surfing," or leaving the area (Skott-Myhre, Raby, and Nikolaou, 2008). Homelessness among refugees, asylum seekers, and recent immigrants may be similarly camouflaged (Haan, 2011; Preston et al., 2011).

The homeless are only the most obvious symptom of inequality in Canada. Behind closed doors are hundreds of thousands more Canadians struggling with poverty, some relying on social assistance or disability income, others depending on minimum wage employment, and all struggling to keep going in a society that too often ignores their plight.

It has always been difficult to draw a clear line between the poor and the nonpoor. After all, between 2002 and 2007, more than one in five Canadians between the ages of 18 and 60 experienced at least one period of low income that lasted at least one year (Human Resources and Skills Development Canada [HRSDC], 2009). More and more Canadians hold only a tenuous grip on financial security. Particularly since 2008, Canadians have resorted to debt to weather difficult economic times. The average Canadian family now carries about $100 000 in debt—a 78 percent increase since the 1990s—and, on average, Canadian households owe $1.53 for every $1 of after-tax income earned (Flavelle, 2012; Olive, 2011a: B1; Rubin, 2011: B1). Nor is the future brighter since one-third of Canadians expect to be paying for their mortgage well past age 65 ("Mortgage Freedom," 2011). In this context, the line between economic survival and marginalization may be narrow.

To keep track of poverty, government agencies, social researchers, and advocacy groups have proposed a number of definitions. Despite these efforts, Canada does not have one official designation for poverty (Broadbent, 2005; Sarlo, 2008; Smith, 2008). Yet definitions of poverty have broad implications. Employing a stricter or looser definition to count the poor may, at the stroke of a pen, dramatically reduce or increase their number. For governments seeking to attack deficits, "reduction by redefinition" is a tempting alternative. In India, for example, the Planning Commission in 2011 applied to the Supreme Court to reset poverty lines and end poverty benefits for citizens who earned more than 68 cents a day in India's urban areas and 53 cents in rural India. Despite protests, the government is intent on lowering the poverty threshold to reduce costs (Westhead, 2011: A3).

Keeping in mind the roots of definitional wrangling, the best-known and most widely used poverty measures in Canada are the three used by Statistics Canada. It established "low-income cut-offs" (LICOs), below which people are considered to live in "straitened circumstances." The cut-offs are based on the idea that poor families must spend 20 percent more than the average family of a similar size on the necessities of food, shelter, and clothing. Since, in 1992, the average Canadian family spent about 43 percent of its after-tax income on food, clothing, and shelter, poor families would be those who spend at least 63 percent of their income on these necessities. Since 1992, the government has used the consumer price index to adjust LICOs to inflation. LICOs are calculated both before taxes (LICOs-BT) and after taxes (LICOs-AT). However, Statistics Canada prefers to employ the after-tax measure since income tax redistributes income and because individuals live on after-tax dollars.

LICOs vary by household size and the size of the community in which one resides, so there are 35 LICOs. For example, a single person in Toronto (a census metropolitan area with 500 000 or more inhabitants) in 2010 who earned less than $18 759 would be living below the LICO-AT line, while a three-person family living on less than $28 430 after taxes in a rural area would fall below the cut-off (Statistics Canada, 2011b: 20). The ultimate result is a gauge of *relative* poverty because the guide establishes a poverty rate by comparing individuals and families relative to the average (HRSDC, 2009).

By using the Statistics Canada LICOs, we can draw a revealing picture of poverty—but a picture with serious limitations. First, the 35 categories do not include Aboriginal reserves, institutional inmates (those in seniors' homes or prisons), residents of the Yukon, the Northwest Territories, and Nunavut, and the homeless. Second, they tell us nothing about the duration of poverty, that is, how long any one individual is poor. Third, many analysts are dissatisfied with the geographical adjustments. According to Statistics Canada, it is 31 percent less expensive to live in rural than in urban areas. However, while research suggests that shelter costs are lower in rural areas, transportation costs are higher. Furthermore, access to subsidized public services, such as child care, health services, and education, as well as competitively priced goods, is restricted in many rural areas. In short, many analysts maintain that the adjustments by location are inaccurate. Fourth, LICOs ignore differences in the actual level of need in particular households. For example, caring for a child with a severe disability and lacking access to subsidized services may significantly increase household economic needs ("Deciding Where," 2005; Ross and Shillington, 2000).

Because of such criticisms, researchers have developed additional measures of poverty. For example, the market basket measure (MBM) establishes the cost of a basic basket of necessary goods and services, and calculates their cost. Specifically, the costs are calculated for food, clothing, shoes, transportation, shelter, and other expenses for a family with two adults ages 25 to 49 and two children ages 9 and 13. It is an "absolute" measure of poverty because it does not compare the economic standing of an individual or a family with the average, and it is more sensitive to regional cost variations than the LICO is. According to MBM calculations (which were extensively rebased in 2010), the threshold for economic and social deprivation would be $28 778 for this family living in rural Ontario and $32 500 for such a family living in Toronto (Statistics Canada, 2011b).

Finally, analysts make use of low-income measures (LIMs). This approach came out of discussions at the Organisation for Economic Co-operation and Development (OECD) in 1989 and is the principle method used in making international comparisons. Put simply, the LIM refers to the median household incomes in a country (half of households lie above the median and half below). For example, in 2009, 50 percent of four-person households in Canada had after-tax income of $37 360 or lower; this figure then represents the LIM for this size household. The LIM is then recalculated to reflect the varying needs of different sizes of households (Statistics Canada, 2011b).

Although Statistics Canada and government agencies in general reject the use of the term "poverty," they are clearly interested in determining what portion of the population has fallen by the wayside. However, the measures just reviewed provide only a snapshot.

Impoverishment and social advancement are dynamic social processes. On the societal level, recession, depression, a public crisis, or a natural disaster may produce shifts in patterns of economic inequality. On an individual level, unemployment, illness, accident, marital breakup, and disability may trigger a sudden slide into the ranks of the poor.

Note also that the poor who are identified by the measures we have discussed are heterogeneous. For example, they are not all on welfare. However, if you are among the 1.7 million Canadians (including almost half a million children) relying on welfare, you are likely surviving on income significantly below the LICOs-AT (Institut de la statistique du Québec, 2010). Thus, in 2009, the annual welfare income for a lone parent with one child living in Ontario was 77 percent of the LICO-AT. A couple with two children living on welfare in Quebec received 65 percent of the LICO-AT. A single employable person in New Brunswick received just 24 percent of the LICO-AT (National Council of Welfare, 2010: A13–A14). Over the past two decades, the value of welfare benefits has steadily declined in some jurisdictions. In Ontario between 1989 and 2009, single employable individuals experienced a 23 percent cut in welfare benefits, and single parents with one child a nearly 3 percent cut. However, in Quebec, Newfoundland and Labrador, and the Yukon, welfare benefits improved during this period (National Council of Welfare, 2010: A27, A28, A29).

In addition to the poor who rely solely on welfare, many others are poor because they earn so little from their paid employment. Indeed, almost two-thirds of poor Canadians are looking for work or are employed (National Council of Welfare, 2012: 10; Luong, 2011). Some 6 percent of the working-age population aged 18 to 64 (excluding students and adults living with family members who support them) had earnings in 2008 that placed them below the LIM (Monsebraaten, 2012a; Stapleton, Murphy, and Xing, 2012: 24). Not surprisingly, with the ongoing loss of well-paid manufacturing employment, the economic recession, and the growth of precarious service-sector work, more and more Canadians, especially in the past decade, are employed but earning below-poverty wages (Stapleton, Murphy, Xing, 2012: 14–25).

As the economy continues to generate short-term, contract, part-time and seasonal employment, many workers are likely to find themselves economically marginalized (Albo, 2010). Between 1996 and 2008, the numbers of individuals who were working yet poor grew by 38 percent (Stapleton, Murphy, and Xing, 2012: 24). Improvements in minimum wage regulations have done little to alter this pattern. In 2011, 5.8 percent of Canadian workers were earning minimum wage (which ranges from a low of $8.75 per hour in British Columbia to a high of $11.00 in Nunavut). However, recent research indicates that in Toronto, a single wage earner working full-time would need to be earning $16.60 an hour (well above Ontario's $10.25 minimum wage) or approximately $33 000 a year to be able to move out of poverty (Monsebraaten, 2012b: 6).

In addition, some individuals combine welfare payments and paid work. Welfare recipients who work may receive monthly "earnings exemptions" allowing them to keep part of their earned income. Exemption rules vary by province and territory (since welfare is a provincial/territorial jurisdiction), the employability of the person, and the size of his or her family. In some provinces, earnings exemptions include work-related expenses, such as child-care costs. Although the provincial and territorial governments' stated intention is to reduce welfare rolls, and despite the already low level of welfare support, all jurisdictions have policies on earnings exemptions that deduct a certain amount of a recipient's earnings from their welfare cheque. For example, in Ontario in 2010, regulations did not allow a lone parent with one child to keep any earned income during the first three months on welfare. After that, the parent could retain only 50 percent of gross earnings. In Alberta, a single employable individual could retain $230 of net income plus 25 percent of any remaining net income (National Council of Welfare, 2010: 7-1–7-4). From this, it is clear that across Canada, combining paid employment with welfare typically does not allow an exit from poverty.

Our portrait of poverty in Canada today is sobering. As the post-recession economic turmoil drags on, and as more recent data become available, it is likely this picture will become grimmer. Between 2007 and 2009, the Ontario poverty rate increased 17 percent and the Canadian poverty rate 6 percent (based on LIM-AT) (Monsebraaten 2011). Certainly, Canada has fared much better than the United States has, where the Census Bureau announced that in 2010, 46.2 million Americans (15.1 percent of the total population) were living in poverty. This was the fourth consecutive annual increase and the highest number of U.S. poor ever reported (Lee, 2011: A23). Even the United States has escaped the 25+ percent unemployment rates and social turmoil reported in Spain, Greece, and Portugal. However, such relative well-being is of little comfort to the single mothers, unattached individuals, Aboriginal Canadians, recent immigrants, people living with disabilities, and others who make up the more than three million Canadians struggling to get by.

THE FEMINIZATION OF POVERTY

Under identifiable circumstances, Canadian women are at high risk of slipping into poverty. In fact, many scholars talk about the "feminization of poverty" insofar as women are much more likely to be poor than men are (Goldberg, 1990; Nelson, 2006; Pearce, 1978). Nor is this a new problem. Deserted, widowed, and orphaned women have long populated the ranks of the poor in disproportionate numbers (Katz, 1975: 60; Simmons, 1986).

While the reasons behind women's impoverishment are complex, they have much to do with traditional gender ideology, inequities in the labour force, family law issues, and the way we typically respond to marriage breakdown. Historically, people have expected women to devote their lives to unpaid duties as wives and mothers. Although in the past many women worked for pay, rules against the employment of married women and the peripheralization and stigmatization of, and low pay scales for, "women's jobs" reinforced the idea that women's proper place was really in the home (Duffy and Pupo, 1992: 13–40; Statistics Canada, 2006a).

This idea came under attack in the twentieth century. The women's movement, increased opportunities for higher education, and the reduction in family size made possible by the legalization of contraception helped to undermine the traditional sexual division of labour. In addition, many Canadian families found it increasingly difficult to live off the income of a single breadwinner. The failure of wages to keep pace with inflation, increased taxation, high unemployment, skyrocketing housing costs, and the loss of high-paying manufacturing jobs made the male-breadwinner family increasingly anachronistic. By 2009, about two-thirds of women with children under the age of three were in the paid labour force, and women composed almost half the Canadian labour force (Ferrao, 2010: 5, 9).

Significant gender differences in work and family life nonetheless persist. Many mothers continue to take time away from paid employment when their children are young or balance family and paid work with part-time or self-employed work (Ferrao, 2010: 13–16). Unless they are well-to-do, women who marry, have children, and assume primary responsibility for domestic work and child care run the risk of impoverishment in the event of divorce or early widowhood—even if they maintain a consistent presence in the part-time labour force (as more than one-quarter of adult Canadian women do) (Ferrao, 2012: 13). Employment in traditional, low-paid women's occupations and time taken off to care for young children can result in economic disaster when a marriage ends in divorce or when women face years of widowhood. Being a recent immigrant, having a disability, or being a member of certain visible minority groups compounds the likelihood of becoming poor.

By the LICOs-AT standard, 22 percent of Canadian single-parent mothers were poor in 2009. While this was a marked improvement over the 40 percent reported in 2000, it means that more than one in five single mothers were living on the economic margins (Statistics Canada, 2011a). While female lone-parent families may result from a variety of situations, fully half of female lone parents are divorced or separated, 30 percent have never been legally married, and 20 percent are widowed. A growing number of female lone-parent families are the result of pregnancy outside of marriage. However, the traditional gender pattern of women assuming custody of children after a divorce or separation remains firm, and lone-parent families are four times more likely to be headed by a woman than by a man (Milan, Keown, and Urquijo, 2011: 12).

The increased risk of poverty after divorce or separation is a result of myriad factors. In the event of divorce, women's pattern of employment, along with earlier periods of withdrawal from the labour force, impede their ability to earn an income. Since women typically become the primary custodial parent, they rely on economic support from their spouse. Despite recent improvements, post-divorce, court-mandated support for children and spouses is difficult to enforce. For example, according to the Ontario Auditor's report, the understaffed and poorly equipped Family Responsibility Office, mandated to enforce court-ordered child support payments, works actively on less than one-quarter of its total caseload and starts action only four months after a case goes into arrears. Despite decades of complaints about this process, if the noncustodial spouse is unable or unwilling to provide economic support, the process of enforcement will likely be lengthy, time-consuming, and frustrating ("Child Support," 2010: IN6).

Given these patterns, it is not surprising that within two years of separation or divorce, 43 percent of women but only 15 percent of men face a decrease in household income while 29 percent of men and 9 percent of women experience an increase (Ambert, 2009: 17). Three years after divorce, women's income remains on average significantly below their income during the marriage and well below their ex-husband's current income. Although Canadian women have made considerable advances in the labour market, divorce patterns still contribute to the feminization of poverty (Ambert, 2009). Despite the needs of single mothers, welfare policy has done little to improve their situation. Although there have been increases in child benefit rates (contributing to improvements in the poverty rate of single mothers), the highest total welfare income in 2009 in Canada for a lone parent with a two-year-old child—$19 297—was in Newfoundland and Labrador. In Ontario, the total 2009 welfare income for such a family (including basic social assistance, other provincial benefits, federal child benefits, other provincial child benefits, HST credit, and provincial tax credits) was $17 372. Except for Newfoundland and Labrador, the provincial welfare support for single mothers was $1000 or more below the LICOs-AT (National Council of Welfare, 2010).

Most significantly, lone mothers, like other welfare recipients, are subject to considerable pressure to enter or return to the labour force as quickly as possible. In the pursuit of reduced provincial deficits, governments have been seeking to reduce welfare rolls and individual welfare payments across the country. Most notoriously, in 1992 the Ontario government under Premier Harris reduced welfare funding by 21 percent. More recently, new regulations in Alberta restrict eligibility for support and amount of welfare payments while mandating that single mothers on welfare search for a job as soon as their youngest child is six months old. In Saskatchewan, single mothers can be required to engage in welfare-to-work programming at the discretion of their caseworker (Cooke and Gazso, 2009).

Unfortunately, this approach fails to address single mothers' responsibilities as caregivers and mothers, and the lack of societal support. In the absence of reliable, low-cost child care and in the face of women's job opportunities being clustered in low-wage, low-skill work, such an approach intensifies the gendered nature of poverty (Breitkreuz, 2005; Cooke and Gazso, 2009). As analysts point out, joining the ranks of the working poor, particularly after being stripped of assets and savings to qualify for social assistance, may leave single mothers stuck at the bottom (Monsebraaten, 2010a; Monsebraaten, 2012a; Stapleton, Murphy and Xing, 2012).

Finally, compounding their plight, single mothers on welfare must also confront the persistent stereotypes that cast them as less worthy of social support than, say, low-income, two-parent families. People often stigmatize single mothers who receive social assistance as promiscuous and irresponsible (Goar, 2008).

Growing old provides no guarantee of relief for women, even though policy initiatives in the 1980s and 1990s reduced much of the poverty burden for seniors (Murphy, Zhang, and Dionne, 2012: 29). Just as being a lone parent puts a woman in economic jeopardy, aging on her own is also problematic. Unattached women over the age of 64— typically widowed, divorced, or separated—face relatively high poverty rates. A recent study found that five years after her husband dies, a woman's income declines on average by more than 15 percent. Meanwhile, a man who loses his spouse experiences a nearly 6 percent *increase* in income. Some 3.6 percent more women than men experience poverty five years after the death of their spouse (Statistics Canada, 2006b).

Senior women are particularly at risk of poverty because they are likely to receive reduced income from occupational pension plans, the Canada/Quebec Pension Plan, and investments. Senior women's after-tax income from all sources in 2008 averaged $24 800 while men's averaged $38 100 (Milan and Vezina, 2011: 21). This is far from surprising since pension entitlements reflect, in part, women's pattern of work interruptions (to take care of family responsibilities), their tendency to work in low-paying jobs with meagre benefits, and their predominance in part-time and contractual work (Gazso, 2005: 59; Statistics Canada, 2006a; Young, 2011).

Based on current trends, most Canadian women can expect to outlive their male partners and spend part of their lives without a male breadwinner in the home. While poverty is highly unlikely for seniors living as couples (an estimated 1.8 percent are poor), 17 percent of senior women living on their own and 12 percent of comparable men live below the LICOs-AT (2008) (Milan and Vezina, 2011: 25).

Despite the dangers associated with ending up unattached, many Canadian women do not plan to maximize financial well-being and autonomy (Duffy, Mandell, and Pupo, 1988). In a culture that perpetuates often unrealistic notions of romantic love, marital life, and parenting, and in an economy premised on relatively low-wage women's work, many women are set up for poverty (McKeen, 2004). With the increasing privatization of pension plans and growing concerns about cutbacks in government-funded pensions, analysts are warning of a resurgence of gendered inequality among seniors. Older, unattached women will be particularly vulnerable if government pensions are reduced or age for eligibility is raised (Young, 2011).

Recent immigrant, visible minority, and Aboriginal women and those with disabilities are at even greater risk of poverty. For example, in 2006, Aboriginal women between the ages of 25 and 54, who are more than twice as likely as non-Aboriginal women to be lone parents and much more likely to be teen parents, earned a median income on average $5000 below that of non-Aboriginal women (O'Donnell and Wallace, 2011: 20, 27). Visible minority and immigrant women are also often disadvantaged because they frequently find that racial and ethnic discrimination, along with language difficulties and inadequate government policy, translate into long hours of precarious, low-wage "women's work," high rates of unemployment, and low income (Chui, 2011; Chui and Maheux, 2011; National Council of Welfare, 2012). Age intensifies the inequality. Older women who are recent immigrants earn incomes below those of their Canadian-born counterparts and rely more on government transfer payments (Statistics Canada, 2006a: 211–38). Aboriginal and visible-minority women are also overrepresented among homeless women. A recent Toronto survey found that more than one-quarter of homeless women belong to a visible minority group, and one in five are Aboriginal (Bacquie, 2008; Street Health Report, 2007).

Finally, disability exacts an added toll on many women's lives. Although most adults with disabilities live on low income, women with disabilities are generally worse off than men with disabilities are. For example, women with activity limitations have an employment rate approximately 10 percent lower than that of their male counterparts (Crompton, 2011: 15). Women over the age of 14 with activity limitations earn on average $24 000 annually, compared with $41 200 for men in the same category. Since the prevalence of activity limitations increases with age, the negative effect of disability on women's economic well-being is likely to intensify over the life course (Crompton, 2011).

CHILD POVERTY

In 2009, almost 1 in 10 Canadian children was growing up in low-income families (Statistics Canada, 2011a). Despite a unanimous vote in the House of Commons in 1989 to eradicate child poverty by 2000, some 634 000 Canadian children are currently poor. While some easing of child poverty took place from 2000 to 2006, the latest low-income figures reveal that the rate increased between 2007 and 2009 (Statistics Canada, 2011a). In an international context, our record seems particularly bleak. According to a recent UNICEF report, Canada ranked 17th out of 24 developed countries in equality of children's material well-being—better than the United States (23) and Britain (19), but worse than the Czech Republic (11) and Germany (10). While Canada ranks much better in terms of educational equality (3) and health equality (9), we are performing dismally in terms of establishing a level playing field for family income and housing (Monsebraaten, 2010b: A16; UNICEF 2010).

Part of the reason for pervasive child poverty is the number of single-mother families and the economic marginalization of some immigrant families. For example, in 2009, almost one-third of poor children lived in a lone-parent family headed by a woman, and almost one-fifth of all children in a mother-headed family lived in low income families (Statistics Canada, 2011a). These children are poor because their parents are poor and their parents' poverty often stems from unemployment, underemployment, inadequate minimum wage standards, and insufficient social welfare support. Predictably, children whose parents are members of at-risk groups—Aboriginal peoples, recent immigrants, and those with disabilities—suffer a greatly increased likelihood of living in poverty. For example, more than one-quarter of visible-minority people living in poverty are children younger than 15 years of age (National Council of Welfare, 2012: 5). Aboriginal children and youth are more likely than other Canadians are to experience the most prolonged and severe poverty (National Council of Welfare, 2007: 21).

STRUGGLING WITH POVERTY: THE PERSONAL EXPERIENCE

Being poor has always meant more than getting by at a certain level of income. Understanding poverty demands more than a statistical overview (Burman, 1988). Poverty often affects people's lives, their sense of self, and their relationships with others. Although the toll of poverty is most apparent in the lives of children, few adults survive impoverishment unscathed. For children and their families, poverty still generally translates into inadequate or insecure housing in unsafe areas. In big cities and on remote reserves, poor children are likely to live in cramped conditions, with substandard heating, too little hot water, improper ventilation, generally unsafe conditions (exposed electrical wiring, and so on), and too little space in which to play and study. Even inadequate housing in large metropolitan areas may gobble up social assistance benefits, leaving little for other necessities, let alone emergencies. As Mel Hurtig (1999) famously titled his book on poverty, the poor often must choose to "pay the rent or feed the kids." Housing problems are frequently compounded by neighbourhoods plagued by high rates of crime and vandalism, inadequate play facilities, high levels of pollution, and hazardous traffic (Baxter, 1993; Goar, 2008; McMurtry and Curling, 2008; Raphael, 2007; Shapcott, 2010; Swift, Balmer, and Dineen, 2010; Welsh, 2008).

Poor families often lack the income to maintain a nutritious diet. High housing costs and the spectre of homelessness mean that food budgets are stretched to the limit. Dental care, even in the face of pain, becomes a low priority. A single mother who is working part-time comments, "I definitely need dental care but it's a matter of finances.... My income just won't cover the extras like going to the dentist ... so the only time I go is when I'm in severe pain" (Wallace and MacEntee, 2012: 35). The net result is a national pattern of health inequity in which the poor—even poor infants and children—are more subject to ill health and frequent hospitalization. For example, the rate of infant mortality in the poorest 20 percent of urban neighbourhoods is 40 percent higher than it is in the wealthiest 20 percent of neighbourhoods. Further, the situation appears to be deteriorating. While in the 1980s there was little difference between wealthy and poor neighbourhoods in the adult death rate from diabetes, today there is an "epidemic" of adult deaths from diabetes among low-income Canadians (Raphael, 2010: 42).

While Canada's food banks and soup kitchens provide a stopgap solution to hunger for many families, many poor children get by on too little food or food with high fat and sugar content (Swift, Balmer, and Dineen, 2010). The homeless are generally plagued by health problems, including malnourishment, chronic respiratory and ear infections, gastrointestinal disorders, sexually transmitted infections, and chronic infections. The psychological health of the poor also reflects the painful social and emotional environment in which they live. A recent study of low-income residents in two large Canadian cities found that almost all the participants felt that they were negatively stereotyped—seen as lazy and irresponsible—by their fellow citizens. Not only did they feel stigmatized, but they also tended to feel they did not belong and that they were socially isolated (Reutter et al., 2009; Stewart et al., 2009).

Predictably, the misery implied in these patterns contributes to family breakdown and dislocation. Life often becomes unpredictable. Being poor means not knowing whether you will be able to continue living in your home and retain custody of your children, or whether your children will have to change schools and make new friends. In these and numerous other ways, the foundations of a person's life may be shattered. Living with profound uncertainty inevitably contributes to stress, depression, and helplessness (Hurtig, 1999; Neal, 2004; Swift, Balmer, and Dineen 2010).

Poverty means more than doing without. It means feeling cut off from the mainstream. With few exceptions, the lives and experiences of the poor are not reflected sympathetically on television or in the movies, if at all. Advertisements in magazines and on subway trains underscore the insufficiencies of their lifestyle. Mothers must scramble to make sure their children have the money to "fit in." As one mother said, "Another thing that comes out [of the monthly budget] that's very important is the children's milk money for school, and their pizza and hot dog money every week, because they won't be ostracized. I won't have other children saying they're too poor to get those." However, meeting these needs means that "sometimes I can afford [heating] oil, sometimes I can't" (Power, 2005: 652).

Relying on social assistance programs further compounds feelings of stigmatization and vulnerability. Even when welfare workers are helpful and supportive, the relationship between worker and client erodes the autonomy, power, and privacy of the poor. The negativity of some welfare workers makes a bad situation worse. One single mother comments, "Every time I come back from there I cry. They make you feel so low, they make you feel like you're worthless, and they think they're God because of what they give you. And they give you nothing. They don't" (Power, 2005: 649). Home visits and personal questions from social assistance workers, along with the constant fear of being "reported to welfare" for not following the rules, further undermine clients' self-confidence.

The negative reaction of the public to welfare recipients complicates their problems with the welfare system. Commonly, property owners will not rent to people on welfare, and women on welfare may find themselves labelled as desperate and sexually available. Degradation becomes part of everyday experience: "And then the taxi driver is looking at you, 'Oh, not another charity case'" (McIntyre, Officer, and Robinson, 2003: 324). Most commonly, the social assistance recipient has to confront the still widespread belief that people on welfare cheat (Blackwell, 2003: 107–08). Informed by the historical notion that many of the poor are not deserving or should be punished for their plight, popular attitudes toward the provision of adequate social assistance remain ambivalent and uninformed.

Despite the enormous pressure to "get back on your feet," endless roadblocks exist on the path to getting off welfare. For many single mothers, adequate child-care support is a major obstacle to employment: "The daycare she went to when she was a baby, every day they called. I had just started this job and every day, I swear, every day they were calling me that something was wrong with her. I'd come in, walk in at 9:00, by 10:00 she's got a rash, or pink eye or something and then I had to leave" (Mason, 2003: 50). A Toronto single mother of three recounts that when her youngest child started Grade 1, she took a part-time job to improve their economic situation. However, her extra income immediately caused her subsidized rent to double. After taxes and employment-related expenses, she found she had not improved her family's economic situation at all (Monsebraaten, 2008: A4).

POVERTY AND THE CHANGING FACE OF SOCIAL INEQUALITY

While the experience of impoverishment may be devastating, the patterns of income inequality in Canada are complex. Certainly, the percentage of Canadians living below the LICOs-AT fell between 2000 and 2007, and then increased for 7 out of 10 provinces between 2007 and 2009 (Statistics Canada, 2011a). This recent shift, along with ongoing economic instability, is particularly concerning in light of the growing chasm between wealthy Canadians and the rest of the population. In the 1950s and 1960s, the wealthiest 1 percent of Canadians earned 8 percent of the total national income, but in 1998–2007 that grew to 30 percent (Olive, 2011b). The growing gap between the haves and have-nots is a global phenomenon, with income inequality hitting a 30-year high across industrialized economies in 2010 (Flavelle, 2011: B2).

Canada is at the forefront of these developments, even relative to the United States, and is experiencing dramatic increases in income disparity ("Canada's Income Gap," 2011: B6). A 2008 study of 30 developed economies reported Canada was second only to Germany in a sharp increase in earnings inequality. By 2009, the richest 3.8 percent of Canadian households controlled 66.6 percent of all financial wealth (excluding real estate), and in the absence of new policy initiatives, this is predicted to reach 70 percent by 2018 (Whittington, 2011: A19). For the poorest portion of the Canadian population, this means that the gap between their real average income and that of the richest Canadians has grown from $92 300 in 1976 to $177 500 in 2009 (Acharya-Tom Yew, 2011: B6).

CONCLUSION

Poverty is an important social issue across Canada. Social inequality is increasing significantly. The victims of poverty include the most vulnerable Canadians. Poverty is rooted in the economic and political systems. While some individuals, such as teenage parents and high-school dropouts, may have made poor decisions, their impoverishment can be traced to inadequate minimum wage legislation, the decline in manufacturing employment in the face of global competition, the unfettered growth in nonstandard employment in the service sector, and the overall weak response from federal, provincial, territorial, and municipal governments in addressing the inequities in our midst. Clearly, as evidenced by past successes in reducing the poverty rates for seniors, policy initiatives—including more progressive taxation and increased social support (especially high-quality, government-subsidized child care)—can address economic inequities. As disparities grow, Canadians will be deciding whether they will demand such actions from their political leaders.

REFERENCES

Acharya-Tom Yew, Madhavi. (2011). "Gap Widens between Rich and Poor." *Toronto Star* 14 July: B6.

Albo, Greg. (2010). "The 'New Economy' and Capitalism Today." In N. Pupo and M. Thomas, eds., *Interrogating the New Economy*. Toronto: University of Toronto Press.

Alphonso, C. (2008). "For Many, Brain Injury at Root of Homelessness." *Globe and Mail* 8 October: A11.

Ambert, A. (2009). *Divorce: Facts, Causes and Consequences*, 3rd ed. Ottawa: Vanier Institute of the Family.

Bacquie, S. (2008). "Homeless Women in Canada." On the World Wide Web at http://section15.ca/features/news/2008/08/22 /homelessness/ (retrieved 6 August 2012).

Baxter, Sheila. (1993). *A Child Is Not a Toy: Voices of Children in Poverty*. Vancouver: New Star Books.

Blackwell, J. (2003). "The Welfare State Rewards Laziness." In J. Blackwell, M. Smith, and J. Sorenson, eds., *The Culture of Prejudice* (pp. 107–12). Toronto: Broadview Press.

Breitkreuz, Rhonda. (2005). "Engendering Citizenship? A Critical Feminist Analysis of Canadian Welfare-to-Work Policies and the Employment Experiences of Lone Mothers." *Journal of Sociology and Social Welfare*, *32* (2), 147–65.

Broadbent, Ed. (2005). "Addressing Child Poverty." *Perception*, *27* (3&4), 9.

Burman, Patrick. (1988). *Killing Time, Losing Ground: Experiences of Unemployment*. Toronto: Wall & Thompson.

"Canada's Income Gap Widening Faster Than in U.S." (2011). *Toronto Star* 14 September: B6.

"Child Support: Too Low a Priority." (2010). *Toronto Star* 11 December: IN6.

Chui, Tina. (2011) "Immigrant Women." *Women in Canada: A Gender-Based Statistical Report.* Ottawa: Ministry of Industry. Catalogue No. 89-503-X.

Chui, Tina and Helene Maheux. (2011). "Visible Minority Women." *Women in Canada: A Gender-Based Statistical Report.* Ottawa: Ministry of Industry. Catalogue No. 89-503-X.

Cooke, Martin and Amber Gazso. (2009). "Taking a Life Course Perspective on Social Assistance Use in Canada: A Different Approach." *Canadian Journal of Sociology, 34* (2), 349–72.

Crompton, Susan. 2011. "Women with Activity Limitations." *Women in Canada: A Gender-Based Statistical Report.* Ottawa: Ministry of Industry. Catalogue No. 89-503-X.

"Deciding Where Poverty Starts." (2005). *Canada and the World, 70,* (5), 4–7.

Duffy, Ann, Nancy Mandell, and Norene Pupo. (1988). *Few Choices: Women, Work and Family.* Toronto: Garamond Press.

Duffy, Ann and Norene Pupo. (1992). *Part-Time Paradox: Connecting Gender, Work, and Family.* Toronto: McClelland & Stewart.

Ferrao, Vincent. (2010). "Paid Work." *Women in Canada: A Gender-Based Statistical Report.* Ottawa: Ministry of Industry. Catalogue No. 89-503-X.

Ferrao, Vincent. (2012). "Paid Work." On the World Wide Web at http://www.statcan.gc.ca/pub/89-503-x/2010001/article/11387 -eng.htm (retrieved 4 August 2012).

Flavelle, Dana. (2011). "Canada Edges above the Global Average in Inequality." *Toronto Star* 6 December: B1, B2.

Flavelle, Dana. (2012). "Borrowing Boomers Pile on More Debt." *Toronto Star* 27 January: B3.

Food Banks Canada. (2012). "Hunger Count 2011: Food Bank Use in Canada." On the World Wide Web at http://www.foodbankscanada .ca/getmedia/dc2aa860-4c33-4929-ac36-fb5d40f0b7e7 /HungerCount-2011.pdf.aspx (retrieved 9 March 2012).

Gazso, Amber. (2005). "The Poverty of Unattached Senior Women and the Canadian Retirement Income System: A Matter of Blame or Contradiction?" *Journal of Sociology and Social Welfare*, 32 (2), 41–62.

Goar, C. (2008). "Abuse Follows in Poverty's Wake." *Toronto Star* 14 November: AA6.

Goldberg, Gertrude Schaffner. (1990). "Canada: Bordering on the Feminization of Poverty." In Gertrude Schaffner Goldberg and Eleanor Kremen, eds., *The Feminization of Poverty: Only in America?* (pp. 59–90). New York: Praeger.

Greater Vancouver Regional Steering Committee on Homelessness. (2011). "Metro Vancouver Homeless Count: Preliminary Report." On the World Wide Web at http://stophomelessness.ca/wp -content/uploads/2011/05/v8_preliminaryreport_may23_ finalversion.pdf (retrieved 9 March 2012).

Haan, Michael. (2011). "Does Immigrant Residential Crowding Reflect Hidden Homelessness?" *Canadian Studies in Population*, *38* (1–2), 43–59.

"Homeless People Die 30 Years Younger, Study Suggests." (2011). *BBC News,* 20 December.

Human Resources and Skills Development Canada. (2008). "Indicators of Well-Being in Canada: Housing—Homeless Shelters and Beds." On the World Wide Web at http://www4.hrsdc.gc.ca/.3ndic.1t.4r@ -eng.jsp?iid=44 (retrieved 3 August 2012).

Human Resources and Skills Development Canada. (2009). "Low Income in Canada: 2000–2007 Using the Market Basket Measure—August 2009." On the World Wide Web at http://www.hrsdc.gc.ca/en/ publications_resources/research/index.shtml (retrieved 9 March 2012).

Hurtig, Mel. (1999). *Pay the Rent or Feed the Kids: The Tragedy and Disgrace of Poverty in Canada.* Toronto: McClelland & Stewart.

Institute de la statistique du Québec. (2010). "Welfare Dependency in Canada—National Statistics." On the World Wide Web at http://www.canadiansocialresearch.net/welfare_dependency.htm (retrieved 17 March 2012).

Katz, Michael B. (1975). *The People of Hamilton, Canada West: Family and Class in a Mid-Nineteenth-Century City.* Cambridge, MA: Harvard University Press.

Lee, Don. (2011). "Record 46.2 Million Americans Live in Poverty." *Toronto Star* 14 September: A23.

Luong, May. 2011. "The Wealth and Finances of Employed Low-Income Families." *Perspectives on Labour and Income* (Autumn), 3–13.

Mason, Robin. (2003). "Listening to Lone Mothers: Paid Work, Family Life, and Childcare in Canada." *Journal of Children and Poverty,* *9* (1), 41–54.

McIntyre, Lynn, Suzanne Officer, and Lynne M. Robinson. (2003). "Feeling Poor: The Felt Experience of Low-Income Lone Mothers." *Affilia, 18* (3), 316–31.

McKeen, W. (2004). *Money in Their Own Name: The Feminist Voice in Poverty Debate in Canada, 1970–1995.* Toronto: University of Toronto Press.

McMurtry, R. and A. Curling. (2008). "Roots of Violence Grow in Toxic Soil of Social Exclusion." *Toronto Star* 15 November: AA6.

Milan, Anne, Leslie-Anne Keown, and C. Robles Urquijo. (2011). "Families, Living Arrangements and Unpaid Work." *Women in Canada: A Gender-Based Statistical Report.* Ottawa: Minister of Industry. Catalogue No. 89-503-X.

Milan, Anne and Mireille Vezina. (2011). "Senior Women." *Women in Canada: A Gender-Based Statistical Report.* Ottawa: Minister of Industry. Catalogue No. 89-503-X.

Monsebraaten, L. (2008). "Having a Job, but Losing Ground." *Toronto Star* 2 April: A4.

Monsebraaten, L. (2010a). "Welfare Vice Crushes Hope of Recovery, Report Finds." *Toronto Star* 14 December: A1.

Monsebraaten, L. (2010b) "Poorest Children Falling Too Far Behind, Report Says." *Toronto Star* 3 December: A16.

Monsebraaten, L. (2011) "Ontario Poverty Rate up Since Last Election." *Toronto Star* 18 June: A14.

Monsebraaten, L. (2012a). "Toronto Ranks of Working Poor Swelling." *Toronto Star* 12 February: A8–A9.

Monsebraaten, L. (2012b). "The Cost of Really Living." *Toronto Star* 11 February: A6.

"Mortgage Freedom Years Away, Poll Finds." (2011). *Toronto Star* 18 November: B3.

Murphy, Brian, Xuelin Zhang, and Claude Dionne. (2012). *Low Income in Canada: a Multi-line and Multi-index Perspective.* Ottawa: Minister of Industry. Catalogue No. 75F002M-No. 001.

National Council of Welfare. (2007). *First Nations, Métis and Inuit Children and Youth: Time to Act.* Ottawa: Ministry of Supply and Services.

National Council of Welfare. (2010). *Welfare Incomes 2009.* Ottawa: Minister of Supply and Services.

National Council of Welfare. (2012). "Poverty Profile: Special Edition—A Snapshot of Racialized Poverty in Canada." On the World Wide Web at http://www.ncwcnbes.net (retrieved 17 March 2012).

Neal, Rusty. (2004). *Voices: Women, Poverty and Homelessness in Canada.* Ottawa: National Anti-Poverty Organization.

Nelson, Adie. (2006). *Gender in Canada*, 3rd ed. Toronto: Pearson Prentice Hall.

O'Donnell, Vivian and Susan Wallace. (2011). "First Nations, Métis and Inuit Women." *Women in Canada: A Gender-Based Statistical Report.* Ottawa: Ministry of Industry. Catalogue No. 89-503-X.

Olive, David. (2011a). "Our Savings Shortfall Threatens Our Future." *Toronto Star* 18 February: B1.

Olive, David. (2011b). "Income Gap HAS Also Widened in Canada." *Toronto Star* 10 September: B1, B3.

Pearce, Diana. (1978). "The Feminization of Poverty: Women, Work and Welfare." *Urban and Social Change Review, 11* (February), 28–36.

Power, Elaine M. (2005). "The Unfreedom of Being Other: Canadian Lone Mothers' Experiences of Poverty and 'Life on the Cheque.'" *Sociology, 39* (4), 643–60.

Preston, Valerie, Robert Murdie, Silvia D'Addario, Prince Sibanda, Ann Marie Murnaghan, with Jennifer Logan and Mi Hae Ahn. (2011). "Precarious Housing and Hidden Homelessness Among Refugees, Asylum Seekers, and Immigrants in the Toronto Metropolitan Area." *CERIS Working Paper Series No. 87.* Toronto: Ceris—The Ontario Metropolis Centre.

Raphael, D. (2007). *Poverty and Policy in Canada.* Toronto: Canadian Scholars' Press.

Raphael, D. (2010). "Health Equity in Canada." *Social Alternatives, 29* (2), 41–49.

Reutter, Linda I., Miriam J. Stewart, Gerry Veenstra, Rhonda Love, Dennis Raphael, and Edward Makwarimba. (2009). "'Who Do They Think We Are, Anyway?' Perceptions of and Response to Poverty Stigma." *Qualitative Health Research, 19* (3), 297–311.

Ross, David and Richard Shillington. (2000). *The Canadian Fact Book on Poverty.* Ottawa: Canadian Council on Social Development.

Rubin, Josh. (2011). "Household Debt Climbs Past Six Figures." *Toronto Star* 18 February: B1.

Salvation Army. (2009). "Poverty Shouldn't Be a Life Sentence: A Report on the Perspectives of Service Delivery in Salvation Army Shelters." On the World Wide Web at http://homeless.samhsa.gov/ResourceFiles/0simvcnv.pdf (retrieved 9 March 2012).

Sarlo, C. (2008). "Measuring Poverty in Canada." *Fraser Forum.* Vancouver: Fraser Institute.

Shapcott, Michael. (2010) "Housing Strategy on the Brink." In Jamie Swift, Brice Balmer, and Mira Dineen, eds., *Persistent Poverty: Voices from the Margins* (pp. 67–74). Toronto: Between the Lines.

Simmons, Christina. (1986). "'Helping the Poorer Sisters': The Women of the Jost Mission, Halifax, 1905–1945." In Veronica Strong-Boag and Anita Clair Fellman, eds., *Rethinking Canada: The Promise of Women's History.* Toronto: Copp Clark Pitman.

Skott-Myhre, H., R. Raby, and J. Nikolaou. (2008). "Towards a Delivery System of Services for Rural Homeless Youth: A Literature Review and Case Study." *Child and Youth Care Forum, 37* (2), 87–102.

Smith, J. (2008). "Definition of Poverty Stalls Federal Committee." *Toronto Star* 16 April. On the World Wide Web at http://www.thestar.com/printArticle/414057 (retrieved 21 August 2009).

Stapleton, J., Brian Murphy, and Yue Xing. (2012). *The "Working Poor" in the Toronto Region: Who They Are, Where They Live, and How Trends Are Changing.* Toronto: Metcalf Foundation.

Statistics Canada. (2006a). *Women in Canada: A Gender-Based Statistical Report,* 5th ed. Ottawa: Ministry of Supply and Services.

Statistics Canada. (2006b). "Study: The Death of a Spouse and the Impact on Income." *The Daily* 10 July. On the World Wide Web at http://www.statcan.gc.ca/daily-quotidien/060710/dq060710a-eng.htm (retrieved 21 August 2009).

Statistics Canada. (2011a). "Income of Canadians 2009." *The Daily.* June 15. On the World Wide Web at http://www.statcan.gc.ca/daily-quotidien/110615/dq110615b-eng.htm (retrieved 21 August 2012).

Statistics Canada. (2011b). *Low Income Lines, 2009–2010.* Ottawa: Minister of Industry. Catalogue No. 75F002M-No.002.

Stewart, Miriam J., Edward Makwarimba, Linda I. Reutter, Gerry Veenstra, Rhonda Love, and Dennis Raphael. (2009). "Poverty, Sense of Belonging and Experiences of Social Isolation." *Journal of Poverty, 13,* 173–95.

Street Health Report. (2007). *Research Bulletin #2: Women & Homelessness.* Toronto: Ontario Women's Health Network.

Swift, Jamie, Brice Balmer, and Mira Dineen. (2010). *Persistent Poverty: Voices from the Margins.* Toronto: Between the Lines.

Toronto Shelter, Support, and Housing Administration. (2011). "Quick Facts." On the World Wide Web at http://www.toronto.ca/housing/pdf/quickfacts.pdf (retrieved 9 March 2012).

UNICEF. (2010). *The Children Left Behind: A League Table of Inequality in Child Well-Being in the World's Richest Countries.* New York: United Nations Children's Fund.

Wallace, Bruce B. and Michael I. MacEntee. (2012). "Access to Dental Care for Low-Income Adults: Perceptions of Affordability, Availability and Acceptability." *Journal of Community Health, 37,* 32–39.

Welsh, M. (2008). "Poorest Areas Also Most Polluted, Report Shows." *Toronto Star* 27 November: A6.

Westhead, Rick. (2011). "Poverty a Numbers Game." *Toronto Star* 9 October: A3.

Whittington, Les. (2011). "Tory Tax Policy May Worsen Disparities." *Toronto Star* 28 May: A19.

Young, Claire. (2011). "Pensions, Privatization and Poverty: The Gendered Impact." *Canadian Journal of Women and the Law, 23* (2), 661–85.

PART 3B

ETHNICITY AND RACE

Sociologists often distinguish **ethnic groups** by ancestry, culture, and social location. **Races** have relatively unique ancestries, cultures, and social locations, too. In addition, races differ from ethnic groups and from each other in terms of visible physical characteristics, such as skin colour, that are socially defined as significant and that are therefore significant in their social consequences.

Some 16.5 percent of Canadians defined themselves as members of a visible minority group in the 2006 census. (The figure excludes Aboriginal Canadians, who constitute another 3.8 percent of the population). The percentage of visible minority group members is higher in large cities, reaching about 25 percent in Montreal, Edmonton, Calgary, and Winnipeg; 40 percent in Vancouver; and 50 percent in Toronto. South Asians (East Indian, Pakistani, Sri Lankan, and so on.) and Chinese each account for roughly a quarter of the racial-minority population, blacks for about 15 percent, and Filipinos for about 8 percent. By some measures, Canada is the most ethnically and racially tolerant country in the world. Still, government-sponsored studies and public opinion polls find that around a third of Canadians are prejudiced at least to some degree against members of an ethnic or racial group. (Note that **prejudice** refers to a negative *attitude* toward members of an ethnic or racial group, while **discrimination** refers to *behaviour* that has negative consequences for such groups.)

Given the existence of ethnic and racial prejudice, most of Canada's racial minorities have fared surprisingly well economically, especially after the immigrant generation. This is a tribute to their resourcefulness and industry, and it is largely a consequence of their social background. Their economic achievements are due largely to the country's selective immigration policy, which favours immigrants who arrive with higher education and money. Credentials and capital help to overcome the worst economic consequences of prejudice and discrimination.

Nonetheless, economic differences among racial and ethnic groups persist. Hugh Lautard and Neil Guppy explore them in depth in Chapter 12, where they analyze Canadian census data from 1931 to 2006. They conclude that occupational differences between ethnic and racial groups have decreased substantially over the period but are still considerable. Why do they persist? Mainly because some groups continue to be augmented by substantial numbers of immigrants, and immigrants suffer more disadvantages than native-born Canadians do. For example, immigrants may lack English-and French-language skills and contacts in the wider community that could help them find better jobs. The Canadian-born children of immigrants are less disadvantaged in this regard, and their movement up the stratification system is therefore somewhat easier, even though discrimination persists, especially for members of some racial minority groups.

Three exceptions cloud the relatively bright picture sketched above:

1. The biggest and most glaring exception is composed of Canada's Aboriginal peoples, who have fared worse than any other ethnic or racial group in the country. European colonization virtually destroyed their way of life. Robbed of land, culture, community, and even children, they now suffer more unemployment, poverty, alcoholism, infant mortality, and day-to-day violence than any other group in the land.

2. A second exception to the generally bright picture regarding trends in ethnic and racial inequality in Canada concerns black men. Their income is typically and substantially lower than we would expect given their level of education, years of job experience, and other factors. What is more, although the economic disadvantages of black men fall after the immigrant generation, they remain significant. This pattern of persistent inequality is unlike that of other immigrant groups—and unlike that of black women, whose earnings are in line with their qualifications after the immigrant generation. It is difficult to escape the conclusion that black men are the victims of prejudice and discrimination so severe that they exert a big impact on their life chances, even if they are born in this country.

In Chapter 13, Scot Wortley and Julian Tanner examine one manifestation of such prejudice and discrimination. Their survey shows that whites and Asians in Toronto enjoy at least three prophylactics against police stops and searches: age, class, and lack of criminal activity. For whites and Asians, being older and better educated, and lacking a criminal record, insulates them from police stops and searches. For blacks, however, age has no such effect. In fact, better-educated and well-to-do blacks are *more* likely to be stopped and searched than are less-educated and poorer blacks; police seem to be especially suspicious of blacks driving expensive cars, for example. And while lack of criminal activity insulates whites and Asians from stops and searches, it does not have such an effect for blacks. If the police kept as close an eye on whites and Asians as they do on blacks, whites and Asians would undoubtedly have a higher crime rate. Conversely, the high black crime rate is at least partly a function of blacks being under closer surveillance than others are.

3. The third exception to the bright picture sketched above concerns immigrants who have arrived in Canada since the 1990s. Overall, they have experienced a lower rate of upward mobility than earlier arrivals. The main reason for their relatively slow economic progress is that their qualifications are insufficiently recognized in the workplace. Recent immigrants are on average better educated than Canadian-born workers are, and their level of fluency in the official languages is not appreciably different from that of earlier arrivals, yet they are experiencing higher levels of unemployment and lower relative earnings than immigrants did before the 1990s. Clearly, Canadian institutions must be changed to use immigrants' skills more effectively. This must be done not just for the sake of immigrants but for the sake of Canadian society as a whole, which loses about $2 billion a year by underemploying highly qualified immigrants and suffers shortages of skilled workers in several fields, most notably medicine.

As measured by per capita annual income, the Québécois used to be a disadvantaged minority in Canadian society but that is no longer the case. Nonetheless, some Québécois still want to opt out of Confederation. Separatism is not, however, either the first or the most recent vision of the ideal future (or "utopia") that has animated Quebec society since the mid-twentieth century. In Chapter 14, Jean-Philippe Warren recaps the utopian visions that have animated Quebec society since that time. These utopias include the desire for (1) the creation of a true democracy, (2) the creation of a culture of openness, (3) the renewal of nationalism (in both federalist and separatist variants), and (4) the establishment of a social democracy in which social justice prevails. Warren evaluates the extent to which it is worthwhile for Quebeckers to continue fighting the battles of their predecessors. He also assesses the extent to which old ideas could usefully give way to a new understanding of Quebec's present condition and ideal future.

GLOSSARY

Discrimination is behaviour that has negative consequences for members of an ethnic or a racial group.

Ethnic groups are social collectivities that are distinguished by relatively unique ancestry and culture.

Prejudice refers to negative attitudes toward members of an ethnic or a racial group.

Races have relatively unique ancestries and cultures but differ from ethnic groups and from one another in terms of visible physical characteristics, such as skin colour, that are socially defined as significant and that are significant in their social consequences.

CRITICAL THINKING QUESTIONS

1. Is it accurate to portray Canada as a vertical mosaic? Justify your answer with material from your readings.
2. Outline the utopian visions that have animated Quebec politics over the past half-century. According to Jean-Philippe Warren, how worthwhile is it for Quebeckers today to fight the battles of their predecessors? What alternative does he propose?

ANNOTATED BIBLIOGRAPHY

Peter S. Li, *Destination Canada: Immigration Debates and Issues* (Toronto: Oxford University Press, 2003). A thorough treatment of immigration in Canada.

Jeffrey Reitz and Raymond Breton, *The Illusion of Difference: Realities of Ethnicity in Canada and the United States* (Toronto: C. D. Howe Institute, 1994). Canadians often think Canada's "ethnic mosaic" differs from the American "melting pot." This book explodes the myth.

Chapter 12

Multiculturalism or Vertical Mosaic?

OCCUPATIONAL STRATIFICATION AMONG CANADIAN ETHNIC GROUPS

HUGH LAUTARD, University of New Brunswick
and NEIL GUPPY, University of British Columbia

INTRODUCTION

Canada is primarily a land of immigrants. Most Canadians trace ancestral roots to Europe or Asia. This has meant, from the origin of the nation, a mixing of people with diverse ethnic roots. How well this mixing has occurred is the focus of this chapter.

The government policy of multiculturalism implies a wholesome mixing of ethnic groups, an equality among peoples of distinct cultural heritages. Canada's diverse cultural heritages are supported through many institutions, including ethnic media outlets, churches, schools, and restaurants. The equality among these diverse cultures is most actively promoted by governments but also by, for example, schools. Multicultural curricula now permeate the school system, in social studies courses, in recognizing different religious holidays, and in celebrating ethnic heritage days (Guppy and Lyon, 2012). Different cultural traditions provide separate ethnic identities within a common, egalitarian framework. Multiculturalism highlights cultural blending and ethnic equality.

A contrasting vision of Canada was proposed by sociologist John Porter (1965). Writing in the 1960s, he championed the imagery of a "vertical mosaic." "Mosaic" highlights distinct ethnic identities, but Porter saw little mixing or blending. He argued that Canada's ethnic groups were vertically arranged. According to Porter, Canada was composed of distinct social groups defined principally by social class and ethnicity. Furthermore, these social groups were vertically ranked according to income, power, and prestige. The vertical mosaic, Porter argued, accentuates distinct cultures and ethnic inequality.

Source: Reprinted by permission of the authors.

How useful are the contrasting images of the vertical mosaic and multiculturalism in understanding modern Canada? Canada's population has grown and diversified since 1965, when Porter published *The Vertical Mosaic*, and since 1971, when Canada adopted multiculturalism as federal government policy.

Section 12.1 of the Canadian Charter of Rights and Freedoms (1985) proclaims: "Every individual is equal before and under the law and has the right to the equal protection and equal benefit of the law without discrimination and, in particular, without discrimination based on race, national or ethnic origin, [and] colour. ..." However, despite the Charter's grounding in multicultural language, the legacy of the vertical mosaic has required additional legislation to help enhance the Charter's equality provisions. So, for example, the Employment Equity Act (1986) seeks to erase the subordinate positions of women, people with disabilities, Aboriginal peoples, and visible-minority groups. The act requires employers to hire according to equity targets to overcome ethnic inequality in the labour force. While proclaiming multiculturalism as official policy, the federal government has had to enact laws simultaneously in an attempt to erode the vertical mosaic. If the key proposition of *The Vertical Mosaic* still holds—that ethnicity shapes inequality—then such legislation as the Employment Equity Act remains important. This implies, though, that multiculturalism remains more ideology than fact, more rhetoric than reality. Is there a causal link between your ethnicity and your socioeconomic fortunes or misfortunes? We present new data that, when compared with trends published earlier, afford the longest historical perspective available on the association between ethnicity and occupation, based on 75 years of census data, from 1931 to 2006. As did Porter before us, we stress both social differences (multiple ethnic groups in a mosaic) and social stratification (vertical alignment of ethnic groups).

IS THE SIGNIFICANCE OF ETHNICITY FOR INEQUALITY DECLINING?

In *The Vertical Mosaic*, Porter described Canada as a nation fractured by ethnicity. He saw the French and the British as two "charter status" groups, commanding greater power and privilege than "entrance status" groups (other immigrants). He analyzed the asymmetry of power favouring the British over the French and claimed that this asymmetry characterized noncharter immigrant groups, too. For Porter, "immigration and ethnic affiliation ... [were] important factors in the formation of social classes" (1965: 73).

Porter focused especially on the economic elite, in which he claimed "economic power belong[ed] almost exclusively to [White Protestants] of British origin" (Porter, 1965: 286). More recent analyses of the wealthiest Canadians show less British dominance. While the Thomson family, with its strong British roots, continues to be the wealthiest Canadian family, the corridors of power are now less WASPish (Nakhaie, 1997; Ogmundson and Doyle, 2001; Ogmundson and McLaughlin, 1990). At one time almost exclusively British, the Canadian elite, almost no matter how it is defined, now contains more people from other ethnic backgrounds. Among current Canadian billionaires are people with ethnic surnames that are very non-British, including Emanuel Saputo (food), David Azrieli (real estate), and Paul Desmarais (finance).

Porter (1965) also used census data from 1931, 1951, and 1961 to make his case. By tabulating ethnic origin and occupation, he showed which ethnic groups dominated which job categories. For example, in the 1931 census, he found British and Jewish groups were overrepresented in professional and financial occupations. Conversely, they were underrepresented in unskilled and primary jobs (fishing, logging, mining). He wrote that the "French, German, and Dutch would probably rank next, followed by Scandinavian, Eastern European, Italian, Japanese, 'Other Central European', Chinese, and Native Indian" (p. 81). His 1961 census data showed that, save for the French who had slid down a little, "the rough rank order [had] persisted over time" (p. 90).

Why were different ethnic groups represented at higher and lower occupational levels? Porter proposed two complementary explanations. First, newcomers to Canada often brought with them different educational and occupational experiences. People of British heritage frequently came with professional qualifications that were officially recognized in Canada, whereas people from other ethnic backgrounds often arrived with little education and no recognized professional skills. New entrants to Canada thus reinforced the link between ethnic ancestry and social class (Porter, 1965: 86, 1985: 40–51).[1]

Second, Porter argued that social mobility was correlated with ethnicity. Ethnic groups, he argued, either varied in how much they valued economic achievement and upward mobility or found that discrimination dampened their labour market success (Pineo and Porter, 1985: 360–61). Indeed, Porter felt that multiculturalism would impede ethnic assimilation and perpetuate the link between social class and ethnicity (Heath and Yu, 2005).

Much social science research has assessed the adequacy of Porter's vertical mosaic imagery. No doubt insightful in his era, is it an accurate portrayal of ethnic inequality through the last half century? Since the end of World War II, the sources of Canadian immigrants have shifted dramatically away from Europe and toward other continents, especially Asia. As well, Canada has changed its immigration policy. Now, greater priority is given to the skills new entrants have, as opposed to their place of birth. For example, more emphasis is now placed on education and fluency in at least one of the two official languages. Occupational experience is more valued than birthplace.

Some researchers have concluded that the vertical mosaic imagery simply needs revising to note its "colour coding." They argue that for people of visible minority background, the association between ethnicity and social class has been retained. Now we have a "new ethnic mosaic ... redrafted along lines of race and colour" (Agocs and Boyd, 1993: 333; Hou, Balakrishnan, and Jurdi, 2009; Pendakur and Pendakur, 2011).

Other research traditions have followed Porter's original lead and compared patterns of association between ethnicity and social class in successive census years. For example, Lautard and Loree (1984: 342) used detailed ethnicity and occupation data from 1931 to 1971 and concluded that "occupational inequality is still substantial enough to justify the use of the concept 'vertical mosaic' to characterize ... ethnic relations in Canada" (Darroch, 1979; Pendakur, 2002). The census data used by Porter and by Lautard and Loree combine both the foreign born and the native born, thus allowing researchers to examine social change by focusing on trends over time. However, the census data that they used provide no test for the two explanations Porter offered about the association of ethnicity and class.

Monica Boyd's (1985) research on the influence of birthplace on occupational attainment offers a test of the immigration interpretation. For foreign-born women and men, Boyd demonstrated that ethnic ancestry was correlated with occupational attainment. Even when immigrants with the same age, education, social origin, and place of residence were compared, the correlation existed. For women who were foreign-born, Boyd found a "double negative" that reinforced the vertical mosaic. She concluded that birthplace and sex are important factors underlying the Canadian mosaic (Boyd, 1985: 441).

The exact nature of the link between ethnicity and inequality turns, at least in part, on issues of definition and methodology. Porter used the best data available to him, but his approach had weaknesses despite his best efforts. The sections that follow describe the three main problems that any analyst must confront in trying to sort out whether the idea of multiculturalism or the image of a vertical mosaic best characterizes modern Canada.

ETHNICITY

Definitions matter. How broadly or finely we choose to define ethnicity is critical in these debates. Historically, male ancestral lineage was the defining feature of ethnicity, at least as used by Statistics Canada for measurement purposes. However, this definition is problematic, not only because it privileges male descent lines. Interethnic marriages occur across generations. National borders change. An increasing number of people consider themselves to be of "Canadian" ancestry since they are descendants of people who arrived in Canada generations ago.

Porter's view of the charter status groups, the French and the British, drew no distinction among the English, the Irish, the Scottish, and the Welsh. Likewise, Statistics Canada for a long time was unable to publish distinct numbers for members of different Asian ethnic groups. That is because the number of Koreans and Cambodians, for example, was too small. Typically, the following ethnic categories have been used in the census, with older census years having even fewer distinct groups: British (English, Irish, Scottish, Welsh), French, German, Italian, Jewish, Dutch, Scandinavian, Eastern European (Polish, Ukrainian), Other European, Asian, and Native Indian.

OCCUPATIONS

Porter originally used five broad occupational categories (professional and financial, clerical, personal service, primary and unskilled, and agriculture). Lautard and Loree (1984) used a more detailed occupational categorization with hundreds of separate job categories for each census.

Occupations are, in important ways, just jobs. To show that members of different ethnic groups concentrate in some jobs and not others says nothing about inequality; it is only a comment about different jobs. Only if those jobs have different rewards attached to them does inequality become an issue. But, what are the most salient rewards—income, working conditions, prestige, authority? The vertical mosaic clearly implies some hierarchy, but what defines that hierarchy is not specified.

HISTORICAL COMPARABILITY

The number and kinds of occupations in Canada have changed over time. Should researchers use older census categories that tend to be broader, or the full range of jobs characterizing the modern division of labour? Likewise, the detail on ethnicity has changed historically, as has the way Statistics Canada collects this information.[2] Should only broad ethnic categories that are strictly comparable over time be used?

MEASURING OCCUPATIONAL STRATIFICATION BY ETHNICITY

With the above limitations in mind, you might conclude that using census data to track labour market changes for members of ethnic groups is highly problematic. Our response to this is fourfold. First, these problems must be recognized and the results interpreted cautiously in light of them. Second, even partial insight is better than ignorance. Third, if the findings of this research complement the findings of other researchers who used different research methods, then the entire body of research is self-reinforcing. Fourth, if better methods exist to answer the question we are pursuing, then we encourage others to do the research.

We use census information for 1971 and 2006 and compare our results to earlier findings, beginning either in 1931 or 1951. Depending on the availability of data, we discuss changes over a period of up to 75 years. The 2006 analysis involves examining the distribution of the members of 17 ethnic groups, by gender, across about five hundred different occupations. This provides enormous detail that we need to summarize. To do so, we measure occupational differentiation by calculating an *index of dissimilarity*, and we examine occupational stratification by using an *index of net difference*.

Here first, by way of analogy, is how to understand the index of dissimilarity. In your college or university, consider the overall percentages of women and men enrolled (assume it is 55 percent and 45 percent, respectively). Now think of the percentage of women and men in each of your classes. How well is the overall gender balance of 55/45 reflected in your individual courses? Extend this to all the courses offered at your institution.

To summarize this detail, begin by calculating, for each course, any difference in the percentage of women (or men) from the overall 55/45 average. This tells you how dissimilar each course is from the overall gender balance. Totalling across all courses provides a convenient summary—the higher the index number, the greater the dissimilarity. Comparing the index of dissimilarity across different faculties or different universities would tell you which has the better gender balance.

In our case, we add the percentage differences between the occupational distribution of each ethnic group and that of the rest of the labour force. Separate calculations are done for women and men. The resulting indexes are the percentages of women and men in each ethnic group who would have to be in a different occupation for there to be no occupational differences among ethnic groups.

For example, say the index of dissimilarity for women of British origin is 11 percent. This means that barely one in ten British women in the labour force would have to be in a different occupation for there to be no difference between their occupational distribution and that of women of other ethnic origins. If the index of dissimilarity for men of Aboriginal origin is 28 percent, this indicates 2.5 times as much difference, with well over one in four Aboriginal men having to be in a different occupation for them to have the same occupational distribution as non-Aboriginal men. Averaging dissimilarity indexes for ethnic groups in two different census years indicates changes in occupational differentiation among ethnic groups. We present such results for 1971 and 2006, and compare them with earlier findings for 1931, 1951, and 1961, for a combined span of 75 years.

Dissimilarity, however, does not necessarily mean disadvantage or inequality. As a method of capturing *stratification*, sociologists have adopted other methods. In this chapter, we use two separate methods to examine stratification among occupations. For 1971, we array occupations on a socioeconomic index that measures the prestige of occupations. These prestige ratings are based on the typical education and income of people in particular occupations. For 2006, where such an index is not available, we use a measure constructed by Statistics Canada to rank the occupational skill requirements of distinct jobs. Occupation data collected from the 2006 census are ranked into one of four skill groups, with the groups arrayed by estimates of educational requirements (university, college, apprenticeship training, and high school or less). To this, Statistics Canada added a "manager" category, which is unranked since the education levels of managers are diverse.

As a way of summarizing occupational inequality, we use the index of net difference. This measure (unlike the index of dissimilarity, which is always positive) may be either negative or positive. An index of net difference with a minus sign indicates the group for which it was calculated is generally lower on the occupational "ladder" relative to the rest of the labour force, while a positive index indicates higher relative position. The greater the absolute size of the index, whether positive or negative, the greater the degree of stratification, while a net difference of zero would indicate overall equality of occupational status. We use this measure to analyze occupational inequality for 1971 and 2006, and compare our results with earlier findings for 1951, 1961, and 1971.

OCCUPATIONAL INEQUALITY BY ETHNICITY, 1931 TO 2006

Table 12.1 contains indexes of occupational dissimilarity for 16 ethnic groups in 1971 and 17 groups in 2006. These scores summarize results based on just fewer than five hundred occupations in 1971 and just more than five hundred occupations in 2006. Generally, ethnic occupational differentiation is lower in 2006 than in 1971. In 2006, average ethnic dissimilarity among men (23 percent) is 7 points lower than in 1971 (30 percent), while it is 9 points lower among women (18 percent, compared with 27 percent). Exceptions to this pattern of declining index scores occur for men and women of German, Dutch, and Scandinavian origin, and for men of Polish origin. There was no change in the score for men of Ukrainian origin and women of Jewish origin.

Table 12.1 also shows that there is a generally consistent pattern of ethnic occupational differentiation. Groups of North and East European origins exhibit below-average occupational dissimilarity, while, with a few exceptions, groups of South European, Jewish, Asian, Aboriginal, and black origins show above-average dissimilarity. The generally lower levels of ethnic differentiation in 2006 compared with 1971 are consistent with the decreases reported by Lautard and Loree (1984) for 1931 to 1971, suggesting an easing of differentiation. Nevertheless, considerable occupational dissimilarity remains among ethnic groups.[3]

Recall that occupational dissimilarity does not necessarily involve occupational stratification. Table 12.2 contains indexes of net difference in occupational status for 1971 and in occupational skill group for 2006 for the ethnic groups discussed previously. In 1971, with the exception of the indexes for men and women of British, Jewish, and South Asian origins, all indexes are negative, indicating the relatively low occupational status of the other groups. Note also that in 1971, both men and women of South European and Aboriginal origin have lower overall occupational status than do the other groups.

TABLE 12.1 OCCUPATIONAL DISSIMILARITY[a] AMONG SELECTED ETHNIC GROUPS AND THE REST OF THE LABOUR FORCE, BY SEX, CANADA, 1971 AND 2006

ETHNIC GROUP	MALE		FEMALE	
	1971	2006	1971	2006
British	15	11	16	11
French	14	10	18	11
German	15	19	11	12
Dutch	16	20	15	16
Scandinavian	17	22	12	16
Ukrainian	15	15	16	12
Polish	15	17	14	13
Hungarian	21	19	20	16
Italian	35	20	38	20
Portuguese	46	27	57	21
Greek	48	30	51	22
Yugoslav	33	22	35	17
Jewish	51	44	32	32
Chinese	52	34	34	26
South Asian	46	28	31	15
Aboriginal	41[b]	28	32[b]	21
Black	NI	26	NI	23
Mean ($\overline{x}$)	30	23	27	18
Number of occupations	(498)	(521)	(464)	(521)

[a] Each figure in the table indicates the percentage of the ethnic group that would have to have a different occupation for there to be no difference between the occupational distribution of that group and the rest of the labour force.

[b] Does not include Inuit.

NI: Not included.

SOURCE: Statistics Canada. Special tabulations of census data. Reproduced and distributed on an "as is" basis with the permission of Statistics Canada.

In 2006, the indexes of net difference are mainly positive. In 1971, they are mainly negative. This is true for both women and men. We conclude that ethnic stratification was less pronounced in 2006 than in 1971.

TABLE 12.2 NET DIFFERENCE[a] IN OCCUPATIONAL STATUS (1971) AND OCCUPATIONAL SKILL GROUP (2006) AMONG SELECTED ETHNIC GROUPS AND THE REST OF THE LABOUR FORCE, BY SEX, CANADA

Ethnic Group	MALE		FEMALE	
	1971	2006	1971	2006
British	0.13	0.05	0.14	0.05
French	−0.06	0.03	−0.02	0.06
German	−0.08	0.02	−0.09	0.00
Dutch	−0.09	0.04	−0.10	0.04
Scandinavian	−0.08	0.06	−0.01	0.03
Ukrainian	−0.09	0.05	−0.13	0.03
Polish	−0.08	0.02	−0.12	−0.01
Hungarian	−0.06	0.06	−0.13	0.02
Italian	−0.22	0.02	−0.35	0.02
Portuguese	−0.38	−0.14	−0.62	−0.14
Greek	−0.27	0.06	−0.48	0.01
Yugoslav	−0.12	0.03	−0.29	−0.01
Jewish	0.36	0.32	0.24	0.25
Chinese	−0.04	0.17	−0.20	0.02
South Asian	0.26	−0.04	0.19	−0.12
Aboriginal	−0.35[b]	−0.14	−0.23[b]	−0.09
Black	NI	−0.10	NI	−0.09
Mean ($|\bar{x}|$)	0.17	0.08	0.21	0.06
Number of Occupational Ranks/Skill Groups	(498)	(4)	(464)	(4)

[a] A negative figure indicates relatively lower overall occupational status/skill group, a positive figure relatively higher status/skill group. Zero indicates overall equality of occupational status/skill group. The greater the absolute size of the index, the greater the inequality.

[b] Does not include Inuit.

NI: Not included.

SOURCE: Statistics Canada. Special tabulations of census data. Reproduced and distributed on an "as is" basis with the permission of Statistics Canada.

Note also that the indexes for 2006 exhibit a pattern more or less similar to that noted above for occupational dissimilarity among ethnic groups. Most men and women of North, East, and South European origin, as well as those of Jewish and Chinese origin, tend to be in higher occupational skill groups than people of South Asian, Aboriginal, and black origin.[4]

FROM VERTICAL MOSAIC TO MULTICULTURALISM?

Has multiculturalism eclipsed the vertical mosaic? Is ethnic inequality, at least as measured by occupational stratification, only a historical curiosity in Canada? Our results show that between 1931 and 2006, a decline in the significance of ethnicity occurred, for both occupational differentiation and stratification. Yet ethnic origin continues to affect occupational inequality.

The trend in occupational dissimilarity indicates a reduction in the ethnic division of labour of about 30 percent for men and 45 percent for women in 70 years (Figure 12.1). Slowly but surely, social differentiation based on ethnicity is eroding. With respect to occupational stratification, there has been a reduction of approximately 50 percent for men and 45 percent for women, although over a shorter span (from 1951 to 2006). From 1971 to 2006, the trend continued. These historical comparisons have the advantage of a 75-year interval of comparison, but such a lengthy interval also makes the specific contrasts cruder than would be ideal.

Do these results imply a "collapse" of the vertical mosaic? No. Between 1971 and 2006, both occupational differentiation and occupational stratification have eroded, but for both women and men, differences persist. Furthermore, these findings are not inconsistent with recent research by Pendakur and Pendakur (2011) that show an increase in the earning gap in the 1990s for both Aboriginal peoples and members of visible minority groups born in Canada, compared

FIGURE 12.1 MEAN OCCUPATIONAL DISSIMILARITY SCORES, 1931–2006

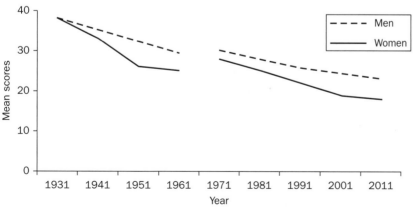

Note: Scores are comparable from 1931 to 1961, using roughly three hundred occupations for women and four hundred for men; between 1971 and 2006, scores increase slightly because more occupations are available for comparison (approximately five hundred for both women and men).

with other Canadian-born labour force participants. Also, work by Hou, Balakrishnan, and Jurdi (2009), shows that recent immigrants to Canada have been faring more poorly than in earlier decades in labour market integration. Based on this research, there is no firm ground on which to conclude that multiculturalism has eliminated the vertical mosaic.

The research design we employed prevents us from investigating which of Porter's two dynamics best explains the continuing level of ethnic inequality: differential immigration or blocked mobility. Our reading of the research literature suggests that differential immigration continues to be the more important factor, especially in terms of visible minorities (Creese and Kambere, 2001; Davies and Guppy, 2010; Sorensen, 1995). That is, ethnicity has less of an effect on inequality for native-born Canadians than it does for immigrants. However, immigration patterns cannot be the sole explanation, because our results are also consistent with research showing that some visible minorities, for example, men of black and South Asian heritage, face earning penalties in the labour market, penalties that are consistent with the blocked mobility thesis (Geschwender and Guppy, 1995; Li, 2000; Pendakur and Pendakur, 2011). Whatever the extent and sources of the vertical mosaic, it coexists with other aspects of ethnic and racial inequality beyond the scope of our analysis, including prejudice, hate, and violence, as well as systematic and systemic discrimination in recruitment, interviewing, hiring, promotion, training, and termination practices.

NOTES

1. For much of Canada's history, foreign-born workers have had a higher level of education than have native-born Canadians (Légacé, 1968; Boyd, 1985). What this average hides, however, is the tendency for immigrants to be either relatively well educated or relatively poorly educated. Note also that earlier in Canadian history, the credentials of immigrants from the United Kingdom in particular were recognized without question. Now, the credentials of immigrants are frequently not accepted as legitimate professional qualifications for the Canadian labour market (Boyd and Thomas, 2001).

2. In the 1971 and earlier censuses, the census question to determine ethnic origin was: "To which ethnic or cultural group did you or your ancestor (on the male side) belong on coming to this continent?" In 1981, the question was: "To which ethnic or cultural group did you or your ancestors belong on first coming to this continent?" Notice how difficult it is for Aboriginal people especially to answer such a

question accurately. Beginning in 1981, multiple ethnic origins were accepted, and the 2006 question read: "What were the ethnic or cultural origins of this person's ancestors?" Our ethnic categories for 2006 are based on single responses and exclude those reporting multiple ethnic or cultural origins, except for multiple origins involving only constituent groups of certain categories. For example, "British" includes persons who report their origin(s) to be British or any one or more of English, Irish, Scottish, Welsh, and so on, but no non-British origin(s). Scandinavian includes persons who report their origin(s) as Scandinavian or any one or more of Danish, Icelandic, Norwegian, Swedish, and so forth, but no non-Scandinavian origin(s). Although the *2006 Census Guide* still made it clear that ethnic origin did not refer to citizenship, "Canadian" was among the examples listed with the question itself. Our data, however, corroborate Li's (2003: 128) observation that "the growth of people reporting Canadian origin ... did not have a measurable impact on the reporting of ethnic minorities." Finally, given the disbanding of the long-form census, this is likely to be the last time this series can be updated.

3. Just as Lautard and Loree's (1984) average dissimilarity for men in 1961 (29) was about double that reported by Darroch (1979), our 1971 averages for men (30) and women (27) are roughly double Darroch's 1971 average for men and women combined. This shows why trend comparisons are so important; the dissimilarity measure is sensitive to the number of occupations used (Lautard and Loree, 1984: 336). The level of dissimilarity reported by other authors is important as a statement about ethnic differences (i.e., how big or small they might be), but it is comparison over time, using a consistent methodology, that answers questions about how ethnic divisions are changing in Canada.

4. Data for the intervening census years, 1981 and 1991, indicate that the overall decline and pattern in ethnic inequality is comparable to those reported by Lautard and Loree (1984), for the census years studied by Porter (1951 and 1961), as well as for 1971 (Lautard and Guppy, 2004).

REFERENCES

Agocs, Carol, and Monica Boyd. (1993). "The Canadian Ethnic Mosaic Recast: Theory, Research and Policy Frameworks for the 1990s."

In J. Curtis et al., eds., *Social Inequality in Canada: Patterns, Problems, Policies* (pp. 330–52). Toronto: Prentice-Hall.

Boyd, Monica. (1985). "Immigration and Occupational Attainment." In M. Boyd et al., eds., *Ascription and Attainment: Studies in Mobility and Status Attainment in Canada* (pp. 393–446). Ottawa: Carleton University Press.

Boyd, Monica and Derrick Thomas. (2001). "Match or Mismatch? The Employment of Immigrant Engineers in Canada's Labor Force." *Population Research and Policy Review, 20* (1–2), 107–33.

Creese, Gillian and E. N. Kambere. (2001). "What Colour Is Your English?" *Canadian Review of Sociology and Anthropology, 40* (5), 565–74.

Darroch, Gordon. (1979). "Another Look at Ethnicity, Stratification and Social Mobility in Canada." *Canadian Journal of Sociology, 4* (1), 1–25.

Davies, Scott and Neil Guppy. (2010). *The Schooled Society: An Introduction to the Sociology of Education,* 2nd ed. Toronto: Oxford University Press.

Geschwender, Jim and Neil Guppy. (1995). "Ethnicity, Educational Attainment, and Earned Income among Canadian-Born Men and Women." *Canadian Ethnic Studies, 27* (1), 67–83.

Guppy, N. and K. Lyons. (2012). "Multiculturalism, Education Practices and Colonial Legacies: The Case of Canada." In C. Kassimeris and M. Vryonides, eds., *The Politics of Education: Challenging Multiculturalism* (pp. 114–35). New York: Routledge.

Heath, Anthony and S. Yu. (2005). "Explaining Ethnic Minority Disadvantage." In A. F. Heath, J. Ermish, and D. Gallie, eds., *Understanding Social Change* (pp. 187–224). Oxford, UK: Oxford University Press.

Hou, Feng, T.R. Balakrishnan, and R. Jurdi. (2009). "The Economic Integration of Visible Minorities in Contemporary Canadian Society Revisited." In E. Grabb and N. Guppy, eds., *Social Inequality in Canada: Patterns, Problems, and Policies*, 5th ed. (pp 253–72). Toronto: Pearson Prentice Hall.

Lautard, Hugh and Neil Guppy. (2004). "Multiculturalism or Vertical Mosaic: Occupational Stratification among Canadian Ethnic Groups." In Robert J. Brym, ed., *Society in Question: Sociological Readings for the 21st Century*, 4th ed. (pp. 165–75). Toronto: Nelson.

Lautard, Hugh and Donald Loree. (1984). "Ethnic Stratification in Canada, 1931–1971." *Canadian Journal of Sociology, 9* (3), 333–44.

Légacé, Michael D. (1968). "Educational Attainment in Canada." *Dominion Bureau of Statistics, Special Labour Force Survey No. 7.* Ottawa: Queen's Printer.

Li, Peter. (2000). "Earning Disparities between Immigrants and Native-Born Canadians." *Canadian Review of Sociology and Anthropology, 37* (3), 289–311.

Li, Peter. (2003). *Destination Canada: Immigration Debates and Issues.* Toronto: Oxford University Press.

Nakhaie, M. Reza. (1997). "Vertical Mosaic among the Elites: The New Imagery Revisited." *Canadian Review of Sociology and Anthropology, 34* (1), 1–24.

Ogmundson, Richard and M. Doyle. (2001). "The Rise and Decline of Canadian Labour/1960 to 2000: Elites, Power, Ethnicity and Gender." *Canadian Journal of Sociology, 27* (3), 413–25.

Ogmundson, Richard and J. McLaughlin. (1990). "Trends in the Ethnic Origins of Canadian Elites: The Decline of the BRITS." *Canadian Review of Sociology and Anthropology, 29* (2), 227–42.

Pendakur, Krishna and Ravi Pendakur. (2011). "Colour by Numbers: Minority Earnings in Canada, 1995–2005." *Journal of International Migration and Integration, 12* (3), 305–29.

Pendakur, Ravi. (2002). *Immigrants and the Labour Force: Policy, Regulation, and Impact.* Montreal: McGill-Queen's University Press.

Pineo, Peter and John Porter. (1985). "Ethnic Origin and Occupational Attainment." In M. Boyd et al., eds., *Ascription and Achievement: Studies and Status Attainment in Canada* (pp. 357–92). Ottawa: Carleton University Press.

Porter, John. (1965). *The Vertical Mosaic: An Analysis of Social Class and Power in Canada.* Toronto: University of Toronto Press.

Porter, John. (1985). "Canada: The Social Context of Occupational Allocation." In M. Boyd et al., eds., *Ascription and Achievement: Studies in Mobility and Status Attainment in Canada* (pp. 29–65). Ottawa: Carleton University Press.

Sorensen, Marianne. (1995). "The Match Between Education and Occupation for Immigrant Women in Canada." *Canadian Ethnic Studies, 27* (1): 48–66.

Chapter 13

The Racial Profiling Debate in Toronto

DATA, DENIALS AND CONFUSION

SCOT WORTLEY and JULIAN TANNER

University of Toronto

For decades African Canadians have complained that they are frequently stopped, questioned and searched by the police for "DWBB":
"Driving While Being Black."[1] Similar complaints have been made
by Aboriginals in the Prairie provinces and South Asians in British
Columbia. Canadian law enforcement officials have rejected such
claims. This controversy reached a boiling point in October 2002 when
the *Toronto Star* published a series of articles on the issue of race and
crime. In addition to reviewing previous research, the *Star* provided its
own analysis of police arrest data. The *Star* analysis reveals that black
people in Toronto are highly over-represented in certain offence categories "including drug possession and 'out-of sight' traffic violations"
such as driving without a licence or driving without insurance. The
Star maintains that this pattern of over-representation is consistent
with the idea that the Toronto police engage in racial profiling. Its
analysis also suggests that blacks are treated more harshly after arrest
than their white counterparts. In particular, white offenders are more
likely to be released at the scene, while black offenders are more likely
to be detained, taken to the station for processing and held in custody
for a bail hearing.[2]

The Toronto Police vehemently denied all allegations of racial bias
in the *Star* series. The Chief of Police for Toronto declared, "We do
not do racial profiling.... There is no racism."[3] Likewise, the president
of the Police Association stated that, "No racial profiling has ever been
conducted by the Toronto Police Service."[4] These sentiments were
echoed by several local politicians. For example, the mayor of Toronto
said, "I don't believe that the Toronto police engage in racial profiling
in any way, shape or form. Quite the opposite, they're very sensitive
to our different communities."[5] Unfortunately, the police have yet to

Source: By Scot Wortley and Julian Tanner in *The Canadian Review of Policing Research*. http://
crpr.icaap.org/index.php/crpr/article/view/26/2. © 2004. Reprinted with permission.

produce concrete data that can lend support to their "no racism" argument. Does racial profiling exist in Toronto? It is the purpose of this paper to briefly discuss the results of two recent Toronto surveys that directly address the racial profiling debate.

RACIAL PROFILING: A DEFINITION

In the criminological literature, racial profiling is said to exist when the members of certain racial or ethnic groups become subject to greater levels of criminal justice surveillance than others. Racial profiling, therefore, is typically defined as a racial disparity in police stop and search practices, in Customs searches at airports and border-crossings, in police patrols in minority neighbourhoods and in undercover activities or sting operations that target particular ethnic groups. It is associated with racial bias in police investigation rather than in arrest decisions or police treatment after arrest. This is not to say that arrest statistics, such as those analyzed by the *Star*, do not reflect profiling. The over-representation of blacks in Toronto arrest statistics could mean that blacks are indeed subject to greater police surveillance; but it could also mean that blacks are more involved in criminal activities. Thus, the racial profiling hypothesis must be tested by examining information on police surveillance activities.

PREVIOUS RESEARCH

Police data from England[6] and the United States[7] suggest that black people come under greater criminal justice surveillance and are more likely to be stopped, questioned and searched by the police than are people from other racial backgrounds. In England, under the *Police and Criminal Evidence Act*, police record the racial background of all people who are subjected to police stops and searches. Statistics from 1997–1998 show that black people in the United Kingdom were stopped and searched at a rate of 142 per 1000, compared to 45 per 1000 for Asians and 19 per 1000 for whites. Overall, the English data suggest that blacks are approximately eight times more likely to be stopped and searched by the police than are whites.[8]

Unlike England and the United States, the police in Canada are not required to record the race of the people they stop or search, so official police statistics cannot be used to investigate the presence or absence of racial profiling in this country. However, a number of field studies have uncovered evidence that racial profiling may exist. For example,

Carl James[9] conducted intensive interviews with over fifty black youth from southern Ontario. Many of these youths reported that being stopped by the police was a common occurrence for them. Robynne Neugebauer's[10] interviews with 63 black and white teenagers from Toronto produced similar results. Although the author finds that teenagers from all racial backgrounds often complain about being hassled by the police, both white and black youth agree that black males are much more likely to be stopped, questioned and searched by the police than are youths from other racial backgrounds. Although these ethnographic studies provide great detail about police encounters and document the lived experiences of black youth, they are based on small, non-random samples. They thus risk being dismissed as anecdotal and not truly representative of police behaviour. However, similar evidence of racial profiling has been found in two recent surveys of Toronto residents.

SURVEY ONE

In 1995, the Institute for Social Research at York University conducted a survey of over 1,200 Toronto adults aged 18 years or older who identified themselves as either black, Chinese or white. Over 400 respondents were randomly selected from each racial group. The survey found that black people, particularly black males, were much more likely to report involuntary police contact than either whites or Asians. For example, 44 percent of the black males in the sample reported that they had been stopped and questioned by the police at least once in the past two years. Thirty percent of black males reported that they had been stopped on two or more occasions. By contrast, only 12 percent of white males and 7 percent of Asian males reported multiple police stops.[11]

Multivariate statistical analyses reveal that these racial differences in police contact cannot be explained by differences in social class, education or other demographic variables. In fact, two factors that seem to protect white males from police contact—age and social class—do not protect blacks. Whites with high incomes and education, for example, are much less likely to be stopped by the police than whites who score low on social class measures. By contrast, blacks with high incomes and education are actually more likely to be stopped than lower class blacks. In fact, black professionals often attribute the attention they receive from the police to their relative affluence. One black survey respondent stated: "If you are black and you drive something good, the police will pull you over and ask about drugs." One weakness with this study, however, is that it does not control for other relevant factors, including criminal behaviour, that may determine who the police stop and search. This issue, however, was addressed by the second survey described below.

SURVEY TWO

The Toronto Youth Crime and Victimization Survey was completed in 2000. Interviews were conducted with a random sample of approximately 3,400 high school students.[12] The results of this study also suggest that black people are much more likely than people from other racial backgrounds are to be subjected to random street interrogations. For example, over 50 percent of the black students report that they have been stopped by the police on two or more occasions in the past two years, compared to only 23 percent of whites, 11 percent of Asians and eight percent of South Asians. Similarly, over 40 percent of black students claim that they have been physically searched by the police in the past two years, compared to only 17 percent of their white and 11 percent of their Asian counterparts. However, the data also reveal that students who engage in various forms of crime and deviance are much more likely to receive police attention than students who do not break the law. For example, 81 percent of the drug dealers in this sample (defined as those who sold drugs on ten or more occasions in the past year) report that they have been searched by the police, compared to only 16 percent of those students who did not sell drugs. This finding is consistent with the police argument that they focus exclusively on suspicious or criminal activity when deciding to make a stop, not the racial characteristics of citizens.

The data further reveal that students who have access to automobiles and spend most of their leisure time in public spaces such as malls, public parks, or nightclubs are much more likely to be stopped by the police than are students who spend most of their time in private spaces or in the company of their parents. This leads to the million dollar question: do black students receive more police attention because they are more involved in crime and more likely to be involved in leisure activities that take place in public spaces?

While our data reveal that white students have much higher rates of both alcohol consumption and illicit drug use, black students do report higher rates of both minor property crime, drug trafficking and violence. Black students are also more likely to report that they are a member of a youth gang. In addition, both black and white students report higher rates of participation in public leisure activities than students from all other racial backgrounds. These characteristics, however, do not come close to explaining why black youth are much more vulnerable to police contact. In fact, after statistically controlling for criminal activity, drug use, gang membership, car use and leisure activities, the relationship between race and police stops actually gets stronger.

Further analysis suggests why this is the case. Racial differences in police stop and search practices are actually greatest among students with low levels of criminal behaviour. For example, 34 percent of the black students who have not engaged in any type of criminal activity still report that they have been stopped by the police on two or more occasions in the past two years, compared to only 4 percent of white students in the same behavioural category. Similarly, 23 percent of black students with no deviant behaviour report that they have been searched by the police, compared to only 5 percent of whites who report no deviance.[13] Thus, while the first survey, discussed above, reveals that age and social class do not protect blacks from police stops and searches, the second study suggests that good behaviour also does not shelter blacks from unwanted police attention.

IMPLICATIONS

These findings have two major implications. Firstly, because the black community is subject to much greater police surveillance, they are also much more likely to be caught when they break the law than white people who engage in the same forms of criminal activity. For example, 65 percent of the black drug dealers in the above high school study report that they have been arrested at some time in their life, compared to only 35 percent of the white drug dealers.

The implication can best be understood by imagining 10,000 people living in a high density community in downtown Toronto. Imagine further that half of the residents of this community are black and the other half are white. Let us also assume that an equal number of the black and white residents (250 from each group) sell illicit drugs on a regular basis. If, owing to racial profiling, black residents are more likely to be stopped and searched by the police, black drug dealers in this neighbourhood will be more likely to be detected and subsequently arrested than white offenders. For example, if 50 percent of the black residents are randomly searched, compared with only 10 percent of the white residents, this searching practice should yield 125 black arrests and only 25 white arrests. Moreover, the race-crime statistics (125 black arrests compared to only 25 white arrests) produced by such biased search practices would probably be used to justify the use of racial profiling. In other words, finding more black than white offenders would tend to reinforce police beliefs that their profiling strategy was correct. Racial profiling, therefore, can become a self-fulfilling prophecy. This example helps illustrate how arrest statistics may have more to do with law enforcement surveillance practices than actual racial differences in criminal behaviour. In sum, racial profiling may help explain the over-representation of minorities in arrest statistics.

The research discussed also suggests, however, that the police almost never arrest citizens who are not involved in some form of criminal activity. This may lead to the conclusion that racial profiling is harmless: if you don't break the law, you will not be arrested. However, the second major consequence of racial profiling is that it serves to further alienate black people from mainstream Canadian society and reinforces perceptions of discrimination and racial injustice. Indeed, our research strongly suggests that black people who are frequently stopped and questioned by the police perceive much higher levels of discrimination in the Canadian criminal justice system than do blacks who have not been stopped. It is of interest that being stopped by the police does not appear to increase perceptions of injustice for whites or Asians.[14] Being stopped and searched by the police, therefore, seems to be experienced by black people as evidence that race still matters in Canadian society, that no matter how well you behave, how hard you try, being black means that you will always be considered one of the "usual suspects."

CONCLUSION

Clearly, the issue of racial profiling requires further research in this country. To date, with the notable exception of the Kingston Police Service in Ontario, Canadian law enforcement agencies have not collected data on this phenomenon. There is a fear that official stop and search data will be misunderstood by the public, used to unfairly label individual officers as racist, increase lawsuits against police services and ultimately result in depolicing (i.e., officers will refuse to respond to situations that involve minority citizens). It should be noted that, in general, these problems have not emerged in England and the United States where this type of data has been collected for years. Canadian police managers need to recognize that there may be major advantages to collecting stop and search data. First of all, it could be an effective means of monitoring police behaviour and might reduce the number of unjustified racial profiling incidents. Secondly, a transparent effort to monitor and eliminate racial profiling, in our opinion, would ultimately improve the relationship the police have with various racial minority communities. By contrast, a refusal to acknowledge and deal with the issue may intensify tensions and ensure that the issue of racial discrimination continues to haunt law enforcement agencies for decades to come.

NOTES

1. Foster, Cecil. (1996). *A Place Called Heaven: The Meaning of Being Black in Canada.* Toronto: Harper-Collins.
2. Rankin, Jim, Jennifer Quinn, Michelle Shephard, Scott Simmie, and John Duncanson. (2002). "Singled Out: An Investigation into Race and Crime." *Toronto Star* 19 October: A1; Rankin, Jim, Jennifer Quinn, Michelle Shephard, Scott Simmie, and John Duncanson. (2002). "Police Target Black Drivers." *Toronto Star* 20 October: A1.
3. "There Is No Racism. We Do Not Do Racial Profiling." (2002). *Toronto Star* 19 October: A14.
4. Porter, Catherine. (2002). "Police Union Blasts *Star*." *Toronto Star* 22 October: A6.
5. "Analysis Raises Board Hackles." (2002). *Toronto Star* 20 October: A9.
6. Bowling, Ben and Coretta Phillips. (2002). *Racism, Crime and Justice.* London, UK: Pearson Education.
7. Shepard Engel, Robin, Jennifer M. Calnon, and Thomas J. Bernard. (2002). "Theory and Racial Profiling: Shortcomings and Future Directions in Research." *Justice Quarterly, 19* (2), 249–73.
8. Bowling and Phillips, 2002.
9. James, Carl. (1998). "Up to No Good: Blacks on the Streets and Encountering Police." In Victor Satzewich, ed., *Racism and Social Inequality in Canada: Concepts, Controversies and Strategies of Resistance* (pp. 157–76). Toronto: Thompson.
10. Neugebauer, Robynne. (2000). "Kids, Cops, and Colour: The Social Organization of Police-Minority Youth Relations." In Robynne Neugebauer, ed., *Criminal Injustice: Racism in the Criminal Justice System* (chapter 5). Toronto: Canadian Scholars Press.
11. Commission on Systemic Racism. (1995). *Report of the Commission on Systemic Racism in the Ontario Criminal Justice System.* Toronto: Queen's Printer for Ontario.

12. Tanner, Julian and Scot Wortley. (2002). *The Toronto Youth Crime and Victimization Survey: Overview Report.* Toronto: University of Toronto, Centre of Criminology.

13. Wortley, Scot and Julian Tanner. (2003). "Data, Denials and Confusion: The Racial Profiling Debate in Toronto." *Canadian Journal of Criminology and Criminal Justice, 45* (3), 367–89; Wortley, Scot, and Julian Tanner. (2004). "The Good, the Bad and the Profiled: Race, Deviant Activity and Police Stop and Search Practices." Paper submitted to the *American Journal of Sociology.* Paper originally presented at the University of Toronto Faculty of Law Conference on Systemic Racism in the Criminal Justice System, November 28, 2002, Toronto.

14. Ibid; Wortley, Scot, John Hagan, and Ross Macmillan. (1997). "Just Des(s)erts: The Racial Polarization of Perceptions of Injustice." *Law and Society Review, 31*: 637–76.

Chapter 14

French Quebec, the Quiet Revolution, and After

GLORIES AND MISERIES OF FOUR UTOPIAS

JEAN-PHILIPPE WARREN, Concordia University

This essay focuses on four visions of the ideal society ("utopias") formulated by the French population in Quebec in the past four decades. My starting point is the Quiet Revolution (1960–70). During the 1960s, Quebec undertook massive reforms aimed at getting rid of what many observers judged to be its backward character. Blaming mostly the Catholic Church's domination of the province, French Canadian intellectuals and militants dreamed of establishing a society in which democracy, tolerance, justice, and openness would prevail. This is how, in the space of just a decade, a largely traditionalist and closed society was transformed by the dreams of a new generation of *Québécois*.[2] This essay relates the story of these dreams and their fate.

The four utopias of the 1960s and the 1970s were as follows:

1. the realization of a thoroughly democratic political system;
2. the achievement of Quebec independence or the construction of a completely bilingual Canada;
3. the establishment of a socialist society ("social democracy"); and
4. the translation of the old language of values into a new humanism adapted to the technological age in the making.

Analysis of these utopias can help us better understand the ideologies and commitments of Quebec social movements during the past four decades, reveal the main political and social tendencies of this period, and, consequently, underline the challenges facing Quebec society today. You will see that, following two decades of struggle and great expectations (the 1960s and 1970s), a period of disillusionment set in. In this respect, Quebec was no different from other countries in the Western world, where the radical 1960s and 1970s eventually gave

Source: © Jean-Philippe Warren (2006).

way to a more conservative era. Reassessing the utopias of the 1960s and 1970s will also serve to emphasize the importance of not forgetting them, even if they must now be understood in a new light.

1. DEMOCRACY

It is easy to forget today, but one of the chief debates that helped Jean Lesage and his Liberal Party get elected in 1960 turned on the question of political morality. The Union Nationale Party, led by Maurice Duplessis, dominated Quebec politics since the 1930s. Duplessis was premier from 1936 to 1939 and from 1944 to 1959. He turned patronage (e.g., hiring and giving government contracts to political friends) and corruption (e.g., accepting bribes) into a political system. Characteristically, Duplessis once started a speech by addressing his audience as "Électeurs, électrices, électricité" ("Male Electors, Female Electors, Electricity"), reminding voters in the small village he was speaking in that they had better vote for his party if they wanted to get connected to the province's electrical grid.

Duplessis organized politics into an efficient machine for reinforcing his personal domination. Companies had to pay a "commission" for every government contract they obtained, and the regime's friends had to contribute to Union Nationale coffers if they expected personal favours. Duplessis was also careful to discredit the provincial Liberal Party. He accused it of being a refuge for French Canada's enemies. Did the Liberal Party not support compulsory military service in 1942, forcing the *Québécois* to fight "England's" war against Germany, as if Quebec were still an English colony, he persistently asked the electorate? Was the Liberal Party not a nest of dangerous socialists, as evidenced by its support for more state intervention in economic life? Duplessis's propaganda tarnished the reputation of everybody who stood in his way. Nor did he stop at words. He took action—often brutal action—to rid himself of opponents. He crushed the prolonged and bitter Asbestos strike (1948) by sending in the police to beat up the strikers. He imposed restrictive new regulations at Laval University that compelled Father Georges-Henri Lévesque to resign as dean of the *Faculté des sciences sociales*. And so forth.

One of the most famous articles published in Quebec in the 1950s was Gérard Dion and Louis O'Neill's "L'Immoralité politique dans la province de Québec" (1956). The authors denounced the "flood of stupidity" that Quebec was witnessing and the complete "perversion of conscience." Their words were harsh for they feared the destruction of democracy in Quebec. This is why, for both of them, an urgent reform of political morals by means of general civic education seemed necessary. "The work has to speed up before demagogues and would-be fascists render the masses so stupid that any effort to right the situation becomes impossible."[3] This was also what the intellectuals grouped around the *Rassemblement* (formed in 1956) and the *Unions des forces démocratiques* (formed in 1958) believed. These two political organizations did not seek to become political parties. Rather, they sought to purify Québec's politics by educating ordinary *Québécois*. "In 1958, French Canadians must begin to learn democracy from scratch," wrote the young Pierre Elliott Trudeau.[4] If the masses were not ready to exercise their political rights, the solution was not to abolish democracy altogether but to elevate political consciousness.

The generation that came of age after World War II was dedicated to establishing liberal democracy in Quebec like no generation before. At last, for instance, Aboriginal peoples gained the right to vote at the federal and provincial levels in the 1960s. To be sure, there were violent elements in provincial politics, including people who thought traditional liberal democracy was a sham and were willing to plant bombs in mailboxes to prove their point. In 1970, the *Front de Libération du Québec* (FLQ) proclaimed: "We wash our hands of the British parliamentary system; the *Front de Libération du Québec* will never let itself be distracted by the electoral crumbs that the Anglo-Saxon capitalists toss into the Quebec barnyard every four years."[5]

Believing Quebec was on the eve of a popular uprising, the FLQ kidnapped and murdered Pierre Laporte, Quebec Minister of Labour, plunging the country into the 1970 "October Crisis," during which martial law was declared, federal troops marched into the province, and arbitrary mass arrests were made. Yet, this outburst of violence cannot make us forget the peaceful and democratic way in which most of Quebec's political disputes were dealt with. Many democratic struggles elsewhere—notably the civil rights movement in the United States, which sought to heal much deeper and more painful wounds—witnessed bitter violence. Most of the members of the postwar generation believed that the people were the sole repository of power and that transparency was the cardinal quality of a democratic regime. This meant an insistence on participatory democracy (universal, mass participation in politics) and the eradication of corruption from public affairs. Notwithstanding the extravagance of most of their claims, the radical groups of the 1970s (the FLQ, the Marxist-Leninists, the Maoists, extremists in labour unions, etc.) attacked liberal democracy for not being democratic enough and extended the critique of the parliamentary system as a system of corruption and favouritism.

In 1978, the ruling party, the *Parti Québécois*, adopted laws restraining companies and trade unions from contributing to the electoral funding of political parties and forcing the latter to state their incomes and expenses. Numerous other provincial laws confirm the commitment of *Québécois* to the health of their democracy.

In Canada, the Trudeau government did not have similar success in its attempt to change the electoral process and political organization in general. Of course, less needed to be done because most of Canada outside Quebec was already a vigorous, albeit imperfect, democracy in the 1970s. It is nevertheless obvious that Bay Street did not lose control over Parliament, that thousands of jobs for political friends were created in the 1970s, and that networks of political patronage remained strong. Characteristically, of the 25 cabinet ministers appointed to Trudeau's first government, 15 were given prestigious federal offices after they left politics.[6] Trudeau's commitment to establishing participatory democracy during his 1968 leadership campaign soon vanished, leaving Canadian politics in pretty much the same state as when he came to power.

This is not to say that Canada is not a democracy and should not, as such, be regarded with envy by the world community. It is to say that democracy, here and abroad, is a work in progress, and that *Québécois*, having made considerable headway in their province, must continue to fight for greater openness of public institutions at the federal and provincial levels. Major changes await us if we want to live up to the dreams of our predecessors. At the provincial level, one of these might involve reassessing the constituency-based, simple majority ballot. In the 1998 Quebec election, fully one-third of the deputies were elected with less than 50 percent of the popular vote in their ridings because so many people voted for losing candidates. Many analysts are now talking about partly adopting a system of proportional representation, as in Western Europe. In addition to the traditional vote for local candidates, this would involve people voting for a province-wide list of candidates established by each political party. It might take, say, 40 000 votes from anywhere in the province to elect each person on a party's list. In that case, few votes would be wasted and representation in the Quebec legislature would much more closely reflect the political will of the people. The fact that the percentage of people exercising their right to vote is slowly but inexorably dropping election after election is one indication among others that democracy in Quebec (and Canada as a whole) is amenable to improvement. The concentration of ownership of the Canadian press in the hands of a few giant conglomerates is another big problem area for Quebec and Canadian democracy.

2. A NATION IN THE MAKING

Jules-Paul Tardivel, the religious owner of the newspaper *La Vérité*, and Henri Bourassa, the founder of the newspaper *Le Devoir*, knew each other well and respected each other's commitments. But, while Jules-Paul Tardivel wrote a novel (*Pour la Patrie*, 1895) in which he predicted an independent Quebec by 1945, Henri Bourassa wrote and spoke to convince English Canadians to help him build a bilingual and bicultural Canada respectful of the two founding nations. When Bourassa died in 1952, neither dream had become reality. The national question remained unresolved. The Quiet Revolutionaries split on this issue, most of the older half joining the federalist camp and most of the younger half joining the nationalist camp.

The historical context nurtured the dreams of both federalists and nationalists. On the one hand, nationalism had been discredited by the horrible atrocities of the fascist regimes during World War II. Furthermore, the Western European countries were trying to unite into a single political body, paving the way, according to optimists, to a world government. On the other hand, colonies around the globe (including, ironically, Canada, which adopted its flag in 1965, its national anthem in 1980, and repatriated its Constitution from London in 1982) were striving for independence from their metropolises while invoking the principle of self-determination recognized by the United Nations.

For French-Canadian federalists, Canada belonged to both francophones and anglophones even if the two founding peoples did not always act like equal partners. With this view in mind they helped to enact the Official Languages Bill (1969) in spite of strong resistance from conservative factions in English Canada, who feared so-called "French power." French-Canadian federalists believed that nearly every Canadian would eventually speak English and French fluently. Moreover, they felt that once Canada was a bilingual country, Quebec would not have the right to speak for all French Canadians.

In contrast, separatists did not believe Canada could ever be a true home for Francophones. English Canadians, they said, had never respected them. They argued, for example, that during World War II the federal government asked the provinces to temporarily hand over their control of income tax but never gave it back. Historically, the federal government even refused things as trivial as bilingual postage stamps, insisting instead on stamps extolling Canada's attachment to the British Empire. French Quebec, said the separatists, shared nothing with the rest of Canada. Moreover, lost in what appeared to be a North American ocean, many *Québécois* felt in danger of being assimilated to the English majority. Securing the *Québécois* nation could only be achieved through the political autonomy of the province, they concluded.

Quebec's last 40 years of history has been summarized by some analysts as a political struggle between sovereigntists and federalists. But, these analysts fail to underline how much both camps came to share as they evolved:

1. *Culture as a state policy.* Despite their continuous quarrelling, Quebec federalists and Quebec separatists were both convinced nationalists, proud of being a citizen either of Quebec or Canada. Jacques Parizeau, leader of the *Parti Québécois* during the 1995 referendum, once said that he and Trudeau agreed on everything except where to put the national capital. And, in fact, while the Quebec government was adopting programs to promote local culture, the federal government, under the guidance of those who exercised "French power," was mounting a campaign to protect Canadian culture from American influence. Artists, magazines, television and radio broadcasting, as well as a host of institutions, associations, groups, and organizations received government funding conditional on promoting "Canadian content." The federal government gave itself the mandate of building a Canadian nation out of British, French, Aboriginal, and other elements, while the Quebec government imagined having a mandate to forge a Quebec nation out of (for the most part) the *Québécois*. Yet, despite heading in different directions, the principles at the crux of Canada's and Quebec's actions were similar. Opposed when they were addressing Canadian cultural issues, they stood shoulder to shoulder at international consultation tables for the protection of local particularities. They tried to save Quebec and Canadian culture from the invasion of

"McWorld" by creating state cultural institutions (Radio Canada, *Télé Québec*), distributing grants to artists and intellectuals (Canada Council for the Arts, *Ministère de la culture*), establishing quotas on "Canadian" and "Quebec" content, and controlling investment in cultural institutions (some companies engaged in cultural production must be two-thirds Canadian-owned by law).

2. *Language as the only legitimate criterion for defining a nation.* A second area of commonality between sovereigntists and federalists involves the criterion they employ for defining a nation. They did not always agree on this matter. In the 1960s, the federal Commission on Bilingualism and Biculturalism had legitimized the "two equal founding nations" idea. In 1972, however, the federal government passed a bill on multiculturalism. Many Quebec nationalists accused Trudeau of betrayal, of watering down the idea of two equal founding nations. To the sovereigntists it seemed that other immigrant groups were now being awarded almost the same status as the *Québécois*. Partly in reaction, the Quebec government passed Bill 101 in 1977. Its aim was to protect not just the French language, but also the values and traditions of the *Québécois*. Yet, in the 1980s and 1990s, more and more Quebec nationalists came to acknowledge that a state can promote only language and that cultural diversity is not a dilution but an enrichment of national traditions. The Quebec nation many *Québécois* have come to believe in is a "nation of cultures"—very much like Canada with its multiculturalist policies—and not a homogeneous nation composed exclusively of people of French descent. For example, historian Gérard Bouchard, a leading separatist thinker, asserts that the *Québécois* should be defined "strictly by a linguistic criterion."[7] As a result of the widespread acceptance of this idea, promoting *Québécois* culture now involves little more than subsidizing the creation of cultural products in Quebec, regardless of their cultural content. This is similar to the situation in the rest of Canada, where cultural products created in Canada are equated with Canadian culture.

3. *Quebec as a people.* A third area of commonality between sovereigntists and separatists concerns the idea that French-Canadian Quebeckers form a *Québécois* people. The *Québécois* have come a long way since the nineteenth century, when they called themselves *Canadiens* to distinguish themselves from the British, and since the turn of the twentieth century, when they called themselves French Canadians to distinguish themselves from Canadians who spoke English. Today, the *Québécois* feel little or no attachment to

their linguistic "brothers" and "sisters" in other provinces. For their part, the leaders of the provincial and federal parties speak of *Québécois* interests without even trying to convince the *Québécois* that they are members of the same family as Francophones outside Quebec. The same recognition was embodied in the ill-fated Meech Lake Accord, which was designed to entice Quebec to recognize Canada's Constitution. The Accord recognized Quebec— not French Canada—as a "distinct society," that is, a society enjoying special status in Confederation.

Today, the national question remains unresolved. The 1980 and 1995 Quebec referenda on sovereignty ended in bitter defeat for the sovereigntists. Trudeau's dream of a bilingual Canada is an almost complete failure, except in the Acadian part of New Brunswick and despite episodic vitality in other French-Canadian communities outside Quebec. Not only is French as a first language not progressing outside Quebec, its only chance of maintaining itself as a first language is to stay within Quebec's borders. The numbers are there to remind anyone of the fragility of the French fact in Canada. In 1971, the percentage of people speaking French at home outside Quebec was a mere 4.4 percent. In 1981, it was down to 3.8 percent. Ten years later, it fell to 3.2 percent. In 1996, it dropped to 2.9 percent. This picture is discouraging for anyone hoping to achieve Henri Bourassa's and Pierre Trudeau's dream of a Canada that would be not just officially bilingual but where French as a first language would flower from coast to coast.

3. SOCIAL JUSTICE

The generation that came of age after World War II committed itself to erecting a welfare state in Canada and Quebec. (A "welfare state" guards citizens from the ravages of the market by providing some level of protection against ill health, unemployment, poverty, etc.) The federal and Quebec bureaucracies were in their infancy in 1940. Twenty years later, things had changed dramatically. Governments were playing a large and growing role in public affairs. In 1950, Quebec was, according to some observers, a "priest-ridden province." In 1980, it was a state-controlled province.

Trudeau made speeches in the 1950s on behalf of establishing socialism in Canada and flirted with the New Democratic Party. He was not alone. In Quebec, many people advocated state intervention in domains previously reserved for the Roman Catholic Church. Soon, education, previously controlled by the Church, came under state jurisdiction and state social programs replaced private charities.

An interventionist state was thought to be necessary for many reasons. The state was a rational institution in an age when efficiency and functionality became watchwords. In an age of universalism, it was viewed as a neutral and inclusive institution in which people of different national origins and religions could be treated equally. The state was regarded, moreover, as a means of "domesticating capital," that is, avoiding recurrent financial and industrial crises. Finally, an interventionist state was widely construed as a means of leading Canadians to the creation of a "just society" in which equality would prevail. Labour unions in particular were fighting for a more equitable distribution of wealth and power.

Many of Trudeau's articles in the 1950s constituted a defence of Keynesian economic theory. (John Maynard Keynes was the leading British economist who first advocated massive state intervention to end the Great Depression of 1929–39.) Thus, it is not surprising that under Trudeau's government, state intervention reached new heights. The federal debt grew nine-fold under his administration. He fostered a national energy policy, restricted foreign investment in Canada, created regional development programs, and so forth. Quebec did not trail behind for long. In the U.S. State Department, Quebec came to be known as "Cuba North." In a little less than a decade, Quebec created or enhanced thousands of municipal councils and regional boards, hundreds of health institutions, innumerable social services, programs for the protection of agricultural lands, giant Crown Corporations such as Hydro-Québec, and so on. The state intervention movement even radicalized itself in the 1970s. Concluding that socialism could never be implemented in Canada, some revolutionaries turned their hopes toward an independent Quebec. Pierre Vallières, for example, the author of the famous *White Niggers of America*,[8] intertwined nationalist sentiments with socialist beliefs.

The deep and prolonged recession of 1981–82, until then Canada's worst economic crisis since World War II, rattled the foundations of the welfare state ideologically and practically. Practically, it meant that the Trudeau spending years were over. In Quebec, the return of Liberal Robert Bourassa to power (1985) brought an end to the liberal spending policies of the *Parti Québécois* years (1976–85). However, privatization of government-owned enterprises and cuts in social programs did not reduce the size of the state as much as is sometimes thought. In fact, in absolute numbers, the state apparatus continued to grow along with Quebec's population. Government transfers (welfare payments, unemployment insurance, etc.) as a percentage of personal income even increased, from 10 percent in 1970 to 17 percent in 1990 to approximately 20 percent in 2000. In comparison with the United States, Quebec and Canada maintained their social-democratic proclivity. The continuation of a national health-care system is testimony to the country's disputed but still strong commitment to social democracy.

Ideologically, the change was more drastic. The state changed its role from arbiter and organizer of the economy to a merchandiser of labour and a servant of the market. The new ideology (known as neo-conservatism in the United States but more accurately called neo-liberalism), does not oppose the state as such. It only wants the state to eliminate all values from its vocabulary save the value of cost-efficiency and let nothing other than the market determine social priorities. The neo-liberal state defines people more as paying clients than citizens with rights. This ideology accompanied the signing of the Free Trade Agreement between Canada and the United States in 1989 (largely supported by the *Québécois*, in contrast with the rest of Canada), its broadening to include Mexico in 1993, and subsequent discussions to eventually create a free trade zone encompassing all of North and South America. This process can only contribute to a further subordination of politics to financial and industrial priorities and interests.

4. A NEW HUMANISM

The first publishing success in Quebec in the second half of the twentieth century was Jean-Paul Desbiens's *Les Insolences du frère Untel*,[9] a book in which the author, a young friar, declared war on Quebec's traditional culture. That 50 000 copies were sold in less than three months reveals how popular and long-awaited Desbiens's criticisms were. Desbiens criticized French-Canadian culture in three ways. First, he said, it was an outmoded island in the midst of a progressive American continent. The French Canadians might use "an American clock" but they lived in "the Middle Ages." The inventions of science, new literary currents, new conceptions in the arts—all this was censored by a clerical authority that associated modernity with evil and erected ideological walls to "protect" French Canadians from the "perverse" influence of an English and Protestant continent. Second, according to Desbiens,

French-Canadian culture imposed a cult of mediocrity on French Canada. "Joual" (the French dialect of the *Québécois*) was for him the self-evident syndrome of this cult. For Desbiens, Joual represented a defeat of the spirit and a laziness of the mind. It was evidence of the abysmal lack of education in the province. Not only did people speak Joual, he complained, they thought Joual. The language crisis was terrible and patent proof of the crisis of French-Canadian civilization, wrote Desbiens. Finally, he argued, French-Canadian culture advocated fear and obedience: "What we are practising here is purity by sterilization, orthodoxy by silence, security by material repetition. We imagine there is only one way to walk straight, to go nowhere, only one way to never be mistaken, never search for anything, only one way to never get lost: sleep. We have invented a radical means of fighting the caterpillars: cut down the trees."[10] The Catholic Church's doctrine was one reason this situation came to prevail in Quebec, according to Desbiens. By insisting continuously on one's duties and not on one's freedom, by exercising its omnipresence and overwhelming authority over almost every field of activity, the clergy served as a sentinel against rebellious, dissident, and deviant attitudes and beliefs, ending up obliterating the very meaning of free will.

Contrary to what has often been stated, however, the Church was not inactive in the secularization of Quebec society. After all, Desbiens himself was a friar in the Mariste order. He was the expression of a new religious ethic that catalyzed the will for social reform and promoted the individual's triumph over authoritarian institutions. It is no coincidence that the Quiet Revolution took place during the reformist Vatican II Council. Abbot Louis O'Neill, Father Lévesque, and committed Catholics like Fernand Dumont and Robert Lalonde drew from this new religious ethic the moral energy to confront the Catholic Church itself.

The search for a new culture took two directions, both closely connected to reform of the educational system. For a century, French-Canadian intellectuals had considered education the core of all reform. "Without school," said early-twentieth-century Quebec nationalist intellectual Lionel Groulx, "nothing is possible. With school, everything is possible." This is close to what many intellectuals of the 1960s believed.

Firstly, some intellectuals tried to adapt the classical colleges' humanism to the new conditions of a technological and modern society. Humanism, they argued, had to incorporate the developments of the human sciences, to be more open to other cultures and beliefs, and to be founded on the rights of the individual. A 1963 government report ratified this perspective: culture was not a catechism of questions and listed answers but a toolkit that enabled every citizen to prepare for the modern industrial world. The creation of the CEGEPs (two-year college) system in 1969 grew out of this report. Spending two years in CEGEPs between high school and university, each student would now have an opportunity to learn the basics of philosophy, humanities, and the social sciences, thus assimilating the lessons of a general but ever-changing humanism.

Secondly, some intellectuals, going further, insisted on a culture that would not only help individuals adapt to the new era, but would encourage them to question society as it was and strive for a better world. Sociologist Marcel Rioux, fearing a world in which all creativity would disappear under the steamrollers of machinery, technology, and computerization, associated education with the imaginative search for new possibilities: "To speak of culture in our modern society is to speak ... of surpassing oneself through values, imagination, and creativity."[11] Rioux insisted among other subjects on the teaching of art in schools so as to introduce students to a world where they could be their own creation.

In the 1960s and 1970s, Quebec's culture flourished like never before, at least quantitatively. The Quiet Revolution brought about the creation of the *Ministère des Affaires culturelles du Québec*, the founding of many publishing houses (the number of titles published annually rose from 260 to 4000 between 1962 and 1977), the release of many films produced by the National Film Board, the popularity of *chansonniers* like Gilles Vigneault and Georges D'or, who were not just singers but cultural icons, and so on. Between 1960 and 1970, the number of university students doubled. The number of artists and art teachers grew from 683 to 3805 between 1951 and 1971.[12] Television transformed itself from a medium of information to an agent of socialization.

More generally, the decline of the traditional nuclear family, the erosion of religious practice, the liberalization of sexual behaviour, and the emancipation of women deeply affected Quebec society. Looking back at the 1950s through the films of the era can be a big shock to anyone who is unaware of the rapid and radical cultural transformations that originated in the 1960s and created a vastly more open and progressive culture in place of the earlier conservatism. Unique to Quebec was the almost complete secularization of social life that was brought about by restricting the Catholic Church to a very narrow role in private affairs. In the 1960s, the "priest-ridden province" rid itself of the widespread influence of the priesthood.

The quest for a new culture—specifically, for a new humanism—ended with the rise of a consumer society. The great celebration of "we-ness" in the 1960s raised hopes of a more fraternal and convivial society. But the 1970s and 1980s opened the way to an increasingly individualistic society in which people were increasingly concerned with their own destiny. The 1960s also raised hopes for an authentic human culture that would enable every person to discover his or her real self. But disillusionment swiftly replaced this optimism. The pervasive influence of American culture—Hollywood cinema, Walt Disney philosophy, a fast-food mentality—jeopardized the formulation of a new humanism. As Rioux put it: "The Americanization of Quebec is, to my eyes, a most important and anguishing question. ... Humanity, which was once condemned to a thermonuclear death ... is now more and more threatened by a cultural death. ..."[13]

Notwithstanding Rioux's condemnation, the consumer society made more and more inroads into Quebec culture. In 2000, 50 percent of Quebec households had two colour television sets, 46 percent owned a gas barbecue, and two-thirds were connected to cable TV. In 1990, 300 000 movie performances were shown on theater screens; in 2000, the number rose to about 650 000—and 85 percent of all movies were American productions. Instead of turning their liberty into an existential or spiritual search, the *Québécois* soon preferred inquiring about the latest car models. Instead of taking advantage of the cultural opportunities offered to them, they became couch potatoes enslaved to their television sets. At least, this is what the generation that came of age in the aftermath of World War II tended to believe. What was missing among the younger generation and in Quebec society as a whole, they said, was what Fernand Dumont called "transcendence." He wrote: "A society is not an aggregate of people pursuing their individual roads according to their interests; nor is it a closed field where factions struggle for their privileges independently of any rules other than the power of numbers or money."[14] A society, continued Dumont, must be capable of judging its inner value by resorting to some abstract transcendence. Failing to achieve such a judgment, a society condemns itself, according to Dumont, to disappearance as a distinct entity.

This cultural revolution had perhaps a deeper impact in Quebec than elsewhere in Canada, for the will to escape a closed and homogeneous religious universe resulted in calling into question all institutionalized authorities. But, in opposition to Rioux's and Dumont's harsh judgments, the general Americanization of French Canadian culture did not only mean the progressive establishment of an atomized and materialist society. It also meant the rise of pluralism, a greater tolerance toward different ways of living, and an attachment to simple and fundamental human values. "Beyond political rhetoric," concluded two sociologists on the basis of a national survey, "Quebec's uniqueness can readily be seen in the province's young people of the 1990s."[15] Among other unique features, Quebec's teenagers, they declared, are more open than teenagers elsewhere in Canada to premarital sex, homosexuality, and abortion, and they enjoy their family life more. Overall, their main characteristic seems to be a "lifestyle flexibility" that regards culture as a series of options and opportunities rather than a set of widely accepted values.

CONCLUSION

The reader has certainly noticed that the four great utopias of the Quiet Revolution did not materialize in contemporary Quebec, at least not completely. This observation allows me to reach three conclusions.

Conclusion 1: If one were obliged to summarize in two sentences the development of Quebec after 1960, one would have to underline two radical social changes that are unique to Quebec history when compared to the rest of North America. First, with the Quiet Revolution, "French Canadians" began to call themselves "*Québécois.*" Second, clerical French Canada gave way to a state-controlled Quebec. But, besides these two changes, the challenges Quebec faces today resemble pretty much those of every other Western society. For example, the fact that Quebec is a minority nation struggling for the recognition of its rights is not unique. In Canada, Aboriginal peoples are also trying to achieve national recognition. Corsicans in France, Basques in Spain, and the Scottish in the United Kingdom are only some of the other small nations searching for a way to preserve their particularities and to promote local autonomy through new political arrangements. It is one of the great lessons of the twentieth century that modern states have to find a way to accommodate basic human rights with the collective ambition of nations. Canada has not yet found all the answers to the dilemma nor the secret to equilibrium. But, it represents one of the greatest social laboratories of what that equilibrium could be like and leads the way for other countries that today confront the same problems.[16]

Conclusion 2: The Quiet Revolution failed to achieve some of its goals. Bare statistics show the failure of the attempt to create a bilingual Canada. A sovereign Quebec now seems a remote dream.

Canadian and Quebec social democracy are on the decline. Democracy is experiencing a crisis. There seems to be little desire to renew humanism. On the other hand, the Quiet Revolution accomplished a complete and largely beneficial transformation of morals and attitudes. For example, in spite of persistent sexism in many quarters, women have gained a status they lacked in the 1950s. Lately, *Québécois* have been found in national surveys to be very tolerant toward immigrants and visible minorities—in spite of a certain level of persistent racism (anti-Semitism, for example, has a long history in Canada, particularly in Quebec). Multiculturalism has brought about a recognition of Canada as a nation of nations. The Charter of Rights and Freedoms is accepted by the vast majority of the provincial population, the only question being whether it should have precedence over the National Assembly in Quebec City. It is worth noting that Quebec passed a *Chartre des droits et libertés de la personne* in 1975 (the provisions of which were extended in 1981) that has quasi-constitutional status and covers not only public law, like its Canadian counterpart, but also private law. The Quebec government was also the first provincial government to sign treaties with First Nations' representatives and has encouraged a new policy of negotiation instead of sterile confrontation.

Conclusion 3: I am not one to believe that a utopia is something that can be fully realized here and now. A utopia is first and foremost a source of inspiration. Obviously, democracy, nationalism, social democracy, and humanism have made inroads in Quebec over the years. But, much more must be done if we want Canada to be a place where justice, tolerance, openness, and transparency prevail. If this lesson in humility is remembered, the utopias of the 1960s and 1970s, with all their excesses and self-evident weaknesses, will not have been dreamt in vain. In this sense, they constitute a useful reminder that if the Canada of 2010 cannot be changed, the Canada of 2060 is yet to be built. That Canada, inescapably, we will have to build together.

NOTES

1. I thank Robert Brym and Valérie de Courville Nicole for their useful comments on a draft of this essay.
2. In this chapter, *Québécois* refers to French Quebeckers and *Quebeckers* refers to the entire population of Quebec.

3. Gérard Dion and Louis O'Neill, "L'Immoralité politique dans la province de Québec," *Le Devoir* (14 August 1956).

4. Pierre Elliott Trudeau, "Some obstacles to democracy in Quebec," *Canadian Journal of Economics and Political Science XXIV:* 3 August 1958: 303.

5. "FLQ Manifesto," on the World Wide Web at http://www.ola.bc.ca/online/cf/documents/1970FLQManifesto.html#top (23 November 2002).

6. Stéphane Kelly, "Pierre Elliott Trudeau et son maître. Une éducation politique," *Argument* (I, 1: Fall 1998) 29–40.

7. Gérard Bouchard, *La Nation québécoise au futur et au passé* (Montreal: VLB, 1999) 69.

8. Pierre Vallières, *White Niggers of America: The Precocious Autobiography of a Quebec "Terrorist,"* Joan Pinkham, trans. (Toronto: McClelland and Stewart, 1971). [First French edition, 1969.]

9. Jean-Paul Desbiens, *Les Insolences du frère Untel* (Montreal: Les Éditions de l'homme, 1960).

10. Ibid., 55–56.

11. Marcel Rioux, Rapport de la Commission d'enquête sur l'enseignement des arts au Québec (Quebec: l'Éditeur officiel du Québec, 1968) quoted in Pierre W. Bélanger et Guy Rocher, dir., École et société au Québec: Éléments d'une sociologie de l'éducation (Montreal: HMH, 1970) 462.

12. Marcel Fournier, *Les Génération d'artistes* (Quebec: IQRC, 1986) 97.

13. Marcel Rioux, "Remarques sur les industries de l'âme," *Question de culture, 7, "La culture: une industrie?"* (Quebec: IQRC, 1984) 50 and 49.

14. Fernand Dumont, *Raisons communes* (Montreal: Boréal, 1995) 218.

15. Reginald W. Bibby and Donald C. Posterski, *Teen Trends. A Nation in Motion* (Toronto: Stoddart, 2000), 115–36. [First non-abridged edition, 1991].

16. Michael Ignatieff, *The Rights Revolution* (Toronto: Anansi, 2000).

PART 3C

SEX AND GENDER

Much prejudice and discrimination exists against sexual minorities—lesbians, gays, bisexuals, and transgendered people—so we may reasonably consider sexuality a basis of social inequality, too. Thus, although Canada legalized same-sex marriage in 2005, three years later 56 percent of Canadians still disapproved of sexual relations between two people of the same sex. Such disapproval is usually silent but sometimes turns into harassment and occasionally into violence.

People commonly justify prejudice and discrimination against sexual minorities on the assumption that there are "naturally" just two, "opposite" sexes. However, research shows that the assumptions of naturalness and opposition are both misguided. One recent research project found it necessary to classify respondents as heterosexual, mostly heterosexual, bisexual, mostly gay/lesbian, gay/lesbian, questioning/uncertain, and other. For each of the sexual orientations, respondents were on average *simultaneously* attracted to same-sex and other-sex partners to varying degrees, and they had had on average at least one same-sex sexual partner. Given the wide variety of sexual orientations and the fact that some self-identified heterosexuals have same-sex attractions and sexual partners, it is difficult to sustain the belief that there are just two, opposite sexes.

In Chapter 15, Michael S. Kimmel and Rebecca F. Plante tackle the idea that sexuality is entirely a natural or biological phenomenon. They note that, until the 1940s, the study of sex was mainly the province of biology and psychology. Researchers in these fields viewed sex largely as a matter of animal desire or irrational impulse. Then, in the 1940s, analysts started investigating sex as a set of behaviours that help people form the wide variety of identities that typify all human populations—a vehicle of meaningful action through which we develop a sense of self. From this point of view, we may not learn sexualities in quite the same way we study the multiplication table, but we learn them nonetheless.

Earlier I mentioned income and occupational inequalities between women and men, but they do not exhaust the bases of gender inequality. Like sexual minorities, women face prejudice and discrimination that can turn into harassment and violence. In Chapter 16, Sandy Welsh and Jayne Baker show that male sexual harassment in Canadian workplace settings is partly the result of learning stereotypical gender roles early in life. They demonstrate that women are unlikely to define unwanted acts as sexual harassment if they have been situated in social locations where stereotypical gender roles are routinely stressed. However, they also show that women are *more* likely to define unwanted acts as sexual harassment if workplaces are organized in certain identifiable ways. We are obliged to conclude that while gender socialization at school and at work is an important source of gender harassment, it is not a straightjacket. Social forces increase the probability that people will act in certain ways, but ultimately people are agents of their own destiny and can organize their social milieux in ways that minimize harassment and violence.

CRITICAL THINKING QUESTION

1. Some people argue that biological differences between women and men necessarily place women at a disadvantage in terms of their occupational choices and earning power. Others argue that custom and power are the main sources of male–female differences in occupational choice and earning power. Outline and justify your position on this issue.
2. How, if at all, do you think that violence against women is related to inequality between women and men?

ANNOTATED BIBLIOGRAPHY

Pat Armstrong and Hugh Armstrong, *The Double Ghetto: Canadian Women and Their Segregated Work,* 3rd ed. (Toronto: Oxford University Press, 2010). An authoritative account of gender inequality in Canada.

Chapter 15

Sexualities

MICHAEL S. KIMMEL,
State University of New York and
REBECCA F. PLANTE, Ithaca College

You won't find a lot of sex in the sociological canon. Most of the founding fathers found sex theoretically discomfiting. Well into the twentieth century, sociologists left sex to the anthropologists, with their seemingly voyeuristic interests in archaic bodily taboos and practices, and to the biologists, with their claims about animals, essences, and evolutionary adaptations. If sociology's project was to chart the rationalizing trajectory of modern society, sex—what Max Weber called "the greatest irrational force of life"—was instinctual and embodied, anarchic and anachronistic, premodern and (Weber again) "externally inaccessible to any rational endeavor."

Weber's contemporary, Sigmund Freud, sealed sex's fate in the social sciences for a generation, declaring sexual desire a primal, indeed foundational, urge, and its sublimation and redirection the basis of civilization. Discussions of sexual behavior, homosexuality, prostitution, pornography, and sexual variations were typically subsumed into the study of crime and deviance—those vestiges of irrationality, those instances of resistance.

While experts had been pronouncing upon and denouncing sexual expression for millennia, the modern social-scientific study of sex began with Alfred Kinsey's massive studies, *Sexual Behavior in the Human Male* (1948) and *Sexual Behavior in the Human Female* (1953). Based on nearly 20 000 of the most intricate and intimate sexual histories imaginable, then or now, Kinsey's major findings rippled through American culture: the ubiquity and centrality of sexual behavior; the near-universality of masturbation among men (without deleterious effects); the apparently high incidence of homosexual acts among men, and of infidelity among both men (50 percent) and women (26 percent); and the significant presence of desire and sexual agency among women. Kinsey also found that sexual behavior varied widely, especially by social class.

Source: "Sexualities" by Michael S. Kimmel and Rebecca F. Plante, *Contexts 6(2)*, pp. 63–65, © 2007 American Sociological Association. Reprinted by Permission of SAGE Publications.

In his effort to normalize sex and legitimate its scientific study, Kinsey mapped sexuality by eschewing moral judgment and studying only behavior, which he characterized in strictly physiological terms: the satisfaction of a biologically based urge, orgasm as a reflex response. Kinsey's strictly behavioral approach—he counted the number of orgasms experienced in each of a variety of situations—separated homosexual acts from homosexual identity. This upended Freudian notions that homosexuality was a gender disorder, a problem of inversion. Nonsense, said Kinsey:

> In studies of human behavior, the term inversion is applied to sexual situations in which males play female roles and females play male roles in sex relations. ... [But] there are a great many males who remain as masculine, and a great many females who remain as feminine, in their attitudes and approaches in homosexual relations, as the males and females who have nothing but heterosexual relations. Inversion and homosexuality are two distinct and not always correlated types of behavior.

Sex is both more and less than a biological drive—it is a primary mechanism by which we constitute our identities, and it is also just another arena of social interaction (and thus becomes "sexuality" or even "sexualities": something bigger and more comprehensive than "sex").

It fell to the next generation of sex researchers, including John Gagnon and William Simon, to carve out a distinctly sociological approach to the study of sex and sexuality. In *Sexual Conduct* (1973), they proposed for the first time that sexual behavior was less about animal desires and more about shared social meanings, and that those meanings were the material through which we built a "self." Their intent, Gagnon later wrote, was "to bring the field of sexuality under the control of a sociological orientation, to lay a sociological claim to an aspect of social life that seemed determined by biology or psychology." Sexuality is socially constructed, built from and by cultures, eras, and institutions.

Whereas Freud had seen a sexual component in all manner of nonsexual activities—he discerned libidinous motives in art, music, political movements, literature—Gagnon and Simon argued that one could find political, economic, cultural, even moral motives in sexual conduct itself. One could "do" sex for social mobility, economic gain, or spiritual transcendence. Sex could become a means to ends much larger than any particular acts—a way to solidify or destroy connections, or to express one's gender role or identity.

Second, contra Kinsey, Gagnon and Simon distinguished behavior from identity. Behavior was far less interesting than the meanings and symbols that became attached to it and through which people understood and accounted for their conduct. Far from the result of blind, seemingly basic biological impulses or anarchic, romantic longings, sexual conduct was normatively organized and coherent, learned through lifelong socialization: "In any given society, at any given moment in its history, people become sexual in the same way they become everything else. Without much reflection, they pick up directions from their social environment. They acquire and assemble meanings, skills and values from the people around them. Their critical choices are often made by going along and drifting."

Sexual behavior is, in this sense, no different from other behaviors in our lives. We learn it from the people and institutions and ideas around us, and assemble it into a meaningful narrative. There are governing rules, hierarchies structuring mobility, and standards of evaluation. Gagnon and Simon coined the phrase "sexual scripts"—the social and cultural blueprints by which we create and express what we typically experience as deeply personal and intimate.

Their insights coincided with the sexual revolution of the 1960s and 1970s, which, coupled with the gay and lesbian and women's movements, generated a fertile new field. In particular, research expanded in four arenas: history, behaviors, identities, and inequalities. Much of this work capitalized on the concept of the social construction of sexuality, the argument that sex and sexuality are not solely hard-wired, essential, animalistic urges and mandates.

Once sexuality and sexual behaviors had been uncoupled from a strictly biological and reproductive agenda, we could begin to examine their history. Historian Jonathan Ned Katz (1995) described the development of the terms *homosexual* and *heterosexual*. At the start of the twentieth century, *heterosexual* referred to someone with a "morbid sexual interest in the opposite sex." Since "normal" sex was defined as reproductive, anything else was abnormal or perverse ("morbid"). As the twentieth century progressed, *heterosexual* evolved to become the taken-for-granted and normal mode of labeling individuals. With the term *homosexual* as its opposite, its dramatic foil, "normal" and "abnormal" were more fully fleshed out. Behaviors attached more intimately to individuals; gradually, the nouns *heterosexual* and *homosexual* were drawn from the adjectives that described behavior.

Such moves were hardly liberating, according to philosopher Michel Foucault (1990). The identification of individuals and classification of behaviors is part of nation-building in the modern era, he argued. The process of normalizing some conduct pathologizes others and subjects all behavior to the legitimate scrutiny of the state. Before the nineteenth century, it was the confessional that provided sexual discourses. In the nineteenth century, the professions—medicine, law, education—expanded their cultural and institutional power over sex, and the production of knowledge about sex became a major instrument in its control: "One had to speak of [sex] as of a thing to be not simply condemned or tolerated but managed, inserted into systems of utility, regulated for the greater good of all, made to function according to an optimum. Sex was not something one simply judged; it was a thing one administered." Contrary to Freud, Foucault insisted that we have no true sexual selves, repressed by morality and institutions. Instead, we can only come to develop sexual selves because of these institutions and their discourses about sex. Thus sex—and sexuality—became a political object.

Research on sexual behavior long suffered from a conceptual apparatus that bore little relation to actual behaviors. A residue of nineteenth-century formulations, the research categories of sexual conduct always referred to marriage—as if all sexual activity were in some way related to that institution. Thus sexual behavior was coded as "marital," "premarital," or "extramarital," even though unmarried, heterosexual people did not think of themselves as having "premarital" sex but simply as having sex.

Much recent research has thus attempted to dislodge the taken-for-granted linkages between sexual behaviors and marriage, to locate sexual activity as it relates to other social institutions, or to disentangle behaviors from their institutional fields. Even heterosexual behavior, long the baseline of comparison, turns out to be varied and complex.

The HIV/AIDS crisis that began in the 1980s provided a new opportunity for research into sexual practices, culminating in the National Health and Social Life Survey (NHSL), carried out by the National Opinion Research Center at the University of Chicago in the early 1990s (Laumann, Gagnon, Michael, and Michaels, 1994). This was the largest and most ambitious study of American sexual behavior ever undertaken, but it was noteworthy largely because of what the researchers did not find. Americans have less sex than we imagined, much of it monogamous and within the context of legal marriage, and enjoy it more. Fewer Americans identified as homosexual than previously believed, and fewer were unfaithful during their marriages than had been feared. This had the opposite effect of Kinsey's studies. Shocked by how little sex we were having, how conventional it was, and how apparently satisfied most us were with these arrangements, the project failed to generate the sort of buzz and outrage that greeted Kinsey.

HIV/AIDS increased research on all aspects of same-sex behavior. Most studies focused on men and risk-reduction, and on the effects of HIV, to the detriment of other aspects of gay or bisexual men's sexualities. Research on lesbians and bisexual women more broadly addressed aspects of identity, politics, and choices.

Cultural understandings exaggerate the differences between other-sex orientations and same-sex orientations. We often believe that the most important thing we can know about a person (after his or her sex/gender) is sexual orientation. In partial explanation for this practice's seductive appeal, Gagnon wrote:

> It is a common, but false, belief that if we know that persons choose same-gender sex partners, we can successfully make inferences about the kinds of families they come from; the kinds of sex lives they lead; their tastes in clothing, art, music, interior decoration; the way they talk; the kinds of work they prefer; and their religious or leisure orientations. We do not believe we can make such inferences about persons who choose opposite-gender sex partners.

Homosexuality (unlike heterosexuality) is a significant label, since it elicits a sequence of interlocked beliefs or judgments which organize our responses to ourselves and to other people.

It is through the other dimensions of identity—race, class, age, religion, and, most important, gender—that we construct our sexualities. These intersections are now the crucial starting point of studies of sexuality.

Although the last thirty years have seen many changes on the sexual landscape, discrimination persists. Heterosexuality remains the standard by which all other forms of sexuality (and gender) are judged. These "boundaries and binary divides" (the hetero/homo dichotomy) characterize the terms of debate about same-sex marriage, for example, revealing the social mechanisms that organize and constrain all sexual expression.

Virtually every country today is confronting new questions about sexual equality, how sexuality should be regulated, and what "the family" will be like in the future. Ken Plummer wonders, Who would have thought at the start of the twentieth century that by its very end we would be seriously discussing

- new forms of publicly recognized "family life";
- the growth of the new reproductive technologies, including surrogate mothers;
- the even wider use of many technologies to transform that most central organ of intimacy: the body;
- the public discussion (and private/public practice) of an array of non-procreative, non-penetrative coital sexualities;
- the development of transgendered worlds;
- the emergence of all sorts of new "private problems and public troubles," including a whole gallery of new "personal types" [such as "sex addict"].

Ironically, worldwide transformations enforce greater homogeneity while also leading to greater inequalities; studies of global sex trafficking, sex tourism, Internet pornography, mail-order brides, and global sexual movements will provide rich sources of research.

Even the body, along with that steadfast, binary, biological opposition between male and female, has been blurred. Studies of transgendered individuals, for example, reveal the ways in which we are alike, patterned by our culture, but also different, individual.

The future of sexuality research is the same as the future of sexualities—as social scientists we will try to understand it, and our society will attempt to name it and tame it. But, sex will always be a little bit messier than our models, lying slightly outside the reach of rationality.

REFERENCES

Foucault, Michel. (1990). *The History of Sexuality.* New York: Vintage Books.

Gagnon, John H. and William Simon. (1973). *Sexual Conduct.* Chicago: Aldine.

Katz, Jonathan Ned. (1995). *The Invention of Heterosexuality.* New York: Plume Books.

Kinsey, Alfred, Wardell Pomeroy, and Clyde Martin. (1948). *Sexual Behavior in the Human Male.* Philadelphia, PA: W.B. Saunders.

Kinsey, Alfred, Wardell Pomeroy, Clyde Martin, and Paul Gebhard. (1953). *Sexual Behavior in the Human Female.* Philadelphia, PA: W.B. Saunders.

Laumann, Edward O., John H. Gagnon, Robert T. Michael, and Stuart Michaels. (1994). *The Social Organization of Sexuality: Sexual Practices in the United States.* Chicago: University of Chicago Press.

Plante, Rebecca. (2006). *Sexualities in Context: A Social Perspective.* Boulder, CO: Westview.

Plummer, Ken. (2001). "The Square of Intimate Citizenship." *Citizenship Studies, 5,* 237–53.

Chapter 16

Sexual Harassment in the Canadian Workplace

SANDY WELSH and JAYNE BAKER

University of Toronto

WHEN IS IT SEXUAL HARASSMENT?

Surveys show that between a quarter and a half of Canadian women in the paid labour force experience unwanted sexual attention at work (Gruber, 1997; Welsh and Nierobisz, 1997). Yet, not all women define unwanted sexual attention—including sexual touching, jokes, and comments—as sexual harassment (Dellinger and Williams, 2002; Giuffre and Williams, 1994; Welsh et al., 2006). Why is this so? In this chapter, we focus on gender socialization as a possible explanation.

To be sure, other factors also play a role. For example, some workplace cultures are less tolerant of sexual harassment than others, and less tolerance may encourage more women to define unwanted sexual attention as harassment (Dellinger and Williams, 2002). In contrast, women from some ethnic and racial groups and women who lack citizenship may be less inclined to define unwanted sexual attention as harassment because of their background and status (Welsh et al., 2006). Women who immigrate to Canada may be initially unaware of what constitutes "sexual harassment" in Canada. They may also be unwilling to label unwanted sexual attention as harassment if it means putting their potential Canadian citizenship status at risk. In our judgment, however, gender socialization plays a primary role in the way women define their experiences and is therefore chiefly responsible for the way women label unwanted sexual attention in the workplace.

Using data from a study of women in Ontario, we demonstrate how gender socialization leads some women to blame themselves for unwanted sexual attention and to dismiss their experiences as unimportant. We begin by defining sexual harassment. We next outline how gender socialization influences women's ability (or inability) to label their experiences as sexual harassment. We then analyze our data, which show how some women in Ontario blame themselves for sexual harassment while others have trouble defining sexual harassment as such. Finally, we demonstrate that gender socialization is not destiny. With the proper social support, some women are able to reevaluate their experience of sexual harassment as unacceptable behaviour and take action to have it corrected.

SEXUAL HARASSMENT

Sexual harassment involves two forms of behaviour: quid pro quo harassment and hostile environment harassment. Quid pro quo harassment involves sexual threats or bribery linked to getting a job, keeping a job, or receiving a promotion or training opportunity. Hostile environment sexual harassment includes sexual jokes, comments, and touching that may create a sexualized environment or one that degrades women. By law, it is up to the person committing the behaviour to know the difference between welcome and unwelcome sexual behaviours (Canadian Human Rights Commission, 2004). At its core, sexual harassment lets women know they are not welcome in certain workplaces and that they are not respected members of the work group (Reskin and Padavic, 1994).

GENDER SOCIALIZATION

Gender socialization focuses on how we learn to become male or female according to the cultural standards of the social collectivities to which we belong. While recognizing the existence of biological differences between boys and girls, gender socialization researchers study how children learn the attitudes, behaviours, and expectations associated with masculine and feminine roles by interacting with teachers, parents, and role models, including the role models portrayed in the mass media. Such interactions reinforce behaviours that fit culturally acceptable forms of femininity and masculinity—and punish behaviours that don't. For example, young girls are often given dolls to play with and encouraged to display affection toward them. Such behaviour conforms to cultural expectations about femininity and nurturance. Yet people typically discourage young boys from playing with dolls, reinforcing expectations about a widely accepted form of masculinity that sees men as less nurturing and affectionate than women.

The aspect of gender roles that is most relevant to sexual harassment concerns the way men learn to become relatively dominant, powerful, and competitive, while women learn to become relatively nurturing, concerned with the quality of social relations, and passive. As a result of this differential learning, most men learn to treat women as sexual objects or "conquests," while most women learn to believe that being treated as such is normal. For example, women generally learn to be nonconfrontational when they are sexually harassed by men; they are inclined not to report such behaviour to the proper authorities. Meanwhile, men come to believe that women want and expect them to flirt, even in the workplace.

Focusing on how people learn gender roles carries with it the danger of emphasizing the existence of only one form of masculinity and one form of femininity—what are often called traditional "gender stereotypes" (Connell, 2002). Said differently, some analysts make it seem as if gender socialization happens to unwitting individuals who lack the capacity to influence, let alone resist, what they are taught. Such analysts downplay the extent to which people enjoy agency and choice. Below, we argue that their determinism is misplaced; people influence and resist traditional gender roles all the time.

GENDER SOCIALIZATION AND SEXUAL HARASSMENT

Early research emphasized how traditional gender role socialization teaches women to tolerate unwanted sexual attention from men and avoid confronting them about it (Gwartney-Gibbs and Lach, 1992; Lach and Gwartney-Gibbs, 1993). From this point of view, by teaching women to avoid conflict and doubt their perceptions, gender socialization makes it more likely that women will not label their experiences as sexual harassment and will not report it (Fitzgerald, Swann, and Magley, 1997; Hotelling and Zuber, 1997).

Researchers then noted that organizational culture contributes to employees' ability and willingness to label certain behaviours as sexual harassment (Folgero and Fjeldstad, 1995). In some masculine work cultures, women may not define their experiences as sexual harassment to ensure that they will be seen as competent team players (Collinson and Collinson, 1996). For example, new female coal miners may consider sexualized hazing rituals part of their initiation into work groups (Yount, 1991). In other workplaces, sexual behaviours commonly understood as sexual harassment may be requirements of the job (Williams, 1997: 4). For instance, restaurants may encourage customers to "talk dirty" to waitresses by promoting drinks with sexually loaded names such as "Screaming Orgasm" (Giuffre and Williams, 1994: 387; Williams, 1997: 22) or by requiring waitresses to wear short tight skirts and revealing tops (Loe, 1996). In these sexually charged or permissive work cultures, degrading sexual behaviours become an expected component of work that may not be considered sexual harassment by employees, be they men or women (Williams, 1997). Yet even in these organizational contexts, gender socialization plays a role since it is part of what leads to the acceptability of sexually harassing behaviours in the first place.

In the remainder of this chapter, we discuss the role that gender socialization plays in how women make sense of the sexual behaviours they experience at work. We show that women's gender socialization affects how women interpret their experience and make decisions about how to respond to it.

METHODS

Our analysis is based on a project designed to evaluate how women define harassment and harassment reporting mechanisms in Ontario. For our study, we selected women with a wide variety of social characteristics so we could learn how race, citizenship, class, language, age, disability, and sexuality help to shape their experiences. In the summer and fall of 2000, we conducted six focus groups, following this up with six additional focus groups and seventeen in-depth interviews in the spring of 2002. Data for our analysis comes from these interviews and focus groups, which included a total of 67 women (for details, see Welsh et al., 2006).

RESULTS

NOT NAMING: NORMALIZING UNWANTED SEXUAL ATTENTION

Several women in our study initially viewed their experiences of sexual harassment as "normal" flirting in the workplace or as sexual attention that they simply had to endure. Consider the experience of one francophone woman who worked in a government office. She experienced touching, suggestive talk, and comments from co-workers suggesting she was a sexual "conquest." She mentioned that she wasn't even aware at first that she was being harassed. Instead she viewed the behaviour as simply flirtatious:

> I welcomed, contributed to, and responded to the flirting. ... It wasn't possible to say anything, to do anything because I was so naive, unaware that it was possible to do something, that it was harassment.

It didn't happen! I was appealing to the guys. Afterward I told myself that the guys were mean, rather than believing that it was harassment. I minimized the situation, though I warned a new employee to be aware of the two men, so I had some kind of awareness. After the physical confrontation, I experienced a great deal of stress and understood that the situation was serious.

The "physical confrontation" that led her to realize that the men's actions were in fact not "normal" involved their trapping her in a room. She concluded:

I minimized, I talked about it to my girlfriends, but as if it was flirtation, and that allowed me to vent. [This was] my way of rationalizing and of minimizing, because if I'd seen the situation clearly, I wouldn't have been able to go in to work.

This woman's experience demonstrates how traditional gender socialization can complicate the ability to identify and label behaviour as sexual harassment. What turned out to be sexual harassment was seen as "normal" flirting between men and women, at least initially.

Some women also had initial difficulty naming the sexual harassment because of their race and/or ethnicity or citizenship status. One example of this comes from the group of Filipina domestic workers in our sample. They came to Canada through the Live-In Caregiver program, which gives them a limited work visa requiring that they hold a domestic worker job for 24 months of a 36-month period to apply for Canadian citizenship. One Filipina who cared and cleaned for an elderly man discussed the conflict between her background and Canadian definitions of sexual harassment:

I remember my first year, he is always telling me why don't you come with me in bed and make me warm? … So I just, I don't know the way to take it in Canada, because in the Philippines if somebody say that to you and they don't touch you, nothing happens, it's just a word, but here in Canada, it's something.

These women also talked about how they were unwilling to file a complaint because it might put their employment and future Canadian citizenship in jeopardy. They were afraid that they would be fired from their job and that they would be unable to find a replacement job that would give them the necessary 24 months of work experience. As one Filipina domestic worker stated: "Even if you don't like your situation, you just wait for the time [when you have more secure status] to leave."

BLAMING ONESELF

As a result of traditional gender socialization, women often take on a passive role when confronting uncomfortable and unpleasant situations. In the case of sexual harassment, this tendency initially leads most women to blame themselves for unwanted sexual behaviour. This is just what we found in our study. In the words of one white respondent: "I used to blame myself for the harassment and ask myself constantly what I was doing to make them want to treat me this way."

Women did not enjoy sexual advances from male colleagues, yet they believed they were the ones to blame for the men's behaviour (Fitzgerald et al., 1997). Other researchers have shown how blaming themselves for harassment reinforces the way in which women are socialized to respond to issues in a nonconfrontational manner. If women blame themselves for the unwanted sexual attention, they will not speak up and attempt to end the harassment.

Like women who experience rape and other forms of sexual violence, the women in our study often blamed their youthfulness or their clothes for inciting men to harass them. Here is what two white women in our study had to say on the subject, the first, anglophone, the second, francophone:

> I did blame myself sometimes for the harassment, asking what it was that made them do this, and also I would think that it was because I was young and the clothes that I wore caused this. I also tried to dress differently so that I wouldn't be attractive at work.

> I asked myself whether the clothes I was wearing were too sexy, even though every day I wore a smock over my clothes since I worked in a hospital setting.

The Aboriginal women in our study also struggled to define their experiences as harassment, especially when the perpetrator was in a position of authority, such as a respected Elder in the Aboriginal community:

> I felt uncomfortable. I don't like doubting myself, I was questioning: maybe that's just the way he is as an Elder but it didn't feel right. Sometimes it's just knowing that something doesn't feel right.

This woman experienced sexual comments, touching, and invasion of personal space. Her case illustrates that the authority of the harasser is an important determinant of the victim's ability to identify her experience as harassment: the greater the authority of the harasser, the more difficult such identification becomes (Carr et al., 2004).

NAMING AND NOT BLAMING: BEYOND GENDER SOCIALIZATION

Some women in our study moved beyond blaming themselves. They redefined their experiences as sexual harassment by talking with someone knowledgeable about the issue. Women began to understand that what they were experiencing should not be tolerated as normal behaviour between men and women. As one white woman said:

> I worked at a bar and I always kept my looks up, you know, that's where your tips come from. I always thought it was because maybe I was wearing the wrong kind of clothes. I was never trashy looking or anything—but I thought maybe that was what it was. Or I thought maybe I was flirting a little bit with him like when I was being nice to him when he first came in, but then I kept thinking to myself, there's no way. I know I wasn't. And especially [after] I got to see [the support worker] from the sexual assault centre—she really helped me. I realized it was about that.

This case demonstrates how some women resist their early gender socialization. The woman in question decided to reevaluate behaviour that at first seemed normal to her and, through the assistance of a support worker, was able to reject her initial beliefs and stop blaming herself.

A black woman who worked in a temporary position demonstrates the same process. She had the following conversation with the interviewer:

> Respondent: How did I cope with it? I started going to talk to [the support worker] a lot. But I, you know how you question yourself. I started thinking it was something that I wore or I had too much makeup on or what was it? You know, I don't know why he started off that way. And I said to her, "You know I had my hair down." Sometimes I wore my hair in a bandanna. I wore a scarf. I wore a T-shirt to cover my body like, you know what I mean, and I didn't wear short, short shorts. And I was like, "Why was he doing that to me?"
>
> Interviewer: So, did you get an answer to that question?
>
> Respondent: Well, she [the support worker] told me that it was nothing that I was wearing or anything. That it didn't have anything to do with that, that it was the person himself.
>
> Interviewer: Do you believe that? Do you believe that it had nothing to do with you?

Respondent: Not at the moment because you know, you question yourself. I guess I questioned myself for a while.

Interviewer: Now how do you look at it?

Respondent: Now how do I look at it? That he was just an ignorant pervert. Stuff like that—he's got some issues he needs to deal with. He's got some problems.

Our interviews show, then, that gender socialization is not the only variable affecting women's ability to define their experience. The nature of workplace culture, the authority of the harasser, the lack of Canadian citizenship, and the intervention of trained support personnel are among the factors that affect the capacity of women to define sexual harassment as such. The fact that some of the women we interviewed first blamed themselves for the harassment they experienced but were later able to reevaluate their experience and report it to the relevant authorities shows that, while gender socialization constrains self-perceptions, it is by no means a lifetime straightjacket (Morgan, 1999). For example, by placing support personnel in the workplace—officials who can discuss incidents of harassment with workers, educate them about what constitutes appropriate and inappropriate behaviour, inform them about their rights and mechanisms for seeking a resolution of grievances—organizations can do much to help women who experience sexual harassment. They can help them to recognize it for what it is and do something about it.

NOTE

1. Research for this project was funded by Status of Women Canada. We thank Jacquie Carr, Barbara MacQuarrie, and Audrey Huntley for collaboration on this project. Michael Schreiner and Robert Brym provided helpful comments on this paper. Finally, we are grateful to the women in our study for sharing their experiences with us.

REFERENCES

Canadian Human Rights Commission. (2004). "Discrimination and Harassment." On the World Wide Web at http://www.chrc-ccdp.ca/discrimination/what_is_it-en.asp (retrieved 31 January 2006).

Carr, Jacquie, Audrey Huntley, Barbara MacQuarrie, and Sandy Welsh. (2004). *Workplace Harassment and Violence. Centre for Violence Against Women and Children.* University of Western Ontario. On the World Wide Web at http://www.crvawc.ca/research_crvawcpubs .htm (retrieved 31 January 2006).

Collinson, M., and D. Collinson. (1996). "It's Only Dick: The Sexual Harassment of Women Managers in Insurance Sales." *Work, Employment and Society, 10,* 29–56.

Connell, R.W. (2002). *Gender.* Oxford, UK: Polity Press.

Dellinger, Kirsten and Christine Williams. (2002). "The Locker Room and the Dorm Room: The Cultural Context of Sexual Harassment in Two Magazine Publishing Organizations." *Social Problems, 49,* 242–57.

Fitzgerald, L.F., S. Swann, and V.J. Magley. (1997). "But Was It Really Harassment? Legal, Behavioral and Psychological Definitions of the Workplace Victimization of Women." In W. O'Donohue, ed., *Sexual Harassment: Theory, Research, and Treatment* (pp. 5–28). Boston: Allyn and Bacon.

Folgero, I.S. and I.H. Fjeldstad. (1995). "On Duty—Off Guard: Cultural Norms and Sexual Harassment in Service Organizations." *Organization Studies, 16,* 299–313.

Giuffre, Patti and Christine Williams. (1994). "Boundary Lines: Labeling Sexual Harassment in Restaurants." *Gender and Society, 8,* 378–401.

Gruber, J.E. (1997). "An Epidemiology of Sexual Harassment: Evidence from North America and Europe." In W. O'Donohue, ed., *Sexual Harassment: Theory, Research, and Treatment* (pp. 84–98). Boston: Allyn and Bacon.

Gwartney-Gibbs, Patricia A. and Denise H. Lach. (1992). "Sociological Explanations for Failure to Seek Sexual Harassment Remedies." *Mediation Quarterly, 9* (4), 363–73.

Hotelling, Kathy and Barbara A. Zuber. (1997). "Feminist Issues in Sexual Harassment." In W. O'Donohue, ed., *Sexual Harassment: Theory, Research, and Treatment* (pp. 99–112). Boston: Allyn and Bacon.

Lach, Denise H. and Patricia A. Gwartney-Gibbs. (1993). "Sociological Perspectives on Sexual Harassment and Workplace Dispute Resolution." *Journal of Vocational Behavior, 42* (1), 102–15.

Loe, M. (1996). "Working for Men at the Intersection of Power, Gender, and Sexuality." *Sociological Inquiry, 66* (4): 399–421.

Morgan, Phoebe. (1999). "Risking Relationships: Understanding the Litigation Choices of Sexually Harassed Women." *Law and Society Review, 33* (1), 67–92.

Reskin, Barbara and Irene Padavic. (1994). *Women and Men at Work.* Thousand Oaks, CA: Pine Forge Press.

Welsh, Sandy, Jacquie Carr, Barbara MacQuarrie, and Audrey Huntley. (2006). "I'm Not Thinking of It as Sexual Harassment: Understanding Harassment across Race and Citizenship." *Gender and Society, 20,* 87–107.

Welsh, Sandy and Annette Nierobisz (1997). "How Prevalent Is Sexual Harassment? A Research Note on Measuring Sexual Harassment in Canada." *Canadian Journal of Sociology, 22,* 505–22.

Williams, Christine L. (1997). "Sexual Harassment in Organizations: A Critique of Current Research and Policy." *Sexuality and Culture, 1,* 19–43.

Yount, K.R. (1991). "Ladies, Flirts, and Tomboys: Strategies for Managing Sexual Harassment in an Underground Coal Mine." *Journal of Contemporary Ethnography, 19* (4), 396–422.

PART 4   SOCIAL INSTITUTIONS

The social structures that compose human societies are nested like Russian dolls or Chinese boxes. There are structures within structures within structures. The smallest are **microstructures**. Microstructures are localized sites of face-to-face interaction, such as families. Social relations in microstructures tend to be emotionally deep and enduring, which is why people value them for their own sake. **Macrostructures**, in contrast, are larger, less localized, and more impersonal. People participate in macrostructures for specific, instrumental reasons—to earn money, get an education, and so on. **Global structures** are even larger, more remote, and more impersonal. They involve relations between whole societies and between nations.

We find **institutions** at both the microstructural and macrostructural levels of society. Institutions are social structures that, to varying degrees, fulfill basic human needs. These needs include the reproduction of the species and the nurturance and primary socialization of small children (a set of functions that is usually performed by the family), the maintenance and renewal of legitimate authority (a set of functions that is performed by the political system), and the production and distribution of material resources (a set of functions that is performed by the economy).

Although institutions fulfill basic human needs, the articles in Part 4 show that these needs are flexible and that a variety of institutional forms may therefore meet them. Moreover, institutions do not always function smoothly. The very term *institution* may suggest a solid and stable establishment, but in reality social conflict is never far below the surface of any institution.

GLOSSARY

Institutions are microlevel and macrolevel social structures that address basic human needs, such as reproduction, nurturance, and primary socialization (the family), the maintenance and renewal of legitimate authority (the political system), and the production and distribution of material resources (the economy).

Global structures are the largest and most impersonal patterns of social relations, sometimes spanning the entire globe, including relations within and between societies and nations.

Macrostructures are large, nonlocalized, impersonal sets of social relations. People participate in them for specific, instrumental reasons.

Microstructures are small, localized, emotionally intense patterns of social relations. People value such relations for their own sake.

CRITICAL THINKING QUESTION

1. Think about your taste in food, music, and style of dress. Do local, regional, national, or global institutions influence you most? Why do different levels of structure exert varying levels of influence on different aspects of your life?

ANNOTATED BIBLIOGRAPHY

Erving Goffman, *Asylums: Essays on the Social Situation of Mental Patients and Other Inmates* (Chicago: Aldine, 1961). This is the classic study of "total institutions," places where people live, work, eat, sleep, rapidly unlearn much of what they knew about how to interact with others in the outside world, and just as quickly learn how to behave as inmates subject to strict institutional norms and the rigid authority of staff members.

Jackie Smith et al., eds. *Global Democracy and the World Social Forums* (Boulder, CO: Paradigm, 2008). This useful study of a global institution in the process of formation documents the rise of the World Social Forum, which promotes global peace, justice, and democracy.

PART 4A

FAMILIES

Notice the italicized terms in the following sentences, taken from this unit's Introduction: "Institutions are social structures that, *to varying degrees,* fulfill basic human needs. These needs include the reproduction of the species and the nurturance and primary socialization of small children (a set of functions that is *usually* performed by the family). ..." The italics signify weasel words allowing me to squirm out of a tight spot. This is the tight spot: The degree to which families fulfill the basic human needs of reproduction and the nurturance and primary socialization of small children has declined in recent decades.

About a fifth of Canadian women between the ages of 40 and 45—women who are near the end of their reproductive years—do not have children, up from about 10 percent circa 1980. The proportion of Canadians who marry is down, the divorce rate is up, and the rate of remarriage after divorce is down. Nonfamily households are more common than they were a few decades ago because more single people, including seniors, can afford to live on their own and because gay and lesbian lifestyles are more widely accepted than they used to be, especially in large urban areas. In Canada, Argentina, Belgium, Iceland, the Netherlands, Norway, Portugal, South Africa, Spain, and Sweden, gays and lesbians can marry. Because of all these factors, the **nuclear family** is no longer the overwhelmingly predominant household form. (The nuclear family consists of a husband and wife who live in the same household and have at least one child.) According to the 2006 census, 14 percent of Canadians lived in nonfamily households and 86 percent in family households. Among family households, 16 percent were lone-parent families, 15 percent were common-law families (55 percent of which had no children at home, and 45 percent of which had children at home), and 69 percent were families of married couples (44 percent of which had no children at home, and 56 percent of which had children at home).

The facts listed above should not lead you to conclude that the family is in a state of collapse. Sociological surveys show that more than three-quarters of Canadians regard their family as the most important thing in their lives, more important than career or religion. The great majority of adults still want to marry and have children. In one poll, more than 90 percent of respondents with children at home said that the family is becoming *more* important to them. What is happening, however, is that people are freer than they once were to establish the kinds of family arrangements that best suit them. For instance, because most adult women are now employed in the paid labour force, and because changes in divorce laws have made the division of property after divorce more equitable, women now have a measure of economic independence that gives them greater freedom to end unsatisfying marriages and seek more gratifying relationships. As this example illustrates, the facts listed in the preceding paragraph do not spell the end of the family but the possibility that family forms better suiting the *diversity* of human needs can take shape.

One alternative family form that is becoming increasingly prevalent is the gay or lesbian family. People are changing laws in some parts of the world to give partners of same-sex unions the same rights and obligations as partners in a marriage. The state compels no religious organization in Canada to bless same-sex unions. However, since July 20, 2005, same-sex unions have been recognized as legal marriages in this country. In Chapter 17, Adam Green places same-sex marriage in social and historical context, analyzes the first (2006) census data containing information on same-sex marriage, and presents fascinating details from his interviews of same-sex couples in Toronto to help us appreciate this new family form.

More than 9.7 million children under the age of 18 lived in Canadian families in 2006. Until they are old enough to take care of themselves, and especially before they start preschool, their parents must arrange some form of daycare for them. In Chapter 18, Jane Beach, Martha Friendly, Carolyn Ferns, Nina Prabhu, and Barry Forer usefully summarize the state of daycare in Canada.

Some parents (mainly mothers) stay at home to take care of their young children. However, most women do not want to be full-time mothers. Families cannot afford to remove a parent from the paid labour force for long anyway. As a result, Canada has developed a patchwork system of daycare involving public and private facilities, as well as nannies for the well off.

In 2008, the average annual cost of childcare in Canada was $7145 per child. There was little variation in cost from one province to the next, with one glaring exception: Quebec. In Quebec, the average annual cost of child care was just $1207 per child. *La belle province* alone has developed a system of universally accessible, high-quality, subsidized daycare. It costs parents just $7 a day. In other ways, too, Quebec is more child friendly than the rest of the country. It has a more generous parental leave policy than the other provinces do, has been paying baby bonuses to parents since 1988, and will soon cover the cost of in vitro fertilization for infertile women. As John Myles detailed earlier (see Chapter 10), these policy innovations have allowed Quebec alone to avoid the kind of rapidly growing income inequality that other provinces have witnessed since the 1990s.

GLOSSARY

A **nuclear family** consists of a husband and wife who live in the same household and have at least one child.

CRITICAL THINKING QUESTIONS

1. What are the major social forces (groups, ideas) for and against gay and lesbian marriage in Canada? Why did the groups and ideas that support gay and lesbian marriage eventually win their struggle in 2005?
2. What are the advantages and disadvantages for children, parents, and society of universally accessible, high-quality, subsidized daycare?

ANNOTATED BIBLIOGRAPHY

Margrit Eichler, *Family Shifts: Families, Policies, and Gender Equality* (Toronto: Oxford University Press, 1997). A penetrating analysis of how Canadian families have changed and how public policies need to be reformed to take account of new realities.

Bonnie Fox, ed., *Family Patterns, Gender Relations*, 3rd ed. (Toronto: Oxford University Press, 2008). The definitive Canadian reader in sociology of the family.

Chapter 17

The Changing Face of Matrimony

SAME-SEX CIVIL MARRIAGE IN THE
TWENTY-FIRST CENTURY

ADAM ISAIAH GREEN, University of Toronto

THE RISE OF CIVIL MARRIAGE FOR SAME-SEX COUPLES

As the second decade of the twenty-first century begins, civil marriage for same-sex couples is a legal option in parts of Western Europe, Africa, and North America, including the Netherlands, Belgium, Canada, Spain, South Africa, Norway, and in two states in the United States: Connecticut and Massachusetts. First legalized in the Netherlands in 2001, same-sex civil marriage is a hot-button issue throughout the Western world, vigorously contested in public discourse and policy. In the United States, for instance, a variety of legal measures designed to prevent same-sex marriage have been put into law, including federal Defense of Marriage Act (DOMA) legislation, which prohibits federal recognition of same-sex civil marriage by defining marriage as the explicit union of one man and one woman, and amendments to state constitutions with the same effect. Some countries sidestep the controversy associated with same-sex civil marriage with legal provisions that are roughly comparable with those of civil marriage. A handful of governments, for instance, grant same-sex couples the right to register as a *domestic partnership*, which confers many of the same rights and responsibilities as civil marriage. Parts of the United States and Western Europe offer *civil unions* for same-sex couples in place of civil marriage, although, like domestic partnership, the benefits of this legal arrangement vary widely from place to place.

Advocates of same-sex civil marriage typically reject these alternative, "marriage-like" measures because they regard them as a kind of second-class citizenship for lesbian and gay couples. They argue that state-sanctioned civil marriage is not just a legal status; it is also a symbolic arrangement that provides a vital source of societal legitimization to which same-sex couples are equally entitled (Hausknecht, 2003; Josephson, 2005; Sullivan, 1997). In contrast, opponents of same-sex marriage marshal a wide range of objections, often rooted in religious belief or historical precedent, to preserve the institution of marriage for opposite-sex couples. Legalizing same-sex marriage, they argue, threatens the sanctity of marriage, offends the moral beliefs of people opposed to homosexuality on religious grounds, and threatens the special social status afforded to the reproductive, heterosexual married couple (Baskerville, 2006; Gallagher, 2003). As well, not all lesbian- and gay-identified activists support same-sex marriage. Some of them argue that the institution itself is inextricably tied to the historical subordination of women and the institutionalization of a heterosexual norm founded on reproduction, monogamy, and the nuclear family (otherwise known as *heteronormativity*) (Warner, 1999; Yep, Lovaas, and Elia, 2003). They see civil marriage as an institution that reproduces inequality and an outdated Judeo-Christian model of a moral intimate life.

These arguments aside, the arc of political history in the modern West bends toward the expansion of civil rights. Younger generations in liberal-democratic societies support same-sex marriage much more strongly than their older counterparts do. The lesbian and gay movements continue to mobilize support for same-sex marriage. Accordingly, same-sex civil marriage provisions are likely to become more widespread over time—albeit not without a fight. The twenty-first century has already witnessed dramatic battles over matrimony, and it is likely to continue to do so.

A BRIEF HISTORY OF CIVIL MARRIAGE AS A SOCIAL CONSTRUCTION

State-sanctioned or *civil* marriage has a thorny past, not least because, throughout history, it restricted *who* could marry, *whom* someone could marry, and the *age* at which a person could marry. In this sense, state-sanctioned marriage has never been a simple entitlement but, rather, one bound to national ideologies concerning class, social status, and citizenship. For instance, Ancient Roman law held that the daughter, granddaughter, or great-granddaughter of a senator could not marry a freedman, an actor, or a man whose father or mother was an actor (Gamsey and Saller, 1987).

Modern civil marriages have been no less restrictive. Besides laws prohibiting same-sex partners to marry, the most common laws restricting marriage involve race, along with gender-specific restrictions on number of spouses and age of marriage. In the early nineteenth century in the United States, for instance, the government prohibited African Americans from civil marriage. Moreover, concern over racial inter-mixing, or *miscegenation*, fuelled a variety of anti-miscegenation laws that made it illegal to marry a person of a different race throughout most of the United States for the greater part of the twentieth century. In fact, a federal decree dissolved the anti-miscegenation only in 1967.

Nazi Germany also institutionalized anti-miscegenation policies to ward off the prospect of "mongrelism." The Nazis first outlawed marriages between Jews and non-Jewish Germans, and then between Germans and Roma ("Gypsies") or blacks. Similarly, under apartheid in South Africa (1948–92), the *Prohibition of Mixed Marriages Act* pro-hibited marriages between whites and blacks, and between whites and "coloureds" (Asians). Both Nazi Germany and apartheid South Africa even criminalized interracial sexual intercourse. In Nazi Germany, it was punishable by imprisonment or death. In both countries, anti-miscegenation laws were repealed only after enormous political upheaval: the demise of the Nazi regime at the end of World War II and the collapse of apartheid in 1992.

Gender-specific restrictions on the number of spouses and age of mar-riage have also been common. For instance, in Utah before 1896, mar-riage was permissible between a man and a woman, or a man and *multiple* women, but never a woman and multiple men. Today, in many parts of the world, women are often encouraged—even coerced—to marry at a younger age than males. For instance, in Ethiopia, it is common for girls under 10 years of age to be married, whereas boys of this age are never married (Haberland, Chong, and Bracken, with Parker, 2005). In Afghanistan, a man must be 18 years old to marry, while a woman can marry at 16, and it is common for girls to be forced into marriage as young as 6 years of age (UNIFEM, 2008). Even in Ohio and Rhode Island, women can marry at 16 years of age, but men must be at least 18 years old.

The history of civil marriage, with its various and changing restrictions, provides sociological clues to the status of the institu-tion of marriage more generally. First, sociologists view marriage as a social construction. The very fact that civil marriage has taken so many historical forms—including, according to some scholars, the inclusion of same-sex couples in early Ancient Rome (Boswell, 1980)—demonstrates the remarkable variety of ways a given society can orga-nize the institution. Civil marriage is constructed out of the norms, values, and political commitments of a given society's policymakers and citizenry. It is not an institution with universal characteristics.

Second, sociologists note that civil marriage helps to institutionalize power relations. People who can marry enjoy advantages over those who cannot marry: certain tax breaks, healthcare benefits, and so on. Moreover, civil marriage serves an implicit legitimating function in that it regards certain two-person arrangements as superior to others and thereby worthy of legal support and protection. For instance, when the United States and Nazi Germany did not recognize interracial marriages, the state was making an explicit statement about which relationships were of value to the nation. Similarly, sociologists typically regard the exclusion of same-sex couples from civil marriage as a form of structural disenfranchisement reflecting national sentiments that devalue gay and lesbian relationships.

Historically, marriage has involved an exchange between spouses' families or clans, in which brides were traded for goods or as payment for debts (Levi-Strauss, 1969). Today, marriage typically institutionalizes gender inequality by relegating women to the roles of mother, domestic worker, and sex provider (Friedan, 1963; Hartmann, 1981; Rich, 1980). Thus, civil marriage often has gender-specific consequences that tend to disadvantage women. For instance, the fact that women can marry at a younger age than men is less a privileged status than a legal mechanism facilitating the institutionalization of women's roles as mothers and wives. When young women and girls are married off to much older men, often without the girls' consent, a husband typically regards his wife as his property, and she faces a relatively poor quality of life (UNIFEM, 2008). Until the twentieth century, women usually married for economic reasons, and even in postindustrial societies they are socialized to believe that marriage and motherhood are essential for a happy, fulfilling life (Rich, 1980). Thus, although, say, Canadian women are rarely forced to marry, neither are they entirely free to reject marriage. And once married, the institution typically cements a woman's subordination to a man, charging her with the responsibilities of bearing and raising children, keeping the household clean and orderly, and tending to her husband's emotional and sexual needs—all without remuneration. In this sense, civil marriage is a *patriarchal* institution of social control that establishes the conditions under which women are systematically disadvantaged and men systematically advantaged.

A third and related stream of scholarly analysis, sometimes called *queer theory*, suggests that widespread civil marriage for same-sex married couples may usher in an era of *homonormativity*, involving the consolidation of new lifestyle norms for lesbians and gays centred on domesticity, monogamy, reproduction, and the nuclear family (Duggan, 2002; Valverde, 2006). From this point of view, same-sex marriage may render lesbians and gays indistinguishable from their heterosexual counterparts, with marriages organized by the institutionalization of husband-wife gender roles, an unequal division of labour, and a conservative sexual politics indebted to Judeo-Christian interpretations of what constitutes a moral intimate life. The traditionalization of formerly queer lifestyles is regarded as problematic to the extent that it stigmatizes or renders less valuable lesbian and gay relationships that are not ongoing, monogamous, married, and reproductive (Johnson, 1996). In this sense, homonormativity threatens to dissolve the critical edge of queer culture, which drew attention to the repressive nature of dominant norms around gender roles and sexual sensibilities in the first place.

Some queer theory scholars are also critical of same-sex marriage insofar as the institution may align with broader transformations in political economy, most notably the transition from the era of centralized, governmental concern for the social welfare of its citizenry to neoliberal reforms that place the burden of social welfare on individuals and private entities (Foucault, 1991). From this perspective, same-sex marriage provisions are less an indication of a nation's social inclusiveness than a consequence of neoliberal reform, whereby the state increasingly cedes the care of citizens to the citizens themselves (Whitehead, 2006). Thus, same-sex civil marriage allows lesbian and gay spouses to look to each other, rather than to the welfare state, for care, support, and financial stability (Lessard, 2007).

I now offer a brief analysis of demographic and interview data to provide a statistical and qualitative portrait of same-sex marriage in Canada today.

A SNAPSHOT OF SAME-SEX MARRIAGE IN CANADA

Popular opinion among Canadians has only recently favoured same-sex marriage. In the first Gallup Canada survey of Canadian attitudes toward same-sex marriage in 1993, 76 percent of those surveyed opposed same-sex marriage. By 2000, that number had fallen to 48 percent.

In 2002, reflecting popular sentiment, the Ontario Supreme Court ruled that the opposite-sex stipulation for common-law marriage was unconstitutional. Similar decisions soon followed throughout Canada, and by 2004, courts in British Columbia, Quebec, Yukon, Manitoba,

Nova Scotia, Saskatchewan, Quebec, and Newfoundland and Labrador fell in line with the Ontario ruling. That same year, the federal government of Canada put forward a request to the Supreme Court of Canada to deliberate on whether the exclusion of same-sex couples from civil marriage was permissible under the Charter guarantees of equality (Nelson, 2008). The Supreme Court ruled that the constitutional definition of marriage did not exclude same-sex couples and that the federal government was within its constitutional rights to redefine marriage to include same-sex couples. Subsequently, Parliament passed Bill C-38, which redefined marriage in line with the Charter. The chief justice of the Supreme Court of Canada signed the Civil Marriage Act into law on July 19, 2005. Same-sex marriage became the law of the land, making Canada only the third country in the world to do so, after the Netherlands and Belgium.

The 2006 census counted 45 345 same-sex couples in Canada, 84 percent of them common law (cohabiting for one year or more) and 16 percent legally married (between July 19, 2005, and the census date) (Statistics Canada, 2008). About 55 percent of same-sex couples were male and 45 percent were female. Eight percent of same-sex couples had children living with them; of these, 82 percent were female couples and 18 percent were male couples. Interestingly, 14 percent of same-sex *married* couples reported having one or more children, compared with just 7 percent of same-sex *common-law* couples. This difference suggests that parenthood may promote civil marriage among same-sex couples—that is, same-sex couples who choose marriage over common-law status may be motivated to do so because they have children or want to have them. Another possibility is that civil marriage promotes parenthood among same-sex couples—marriage may encourage same-sex couples to want to have children. A third possibility is that both circumstances prevail.

The census is mute on such complex questions as whether and to what degree marriage promotes parenthood or vice-versa among same-sex couples. Until sociologists conduct more surveys and interviews of same-sex couples in Canada, we must rely partly on data from other countries to gain insight into many aspects of same-sex marriage. For example, one study found that nearly half of 812 married and registered gay and lesbian individuals in Denmark reported "legal rights" as the chief motivation for having their relationship formally recognized by the state (Eskridge and Spedale, 2006: 134). These legal rights include inheritance rights, tax breaks, and health and employment benefits. The Danish research also found that important intangible benefits derive from marriage, including increased commitment to the relationship, increased legitimacy, and increased social support from family and friends. Taken as a whole, these benefits seem to increase the durability of same-sex relationships.

My study of same-sex marriage in Ontario among 30 spouses, divided evenly by sex, yielded similar results (Green, 2008). Married spouses—men and women—were overwhelmingly surprised about the degree to which civil marriage conferred a sense of legitimacy and permanence to their relationship. In addition, some of these spouses found that the new sense of legitimacy extended beyond their immediate friends and families to the workplace. Co-workers and employers respected the individuals I interviewed—and their intimate relationships— more once they got married. In turn, marriage may produce conditions under which lesbian and gay employees can build better relationships with employers and clients. As one male respondent put it:

> There are honestly work benefits for us being married. When I interact with the partners (of the firm) in general ... it's probably more comfortable if they had us over for dinner. We could get invited as a couple. It's a different comfort aspect to it ... even how people interact and so on, even the signs of stability which is important to them when you get to the next level.... And in contrast to the gay village boys that are at work who might even be at the same career level (but) can't talk about their (partners) at all.... For sure, there's a difference, the whole perception of stability is different between the two. Because even small-talk wise, even if you were gay and kind of semi-in, semi-out at work, you just don't talk about your personal life.... And part of the way you develop rapport with anyone is to talk about your personal life: "Are you married and do you have kids?" It's the standard small-talk question.

Although civil marriage may provide same-sex couples with benefits similar to those enjoyed by heterosexual couples, marriage forms are unlikely to be identical in the two cases. In particular, civil marriage may not produce the same level of monogamy as opposite-sex marriages, especially among male couples. In the United States, nearly all married couples expect sexual exclusivity from their spouses, and the situation is probably not very different in Canada (Laumann, Gagnon, Michael, and Michaels, 1994). In contrast, the Danish study cited earlier found that although some married same-sex male couples embraced monogamy, some did not. In my study, 40 percent of the women and 60 percent of the men reported that they do not believe that marriage must always be monogamous. Some 47 percent of male respondents reported an *explicit* policy of non-monogamous practice, as did a lone female same-sex spouse. However, half of the respondents with explicitly monogamous marriages believed that it is acceptable for marriages to be non-monogamous, while about one in five monogamous males and one in 10 monogamous females remained open to the possibility that their own marriages might one day become non-monogamous. Most interestingly, nearly half of the men with openly non-monogamous marriages decided to have an open marriage *after* getting married. Although my small sample size does not permit generalizing to the broader population of same-sex marriages in Ontario, much less Canada as a whole, the findings are consistent with research on the sexual norms of gay men and gay subcultures (Weeks, Heaphy, and Donovan, 2001; Woolwine and McCarthy, 2005). According to one study, gay men do not articulate a single moral code around sexual fidelity but rather a kind of "morally pragmatic stand" arising in the historical context of anti-homosexual sentiment and associated stigmatization (Woolwine and McCarthy, 2005: 399–400). Put another way, becoming gay is marked by a process of "unlearning" heterosexuality, including the expectation of a heteronormative lifestyle (Herdt and Boxer, 1992). In this light, it is perhaps not surprising that same-sex married couples, historically excluded from the institution of civil marriage, would draw from their prior experience in constructing married life.

If norms and practices around marital fidelity are, on average, different for same-sex couples and their heterosexual counterparts, norms and practices around the domestic division of labour might also represent a departure. In fact, the literature suggests that same-sex couples in general reject "husband-wife" roles in favour of a more egalitarian model of domestic work founded on choice and interest (Blumstein and Schwartz, 1983; Dunne, 1997; Green, 2008; Patterson, 1995). Thus, almost all the same-sex couples in my Ontario study reported sharing equally in housework and child care. On occasion, housework was apportioned according to financial contributions; the partner who earned more money did less housework. However, in these circumstances, it was common for the partners to reverse roles when, for instance, the higher-earning partner lost his job or returned to school. In short, rather than accepting fixed husband-wife roles, the same-sex couples in my study negotiated domestic work on an ongoing basis determined by pragmatic concerns and personal interests. The heavy hand of patriarchy was nowhere to be found. In sum, although more research is needed to explore whether the division of domestic labour among same-sex couples is consistent with their self-reports, preliminary findings suggest that same-sex marriage may differ significantly from heterosexual marriages in this way, too.

REFERENCES

Baskerville, Stephen. (2006). "The Real Danger of Same-Sex Marriage." *The Family in America* [Online Edition], *20* (5), 6. On the World Wide Web at http://www.profam.org/pub/fia/fia.2005.6.htm (retrieved 13 November 2008).

Blumstein, Philip and Pepper Schwartz. (1983). *American Couples: Money, Work and Sex*. New York: William Morrow.

Boswell, John. (1980). *Christianity, Social Tolerance and Homosexuality: Gay People in Western Europe from the Beginning of the Christian Era*. Chicago: University of Chicago Press.

Duggan, Lisa. (2002). "The New Homonormativity: The Sexual Politics of Neoliberalism." In Russ Castronovo and Dana Nelson, eds., *Materializing Democracy: Toward a Revitalized Cultural Politics* (pp. 175–94). Durham, NC: Duke University Press.

Dunne, Gillian A. (1997). *Lesbian Lifestyles: Women's Work and the Politics of Sexuality*. Toronto: University of Toronto Press.

Eskridge, William Jr. and Darren Spedale. (2006). *Gay Marriage: For Better or for Worse? What We've Learned from the Evidence*. New York: Oxford University Press.

Foucault, Michel. (1991). "Governmentality." In Graham Burchell, Colin Gordon, and Peter Miller, eds., *The Foucault Effect: Studies in Governmentality with Two Lectures by and an Interview with Michel Foucault* (pp. 87–104). Chicago: University of Chicago Press.

Friedan, Betty. (1963). *The Feminine Mystique*. New York: W.W. Norton and Company.

Gallagher, Maggie. (2003). "The Divorce Thing: A Diversion in the Marriage Debate." *National Review Online* (August 13). On the World Wide Web at http://www.dadi.org/divthing.htm (retrieved 13 November 2008).

Gamsey, Peter and Richard Saller. (1987). *The Roman Empire: Economy, Society and Culture*. Los Angeles: University of California Press.

Green, Adam Isaiah. (2008). "Same-Sex Marriage: Lesbian and Gay Spouses Marry Innovation and Change." Paper presented at the Annual Meeting of the American Sociological Association, August 1–4, Boston, Massachusetts.

Haberland, Erica, L. Chong, and Hillary J. Bracken, with Chris Parker. (2005). "Early Marriage and Adolescent Girls." *Youth Lens, 15* (August).

Hartmann, Heidi. (1981). "The Family as the Locus of Gender, Class and Political Struggle: The Example of Housework." *Signs: Journal of Women in Culture and Society, 6*, 366–94.

Hausknecht, Murray. (2003). "Gay Marriage and the Domestication of Sex." *Dissent* (Fall), 8–10.

Herdt, Gilbert and Andrew Boxer. (1992). "Introduction: Culture, History, and Life Course of Gay Men." *Gay Culture in America: Essays from the Field.* Boston: Beacon Press.

Johnson, Fenton. (1996). "Wedded to an Illusion: Do Gays and Lesbians Really Want the Right to Marry?" *Harper's* (November), 41–50.

Josephson, Jyl. (2005). "Citizenship, Same-Sex Marriage, and Feminist Critiques of Marriage." *Perspectives on Politics, 3*, 269–84.

Laumann, E.O., J.H. Gagnon, R.T. Michael, and S. Michaels. (1994). *The Social Organization of Sexuality: Sexual Practices in the United States.* Chicago: University of Chicago Press.

Lessard, Hester. (2007). "Family, Marriage, and Children: Neo-Liberal Choices and Conservative Values." Paper presented at the Annual Meeting of the Law and Society Association, July 25–28, Berlin, Germany.

Levi-Strauss, C. (1969). *The Elementary Structures of Kinship.* London: Eyre and Spottiswoode.

Nelson, Adie. (2008). "What Is a Family? New Challenges in Defining an Everyday Term." In Robert J. Brym, ed., *Society in Question*, 5th ed. (pp. 145–51). Toronto: Nelson.

Patterson, Charlotte, J. (1995). "Families of the Lesbian Baby-Boom: Parents' Division of Labour and Children's Adjustment." *Developmental Psychology, 31*, 115–23.

Rich, A. (1980). "Compulsory Heterosexuality and Lesbian Existence." *Signs, 5* (Summer), 631–60.

Statistics Canada. (2008). "Status of Same-sex Couples (3), Sex (3) and Presence of Other Household Members (5) for the Same sex Couples in Private Households of Canada, Provinces and Territories, 2006 Census—20% Sample Data." On the World Wide

Web at http://www12.statcan.ca/english/census06/data/topics /RetrieveProductTable.cfm?Temporal=2006&PID=89034&GID=614 135&METH=1&APATH=3&PTYPE=88971&THEME=68&AID=&FREE =0&FOCUS=&VID=&GC=99&GK=NA&RL=0&TPL=NA&SUB=&d1=0 (retrieved 13 November 2008).

Sullivan, Andrew. (1997). *Same-Sex Marriage. Pro and Con.* New York: Vintage.

UNIFEM. (2008). *United Nations Development Fund for Women: Afghanistan Fact Sheet 2008.* Kabul, Afghanistan: UNIFEM.

Valverde, Mariana. (2006). "A New Entity in the History of Sexuality: The Respectable Same-Sex Couple." *Feminist Studies, 32,* 155–63.

Warner, Michael. (1999). *The Trouble with Normal: Sex, Politics and the Ethics of Queer Life.* New York: Free Press.

Weeks, Jeffrey, Brian Heaphy, and Catherine Donovan. (2001). *Same-Sex Intimacies. Families of Choice and Other Life Experiments.* New York: Routledge.

Whitehead, Jaye. (2006). "Same-Sex Marriage as Risk Management." Paper presented at the Annual Meeting of the American Sociological Association, Montreal Convention Centre, August 11, Montreal, Quebec.

Woolwine, David, and E. Doyle McCarthy. (2005). "Gay Moral Discourse: Talking About Identity, Sex and Commitment." *Studies in Symbolic Interaction, 28,* 379–408.

Yep, Gust A., Karen E. Lovaas, and John P. Elia. (2003). "A Critical Appraisal of Assimilationist and Radical Ideologies Underlying Same-Sex Marriage in LGBT Communities in the United States." *Journal of Homosexuality, 45,* 45–64.

Chapter 18

The State of Early Childhood Education and Child Care in 2009

JANE BEACH

MARTHA FRIENDLY, CAROLYN FERNS, and NINA PRABHU

Childcare Resource and Research Unit; and

BARRY FORER, University of British Columbia

Over the last three decades, participation in an early childhood education and care program has become the norm for older preschool-aged children in Canada. Early childhood education and care, or ECEC, refers primarily to kindergarten and regulated child care programs. National data show that nearly 80% of preschool-age children with employed or studying mothers are regularly in some form of non-parental child care or early childhood program with almost 50% in an organized ECEC program, although data that indicate whether these meet parents' needs for "care," and whether they are high quality enough to be defined as "early childhood education," are not available (Cleveland, Forer, Hyatt, Japel and Krashinsky, 2008). Between the 1980s and 2009, the proportion of children aged six months to five years who were in some form of extra-parental child care increased significantly, while more child care-using families shifted to child care centres and relative care (Statistics Canada, 2005). At the same time, kindergarten programs developed across Canada to cover virtually all five year olds and some four years, although kindergarten is usually a part-time program, ordinarily covering two and a half hours a day. Of the more than 70% of children with both parents or a single parent in the paid labour force, many or most were presumed to be in family child care provided by an unregulated family child care provider, an in-home caregiver or a relative for at least part of their parents' working hours.

The range and quality of early childhood education and care services and access to them vary enormously by region and circumstances.

Source: Originally published as "The State of Early Childhood Education and Care in 2009," *Early Childhood Education and Care in Canada 2008* (Toronto: Childcare Resource and Research Unit, 2009). http://www.childcarecanada.org/sites/default/files/ECEC08_State_of_ECEC_2009.pdf. Reprinted by permission.

Organized ECEC services across Canada are in short supply or, like public kindergarten, not sensitive to the labour force needs of parents and are available for only a minority of preschool-aged children. Regulated child care is often too costly for ordinary families or not sufficiently high quality to be considered "developmental." Young school-aged children may be alone after school or attend recreation or other community programs that are not intended to provide "care." Overall, no region of Canada provides a system of well-designed, integrated and adequately funded early childhood education and care services to meet the needs of a majority of families and children.

One of the most salient pieces of information about Canada's early childhood education and care situation is that, although participation in the paid labour force has become the norm for mothers of young children, and the evidence about the benefits of quality early childhood programs for young children has accumulated, the situation has failed to progress significantly. International comparative studies such as the OECD's Thematic Review of Early Childhood Education and Care1 and UNICEF's 2008 report card on provision of early childhood education and care indicate that while—as the OECD has described it—"Policy makers have recognized that equitable access to quality early childhood education and care can strengthen the foundations of lifelong learning for all children and support the broad educational and social needs of families" (OECD, 2001, p. 7), Canada has fallen farther and farther behind most other affluent countries, ranking—according to UNICEF's 10 benchmarks—at the very bottom (UNICEF, 2008).

HOW EARLY CHILDHOOD EDUCATION AND CARE IS ORGANIZED IN CANADA

Each of Canada's 14 jurisdictions—10 provinces, three territories and the federal government—has a number of programs for care and early childhood education as well as for meeting other objectives such as supporting parents and ameliorating the effects of poverty.

Each province and territory has a program of regulated child care that includes centre-based full-day child care, regulated family child care, school-aged child care and, usually, nursery or preschools. The provincial/territorial child care programs provide legislated requirements for operation of services and a variety of funding arrangements, usually under a social or community services ministry.

Provincial/territorial governments also have responsibility for public kindergartens that primarily operate part-time—usually 2.5 hours a day—for five year olds under ministries of education.

Generally, kindergarten programs for five year olds (or fours in Ontario) are a public responsibility while "care" and early childhood education for children younger than age five is a private family responsibility. In addition to these provincial/territorial programs, a variety of care and education programs—for example, Aboriginal Head Start and Military Family Resource Programs—operate under the aegis of the federal government.

ECEC (or early learning and child care) in Canada consists of regulated child care and kindergarten, supplemented by family resource programs that are primarily intended to support parents and by an assortment of cash payments, complemented by maternity and parental leave.

ROLES AND RESPONSIBILITIES FOR ECEC

That Canada has a federal system is key to the definition of responsibilities for the country's ECEC. The division of powers between federal and provincial governments was originally defined in the Constitution Act of 1867 and has evolved over the years. The 1990s and 2000s have been periods of devolution of roles and responsibilities for social programs, primarily from the federal to the provincial level. The Social Union Framework Agreement (SUFA) of 1999 shaped Canada's social policy for some years although its status is unclear at this time.

A new role that developed in the 2000s for the federal government is that of financing some ECEC costs. For the first time, the federal government began to transfer earmarked funds to the provinces and territories to spend on regulated child care in 2003. These specifically earmarked funds flow through several intergovernmental agreements (see Federal ECEC section). Earmarked federal transfers reached as high as $950 million annually for a short period in the mid-2000s and totaled $600 million in 2007/08.

Thus, with few exceptions, ECEC services—child care, nursery schools, kindergarten—are, like health, social services, and elementary, secondary and post-secondary education—under the jurisdiction of provinces and territories. Each of Canada's 10 provinces and three territories has developed a program of regulated child care and—in most cases—a separate public kindergarten program.

Canadian municipalities do not have powers assigned by constitutional arrangements but are subordinate to the provinces, which delegate powers, including taxing powers, to them. Outside Ontario, where they play several important roles in child care (funding, operation of services [about 10% of regulated child care services are municipally operated] and policy-setting), local governments generally have no function in regulated child care, although the City of Vancouver has adopted a key planning role. Local school boards (or school divisions) are also subordinate to provincial governments; these usually have primary responsibility for operation of elementary schools, including kindergarten, and may host child care programs as landlords as well.

Parent-users, non-governmental organizations and other community-based actors are a key part of Canadian ECEC. At the service delivery level, the bulk of the supply of regulated child care is initiated and maintained by parent and/or voluntary boards of directors; these child care programs comprise most of the nonprofit child care sector, which represents 75% of the total supply. Otherwise parents generally have little specific role in regulated child care, although the bulk of child care services and private arrangements are paid for by parent fees; a national study in 1998 found that an average of 49.2% of revenue for full-day child care centres came from parent fees.

In most parts of Canada, advocacy, professional and service groups, researchers and, to some extent, organized parent groups where they exist, make up what is often called "the child care community." These groups are important providers of services like professional development and in-service training. In addition, advocacy for more and better child care—and now ECEC—has been a visible feature of the Canadian ECEC landscape for decades. Alliances with other groups with an interest in ECEC—for example, the labour movement, anti-poverty activists, feminists and other sectors—have long been a fundamental element of Canadian advocacy for child care. At the present time, professional, service and advocacy groups are considerably weakened as the federal funds that have traditionally supported their activities have been withdrawn.

SERVICE OVERVIEW

Most of Canada's ECEC programs are under provincial jurisdiction. Generally, regulated child care includes centres, usually (except in Quebec, Saskatchewan and the Yukon) nursery schools, preschools or part-day centre-based programs and regulated family child care under the same legislation. Almost all jurisdictions now require at least some of the staff working in child care with children to have some training in early childhood education; however, Canadian requirements for early childhood training are generally acknowledged to be less than adequate (UNICEF, 2008).

All jurisdictions subsidize at least some of the costs of regulated child care for low-income, usually employed, parents. However, in some cases, limitations on the number of these subsidies exclude many eligible parents; in other cases, the subsidy provided does not cover the whole fee; sometimes there is a significant gap between the subsidy rate and the parent fee. As well, in most provinces/territories, the income level that determines eligibility is too low to cover modest and middle income families (Beach and Friendly, 2005). In much of Canada, middle class or modest income families do not qualify for a fee subsidy and cannot afford regulated child care.

Some provinces also provide funds to support the overall operation of child care services; this may be in the form of wage grants to raise staff wages. Overall, though, except in Quebec, child care is primarily a fee-paying service with many families not able to access services due to costs. Only Quebec has set out designated substantial public funding.

All the provinces and territories provide public kindergarten. In most cases kindergarten is part of the public education system and in most jurisdictions, it is treated as an entitlement with no fees. All provinces/territories provide kindergarten for five year olds; in Ontario, four year old kindergarten is available universally too. Most kindergarten is part-day or part-time with three provinces offering full-day kindergarten (for the length of a school day). Attendance at kindergarten is compulsory in two jurisdictions; however, almost all age-eligible children attend public kindergartens when they are offered. Three provinces and the territories maintain more than one publicly funded school system (public and Catholic). All offer kindergarten in both official languages where population warrants. Some jurisdictions, such as Nunavut, provide kindergarten in regional First Nations or Inuit languages.

EARLY CHILDHOOD EDUCATION AND CARE IN THE 1990S

Between 1984 and 1995, there were three significant attempts to develop a national approach to child care as successive federal governments announced a national strategy. Each of these—the Task Force on Child Care set up by the Trudeau government (1984), the Special Committee on Child Care of the Mulroney government (1986), and the initiative based on Jean Chretien's 1993 Red Book election commitment—recognized the primacy of the provinces in social or educational services such as child care. However, none of these efforts was successful in producing a pan-Canadian strategy or approach to early childhood education and care.

In the mid-1990s, Canada's political arrangements, which had historically featured tensions between federal and provincial roles, tilted toward provincial primacy. This shift had a strong impact on the future of early childhood education and child care. The Canada Assistance Plan was abolished in 1996 (and never re-established) and all federal dollars for provincial health, education and welfare programs were subsumed in a block fund, the Canada Health and Social Transfer (CHST). Social policy experts feared that, without conditions like those that had been part of the CAP agreement, provincial spending of the substantially reduced federal dollars in the CHST would become less accountable both to the federal government and to the public.

A debate about what was termed "social policy renewal" arose in a climate of anxiety about Quebec separation and the fiscal deficit. This was formalized in February 1999 as the federal government and the nine provinces comprising "the rest of Canada" outside Quebec signed the Social Union Framework Agreement (SUFA). These features of politics vis-à-vis Canadian federalism continued to play key roles in the development of a national early learning and child care program after 2000. While there was interest in young children and in "child development" as manifested in the National Children's Agenda (1997) and the Early Childhood Development Agreement (2000) which carried new federal funds for provincial children's programs, early childhood education and child care per se was off national policy agendas throughout this period and, indeed, lost ground in some provinces such as Ontario, Alberta and British Columbia (Friendly, Beach and Turiano, 2002).

In 2001, the federal government increased the parental leave portion of the Employment Insurance benefit to 35 weeks, making a total benefit covering 50 weeks combined maternity/parental leave available to eligible new parents. In response, all provinces/territories eventually amended their employment legislation to allow for an extended parental leave to match or exceed the federal benefit period.

EARLY CHILDHOOD EDUCATION AND CARE IN THE 2000s

Child care remained off the national policy agenda and while it remained off most (not all) provincial/territorial agendas, Quebec took a giant step forward. With a process that began in 1997, Quebec started to bring in a publicly funded universal ECEC program. The evolution included moving from reliance on parent fee subsidies (like other provinces) to a public funding model; introduction of full-day kindergarten for all five year olds; expansion of spaces—supported by capital funding—to provide much greater availability through community-based *centres de la petite enfance* (CPEs) that include centre-based and family day care; a $5-a-day parent fee for all families regardless of income; and a commitment to improved maternity/parental leave (Tougas, 2002). The process continued into the 2000s, although it shifted gears somewhat when a Quebec election brought in a new government.

Canada-wide, it was not until 2003 that another intergovernmental agreement—the Multilateral Framework on Early Learning and Child Care—was put in place by Federal Human Resources Minister Jane Stewart and provincial/territorial social services ministers. The ministers' communiqué said that, "This early learning and child care framework represents another important step in the development of early childhood development programs and services" (Government of Canada, 2003), while Minister Stewart called the Agreement "the beginning of a very solid national day-care program for Canadians" (Lawton, 2003).

But it was the next step towards a national early learning and child care program that was historic as it was the first time that a national child care program had been promised since Brian Mulroney's Progressive Conservative government considered it in 1986. This commitment came in the 2004 election campaign when the federal Liberals promised to develop a national early learning and child care system based on four principles— Quality, Universality, Accessibility and Developmental [programming] (QUAD). The campaign platform promised 5 billion new dollars over five years to begin to build the system. Most of this money was to be transferred to provinces/territories using the CST formula; $100 million was to be used for "accountability and data" and $100 million for early learning and child care for First Nations communities (on-reserve).

After the Liberals won the 2004 election, they began negotiations with provinces to secure agreement to participate. The federal government's conditions were (a) provinces were to produce Action Plans before a five-year funding agreement was finalized; (b) federal funds would be used only for regulated early childhood education and care programs; (c) provinces would publicly report on the use of funds. By December 2005, nine provinces had signed bilateral agreements-in-principle with the Government of Canada on early learning and child care and two—Ontario and Manitoba—had published provincial action plans. These two, along with Quebec, which did not sign an

agreement-in-principle or publish an Action Plan, moved on to nego-
tiate full five-year funding agreements with the federal government.

These agreements marked the first time that a Canadian government had followed through with an election commitment to improve
child care across Canada. While there was some variation in the
provinces' directions as described in the agreements-in-principle, in
signing them, the provinces committed to developing detailed Action
Plans based on the four QUAD principles. In addition, all agreements
included provincial commitment to collaborative infrastructural work
in such areas as a national quality framework and data systems.

NEW DIRECTIONS

In January 2006 a minority Conservative government was elected.
The new government announced that the processes set in motion by
the bilateral agreements would be terminated; that all jurisdictions—the
three provinces with five-year funding agreements (Quebec, Ontario
and Manitoba), the seven provinces that had not yet released their
Action Plans, and the three territories—would get one year's worth of
federal funding; it would end March 31, 2007.

The new federal government promised an individual cash payment to parents—the Choice in Child Care Allowance, later renamed
the "Universal Child Care Benefit"—an annual payment of $1,200 to
all parents with children under age 6, taxed in the hands of the lower-
income spouse. In addition, the Conservatives said that they would
initiate a Community Childcare Investment Program, later renamed
the Spaces Initiative (capital funding to set up child care) to "help
employers and communities create child care spaces in the workplace
or through cooperative or community associations by establishing a
tax credit for capital costs of $10,000 per space; funding of $250 million a year was identified for this initiative and—in the 2007 federal
budget—was subsequently included as a transfer payment to provinces
in the Canada Social Transfer.

The Universal Child Care Benefit cheques began to flow to
parents in July 2006. An advisory committee was established to
advise the Minister on the Child Care Spaces Initiative and consulta-
tions were held across Canada on this initiative. The advisory committee released a report and recommendations (Ministerial Advisory
Committee on the Government of Canada's Child Care Spaces
Initiative, 2007); $250 million in transfer payments were announced
in the 2007 federal budget.

After the January 2006 election and the cancellation of the national early learning and child care program, the focus of ECEC policy shifted to the provinces and territories.

While growth in regulated child care continued, between April 2006 and April 2007 there was limited growth in the number of regulated child care spaces in most provinces/territories, with expansion in Quebec slowing sharply. The increase—26,661 spaces—was the smallest in several years; between 2007 and 2008, the increase was 29,271 spaces. In comparison, supply grew by 65,337 (an average of 32,668 in each year) between 2004 and 2006, and by 152,493 between 2001 and 2004 (an average of 50,831 a year in each of those three years) (Childcare Resource and Research Unit, 2008). The increase in spaces between March 2007 and March 2008 was again quite small—an additional 29,271 spaces.

In May 2006, an NDP-sponsored private member's bill, Bill C-303 was introduced. The "Act to establish criteria and conditions in respect of funding for early learning and child care programs in order to ensure the quality, accessibility, universality and accountability of those programs, and to appoint a council to advise the Minister of Human Resources and Skills Development on matters relating to early learning and child care" was supported by the New Democrats, the Liberals and the Bloc Québécois and—although ruled a "money bill," made its way through committee hearings to Third Reading, when the government was prorogued in November, 2008. The NDP Critic for child care, Olivia Chow, reintroduced the bill in April 2009.

In 2008, UNICEF published the first international study to rank the quality, access, financing and policy of ECEC programs using measurable benchmarks pegged to the average level of OECD achievement. Canada's provision of early childhood education and care ranked at the very bottom of 25 developed countries, tied with Ireland, as Canada achieved only one of ten minimum standards (UNICEF, 2008).

While Canada has a long way to go to reach the coverage, funding, policy, and infrastructure levels of other countries, there have been some promising, modest provincial initiatives since 2006. Several provinces have attempted to strengthen the ECEC workforce by helping to support training and education of staff; some have introduced recruitment and retention initiatives, and some have increased levels of operating funding for regulated programs. Some small capital grants have been made, largely to enable centres to repair and refurbish facilities; while not necessarily increasing the supply of child care, they have improved physical environments for children. In a few instances, incentives to increase the supply of spaces have been initiated. In some provinces, notably Ontario, ministries of education have begun to take an increased interest in early childhood education and have begun discussion with social/community services ministries on issues related to curriculum, expanded full-day programming or full-day kindergarten and school delivery of other early childhood initiatives.

REFERENCES

Beach, J. and Friendly, M. (2005). *Quality by Design working documents: Child care fee subsidies in Canada.* Available online at: http://www .childcarequality.ca/wdocs/QbD_FeeSubsidies_Canada.pdf

Childcare Resource and Research Unit. (2008). *Child care space statistics 2007.* Toronto: Author. Available online at: http://www.childcarecanada.org/pubs/other/spaces/ccspacestatistics07.pdf

Cleveland, G., Forer, B., Hyatt, D., Japel, C., and Krashinsky, M. (2008). New evidence about child care in Canada: Use patterns, affordability and quality. *Choices, 14*(2). Montreal: Institute for Research on Public Policy.

Friendly, M., Beach, J. and Turiano, M. (2002). *Early childhood education and care in Canada 2001.* Toronto: Childcare Resource and Research Unit.

Government of Canada. (2003*). Federal/provincial/territorial agreement on early learning and child care.* Available online at: http:// www.socialunion.gc.ca/elcc_e.htm

Lawton, V. (2003). Ottawa, provinces sign day-care deal: 50,000 new spots over five years, $900M program "essential first step." *Toronto Star.* March 13. Available online at: http://action.web.ca /home/crru/rsrcs_crru_full.shtml?x=33627

Ministerial Advisory Committee on the Government of Canada's Child Care Spaces Initiative. (2007). *Child care spaces recommendations: Supporting Canadian children and families: Addressing the gap between the supply and demand for high quality child care.* Ottawa: Government of Canada. Available online at: http://www .hrsdc.gc.ca/eng/publications_resources/social_policy/mac _report/child_care_spaces_strategy.pdf

Organisation for Economic Co-operation and Development. (2001). *Starting Strong: Early childhood education and care.* Paris: Author.

Statistics Canada. (2005). Child care: 1996–2001. *The Daily.* Ottawa: Author. Available online at: http://www.statcan.ca/Daily /English/050207/d050207b.htm

Tougas, J. (2002). *Reforming Quebec's early childhood education and care: The first five years.* Toronto: Childcare Resource and Research Unit. Available online at: http://www.childcarecanada.org/pubs /op17/op17ENG.pdf

UNICEF. (2008). *The child care transition, Innocenti Report Card* 8, 2008. Florence: UNICEF Innocenti Research Centre.

PART 4B

POLITICS

Voters are unhappy, in Canada no less than in other democratic countries. Surveys repeatedly show that Canadians are growing increasingly cynical about politics and distrustful of politicians. As a result, fewer Canadians are voting; while 80 percent of eligible voters cast ballots in the 1958 federal election, 61 percent did so in 2011. In addition, political loyalty is antique. Voters are more willing than ever to switch allegiance from one party to the next in succeeding elections. Ideologies, principles, and programs sway them less than personalities and fleeting issues do. Consequently, Canada's political landscape gyrates from one election to the next. The fortunes of some parties rise as quickly as the fortunes of other parties decline.

According to some commentators, widespread discontent with politics resulted in a fundamental shift in the Canadian party system in 1993. For three decades before the federal election of that year, Canada was a "two-and-a-half party system." Strong Liberal and Progressive Conservative parties vied for power while a weak NDP usually captured about a seventh of the popular vote. These parties failed to represent strong regional voices, however, so in 1993 two new parties emerged—the Parti Québécois and the Reform Party. They placed second and third, respectively, as half the electorate switched parties from 1988, and they had strong regional bases of support, the PQ in Quebec and Reform in the West. Federal elections since 1993 have proven to be just as volatile—in 2011, for example, the Liberal party was practically wiped off the electoral map while the NDP almost swept Quebec and became the Official Opposition.

In Chapter 19, Lawrence Leduc, writing from the perspective of the 2011 federal election, argues that, despite the volatility, the Canadian party system today is little different from what it has been since the end of World War II: a system of "brokerage politics" and "dealigned voters."

Brokerage politics involves party leaders organizing focus groups, public opinion polls, and informal canvasses of voters to determine the hot issues of the day. With this information in hand, they delineate the varied interests of the electorate. They then work out a strategy for organizing a coalition of diverse interests that, they hope, will support their party. They use advertising firms, public relations experts, and "spin doctors" to help them project an image of the party and its leaders that will appeal to the diverse interests in their desired coalition. In this way, party leaders "broker" a coalition of supporters.

The components of the brokered coalition change over time. That is because new political exigencies emerge, and they often require that parties strengthen their ties to some interest groups and weaken their ties to others. As a result, party policies are also in flux. The goal of parties in a system of brokerage politics is not to adhere to relatively fixed sets of principles but to manipulate the electorate to gain and maintain power. The system of brokerage politics seems highly democratic because parties listen intently to the opinions of groups of voters. However, the system is in fact unresponsive to voters' group interests, which are likely to be watered down or sacrificed entirely as parties seek to broker coalitions between diverse groups. Brokerage politics is a major source of voter cynicism. It produces a **dealigned electorate**, voters whose allegiances are easily swayed from one election to the next in response to the issues of the day and the appeal (or lack of appeal) of party leaders. Leduc's review of recent voter surveys demonstrates that the Canadian electorate remains dealigned. As a result, we can expect dramatic swings in voter support in future federal elections without any fundamental change in the Canadian party system.

Conventional politics takes place through the ballot box. Unconventional politics takes place through demonstrations, riots, suicide bombings, wars, and so on. In the twentieth century, wars started to involve mainly civilian casualties. Thus, only 5 percent of casualties in World War I were civilians. By the 1990s, the figure rose to 90 percent. Chapter 20 examines civilian mass killings and what can be done to make them less common. In Michael Mann's account, European (later American and Japanese) overseas imperialism emerges as a major culprit; imperialist powers often sought to conquer territory and control resources by killing natives en masse. Then, after World War II, many new states lacking strong central authority were established. Since the big and not-so-big powers (the United States, Russia, China, and Cuba) were often willing to fund and arm rival ethnic groups in weak states to further their own interests, the scale of civilian casualties rose. In recent decades, "terrorism" and "state terrorism" have also contributed to the slaughter of innocents.

Since the early 1990s, the global human rights movement has grown enormously. It is devoted to documenting, analyzing, publicizing, and protesting abuses of **personal integrity rights**: mass murder, arbitrary imprisonment, and torture. As James Ron shows, the efforts of human rights activists seem to have been most successful in Latin American countries with relatively strong democratic movements, economies, states, and international ties. They have been less successful in countries that lack these characteristics. This is a sobering finding because it suggests that human rights efforts are likely to be least effective in the countries of sub-Saharan Africa, where human rights abuses are most widespread.

GLOSSARY

Brokerage politics involves parties that lack clear ideological and issue differentiation and stable bases of voter support. They cobble together new coalitions of support in every election, basing their platforms on the results of public opinion polls, focus groups, and informal canvasses of voters, and swaying public opinion by using advertising firms, public relations experts and "spin doctors."

A **dealigned electorate** comprises voters whose allegiances are easily swayed from one election to the next in response to the issues of the day and the appeal (or lack of appeal) of party leaders.

Personal integrity rights include the right not to be tortured, arbitrarily imprisoned, or murdered.

CRITICAL THINKING QUESTIONS

1. Which is more democratic—a system of brokerage politics or a system in which various group interests are firmly aligned with specific parties?
2. What are the major factors that account for increasing civilian casualties in warfare? Can the slaughter be stopped? If so, how?

ANNOTATED BIBLIOGRAPHY

Doug Baer, ed., *Political Sociology: Canadian Perspectives* (Toronto: Oxford University Press, 2002). Covers the major issues in the study of Canadian politics from a sociological perspective.

Rod Bantjes, *Social Movements in a Global Context* (Toronto: Canadian Scholars' Press, 2007). A unique and valuable Canadian perspective on the global resurgence of social movements in the twenty-first century (including Internet protest, Islamism, and indigenous peoples' movements) and state reactions to protest.

Charles Tilly, "Violence, Terror, and Politics as Usual." *Boston Review*, 27 (3), 2002. http://www.bostonreview.net/BR27.3/tilly.html. The best short account of the sociological and historical underpinnings of modern "terrorism" and other forms of civilian killings.

Chapter 19

The Canadian Voter in a New Conservative Era

LAWRENCE LEDUC, University of Toronto

Analysts have called electoral choice and its consequences a grand Canadian puzzle.[1] The Canadian electorate is volatile, sometimes causing dramatic electoral setbacks for one or more political parties, sharp movements in public opinion polls, and significant variations in the outcomes of federal and provincial elections. Paradoxically, volatility has not prevented political parties or leaders from holding on to power for substantial periods. Mackenzie King's 22 years as prime minister (1921–1930; 1935–1948) or Pierre Trudeau's fifteen years (1968–1979; 1980–1984) demonstrate that successful political leaders have been able to construct "dynasties" that create the illusion of a dominant partisan alignment.[2]

History also shows us that both of these successful leaders endured major electoral setbacks during their tenure (King in 1930, Trudeau in 1979), in both instances the main cause being economic adversity. Yet both survived and ultimately returned their parties to power. With the Conservative victory in the 2011 federal election, we appear to be once again entering an era of individual volatility and aggregate continuity. Understanding the persistence of these two seemingly contradictory patterns in Canadian electoral politics is the subject of this chapter.

THE 2011 ELECTION

Although it was achieved with just 39.6 percent of the vote (the second-smallest plurality in Canadian history[3]), the Conservative majority victory in 2011 was convincing, following two minority outcomes (2006, 2008). Adding 22 seats in Ontario to its established base in the West, the Conservatives under Stephen Harper benefited both from the collapse of the Liberals and the splitting of votes between the two main opposition parties, as the NDP surged in Quebec. However, despite the political turbulence of recent years, and three successive election

Source: Reprinted by permission of the author.

victories by the Harper Conservatives, the fundamental nature of the Canadian electorate has remained much the same.[4]

The outcome of the 2011 election all but guarantees that the Conservatives will remain in office until 2015. By the time of the next federal election, Harper's tenure in office will have approached that of Jean Chrétien, who likewise presided over a period of volatile electoral politics and successive election victories (1993, 1997, 2000) for more than a decade. Another victory would thus place Harper among Canada's most enduring and politically successful leaders. I will argue, however, that such success has often been mistaken in the past for a pattern of stable political alignments and dominant parties. Rash proclamations of the demise of the Liberal Party are almost certainly wrong, just as past judgments following dramatic elections have typically proven to be.[5] Even in periods where one party or leader appeared dominant for a substantial period, the possibility of a rapid reversal in fortune was always present. The dramatic political events of the past two decades, which first saw the collapse of the old Progressive-Conservatives in 1993 and then the reduction of the once dominant Liberals to third-party status in the more recent (2006–11) period, have done surprisingly little to alter the fundamental nature of Canadian electoral politics. Relatively weak but broadly inclusive political parties compete for much of the same political space, acting as "brokers" among different groups, regions, and interests.

BROKERAGE POLITICS

Canadian political parties have traditionally been brokerage parties. Lacking stable support groups in the electorate, and generally avoiding clear ideological and even issue differentiation from their competitors, the parties and their leaders approach each election anew, hoping to put together a winning coalition of support across the electorate.[6] Brokerage parties do not seek to appeal to voters' long-standing principles or ideological commitment. They embrace issues, such as "the economy," "healthcare," or "national unity," and promise to confront the current set of challenges more effectively than their opponents.[7] They are not bound by positions or actions that they have taken in the past, and they sometimes appear inconsistent as they search for electorally successful formulations or respond to new versions of old problems. They organize around leaders rather than around principles or ideologies and expect the leader to work out the multitude of compromises required for electoral success. A variety of conflicting and contradictory policy stances may coexist in a brokerage party.

Some analysts suggest that the Canadian preoccupation with issues of national unity, ethnic/linguistic relations, and federal-provincial divisions of responsibility has prevented the emergence of an electoral politics of social class or ideology.[8] In the past, the major parties have generally attempted to accommodate interests on the opposing sides of important social, linguistic, or regional cleavages. On this interpretation, the success of the Liberals throughout Canadian history came not from the "natural" dominance of the party but from its success at fashioning new coalitions of support, constructed and maintained by effective leaders.[9] However, brokerage politics, by its very nature, leads to weak parties, limited commitments from voters, and considerable volatility, or at least the potential for volatility, in elections.[10] For a time following the political "earthquake" of 1993, in which the then-governing Progressive-Conservatives were reduced to 16 percent of the vote and two parliamentary seats, Canadian politics appeared to be charting a markedly different course. Certainly, the rise and persistence of the Bloc Québécois made the task of weaving together a national majority more difficult. Reassembling the pieces of the old Progressive-Conservative Party turned out to be more arduous and complicated than anyone might have imagined, as three successive leaders sought to construct a new vehicle that might prove to be competitive with the Liberals in the federal political arena—first as the Reform Party, then the Canadian Alliance, and finally the new Conservative Party of Canada. However, the 2003 merger of the Alliance with the remnants of the old Progressive-Conservative Party provided the framework for the construction of a new brokerage party with a potentially broader range of appeal than its immediate predecessors had. As the 2004 and 2006 campaigns waged by the new party demonstrated, the key to its victory lay in refashioning old political coalitions and mobilizing short-term discontent.[11] Its success in the 2011 election, together with the sudden demise of the Bloc, appears to have returned the Canadian political landscape to a more familiar shape, even allowing for the setback suffered by the Liberals and the sudden surge of the NDP.

ENTERING THE HARPER ERA

At first, the post-1993 world seemed different from the traditional brokerage model to which Canadians had long been accustomed. With the Canadian Alliance promoting an agenda of a "united right" and the Bloc Québécois committed to achieving sovereignty for Quebec, Canadian federal politics in the 1990s appeared to have become segmented into parties and groups representing narrower and more specific ideological, interest, or issue positions than had been the case in the past. Even the Liberals, with weaker representation from Quebec and the West, appeared increasingly to speak largely for the interests of Ontario or the major urban centres. Some scholars interpreted the 1993 election as the start of a major political realignment in which the foundations of an entirely new party system were being formed.[12] However, this "new" party system, if indeed it ever really existed, proved to have little staying power. With hindsight, we can see that the past two decades of Canadian politics have witnessed continued dealignment rather than the solidification of strong, new partisan alignments. Voter volatility has remained high. The present period may prove to be similarly deceptive, as predictions of the death of the Liberal Party, the establishment of a new and more cohesive Conservative majority, or greater polarization between left and right are commonly put forward. Little firm evidence exists to support such predictions. Even with a different party in power, and the NDP in Opposition, the future may well look like the past.

No stunning electoral victory inaugurated the Harper era. Rather, the construction of the Conservative majority was incremental. Preston Manning established the dominance of the Reform party in the West but he was unable to extend that success significantly beyond his regional base. Under the banner of Reform's successor party, the Canadian Alliance, Stockwell Day did somewhat better, obtaining 24 percent of the vote in Ontario in the 2000 federal election but only two seats. With the merger of the Alliance and Progressive Conservatives in 2003, Harper was well positioned to build on this base. Aided by the sponsorship scandal in 2004, the Conservatives' vote share in Ontario improved to 31 percent, yielding 24 parliamentary seats. Nearly all of these were in rural areas. The 2006 election, which brought the party to power, added a breakthrough in Quebec, with the Conservatives obtaining 25 percent of the vote and 10 seats in that province. Thus, each election saw another building block added, while at the same time retaining all or most of the gains realized previously. One of the weaknesses of the Conservatives in the 2006 and 2008 elections had been their failure to win a seat in any of Canada's three largest cities. This deficiency was overcome in 2011 with the party's breakthrough in metropolitan Toronto, taking a number of urban seats previously held by Liberals.

The 2006 election also saw a return to the practice of brokerage politics and yielded a result that largely revived and reaffirmed the attraction of the brokerage model. Stephen Harper fashioned his victory not by "uniting the right" but by deliberately positioning his party closer to the centre of the ideological spectrum and appealing to interests outside of his secure Western base. The Bloc, although running candidates only in Quebec, sought to broaden its appeal to federalists and other voters, emphasizing not the sovereignty agenda but rather the sponsorship scandal. Both the NDP and the Liberals pitched large parts of their 2006 and 2008 campaigns to each other's voters, deemphasizing issue and ideological positions and appealing instead for "strategic" votes to defeat the Conservatives.

The Conservatives' 2004 campaign experimented with a tactic that was to become more prominent over the decade: promising small but targeted policies in an effort to make direct personal connections with voters. In 2004, the Conservatives promised to raise the child tax credit and establish tax-free savings plans. Although these initiatives generated a positive response, they were dwarfed by the larger issues of tax cuts and increased healthcare spending. The Conservatives quickly learned that the public reacted well to such pocketbook promises.

In 2004, Conservative strategists were also well aware that the Liberals had an advantage in the area of social policy and they attempted to counter this advantage by offering even more money for healthcare than the Liberals did. The Conservative health policy reflected the Harper strategy of presenting a more moderate image for the party by underlining its commitment to the public provision of health services. As it played out during the campaign, the commitment to increased spending on health coexisted uneasily with a continuation of the party's promise of tax cuts. In the successful 2006 campaign, however, the Conservatives retreated from the large-scale funding and tax-cut pledges that had caused them difficulty in 2004 and embraced smaller-scale targeted programs in both areas: reduction of hospital wait times and a 2 percent reduction in the GST.

The incremental gains made by the Conservatives between 2004 and 2006 persuaded Stephen Harper that the same approach would produce a majority two years later. Although the 2008 campaign was highly negative, consisting largely of attack ads against the Liberal leader, Stéphane Dion, and his environmental ("Green Shift") policy, it pursued other issue strategies similar to those that had been successful in 2006. The Conservatives also asserted their overall competence in managing the economy and offered assurances that a Harper administration would continue to pursue balanced budgets, lower taxes, and job creation. While these positions were nearly overtaken by the deepening global economic crisis, they were enough to produce a second Conservative minority government, with modest increases in both the party's vote share (from 36 to 38 percent) and parliamentary seats (a net gain of nineteen). In government, the Harper Conservatives continued to undertake small-scale initiatives, including census reform, getting rid of the gun registry, and revamping the criminal justice system. The stimulus package (the "Economic Action Plan"), belatedly brought in as a response to the global economic crisis, became the centrepiece of the government's economic policy. A renewal of attack advertising against new Liberal leader Michael Ignatieff kept the focus on the negative characteristics of the opposition and away from the sparseness of the government's legislative program and the limited nature of its vision. With the likewise modest gains in both vote share and parliamentary seats in 2011 noted earlier, the incremental march to power of the Harper Conservatives was complete.

A DEALIGNED ELECTORATE

Canadian voters have not generally been constrained in their voting choices by powerful social or ideological cleavages or by strong partisanship. This circumstance has allowed the parties to appeal to voters across lines of ethnicity, regionalism, and social class, even though such appeals are not always successful in any given election. Since the time of the first survey-based national election studies in 1965, scholars have observed that the Canadian electorate as a whole has tended to exhibit relatively weak ties to political parties and therefore considerable volatility in elections.[13] Unhindered by past feelings of party loyalty, many voters feel free to choose which party to support on the basis of such short-term factors as the particular issues of the day, their assessment of the state of the economy, the characteristics of the party leaders, or the likelihood of effective representation from a local candidate. Such a pattern contrasts with some of the more ideologically driven party systems of Europe or with the more party-identified electorate of the United States. In their study of the 1974 Canadian electorate, Clarke and associates classified only about a third of the Canadian electorate as *durable* partisans, whose support parties could rely on. The remaining two-thirds were *flexible* partisans. Parties could win or lose their support based on short-term factors.[14] The movement of voters between elections is often less than these figures imply. However, given the implications of a weakly aligned electorate, political parties have long been aware that they cannot count on the continued support of a loyal band of followers to win elections. The sudden reversals of party fortunes that have occurred in many elections demonstrate this point. The relative freedom from sociodemographic constraints that Canadian parties enjoy is thus a mixed blessing. On the one hand, they are able to fashion new appeals and seek new sources of support as opportunities arise. On the other hand, they know that even many seemingly "loyal" supporters can quickly turn against them if they become disillusioned. This explains both the periodic tendency toward sudden and sharp electoral reversals and the ability of parties over time to recover from adversity and adapt to new political circumstances.

Figure 19.1 shows the continued weakness of partisan ties, and the electoral unreliability of supporters of the major parties.[15] Support for the Conservative party, while it has now surpassed that of the Liberals, is nevertheless much lower than the Progressive-Conservatives enjoyed during the 1980s under Brian Mulroney and now rests at about the levels enjoyed by the PCs under Joe Clark in the late 1970s (see Figure 19.2). Core support for the party is still less than the sum of its former parts—Reform/Alliance and the Progressive Conservatives—and about 8 percent less than the number of votes that it received in the 2011 election. This, of course, did not prevent the Conservatives under Stephen Harper from winning the last three federal elections, and it does not mean that they cannot win another under these same conditions. It means simply

FIGURE 19.1 FEDERAL PARTY IDENTIFICATION, 2011

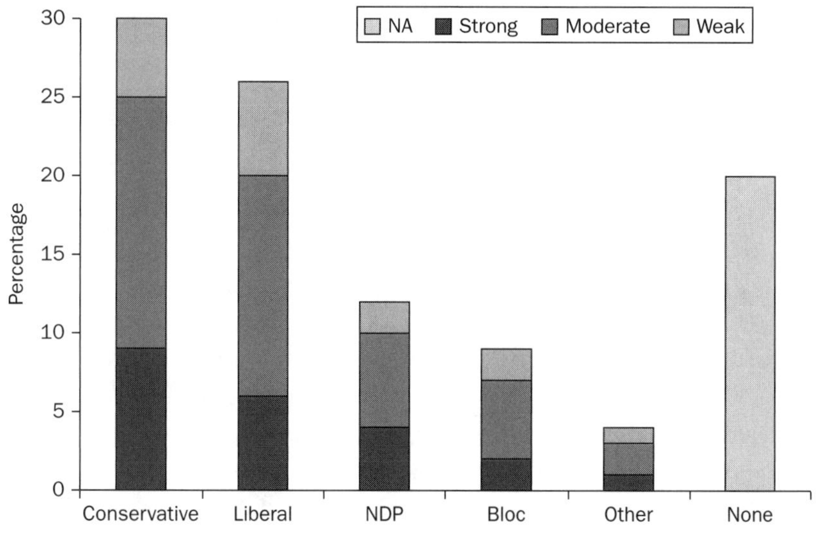

SOURCE: 2011 Canadian Election Study (N = 4041).

FIGURE 19.2 PARTY IDENTIFICATION IN THE CANADIAN ELECTORATE, 1974–2011

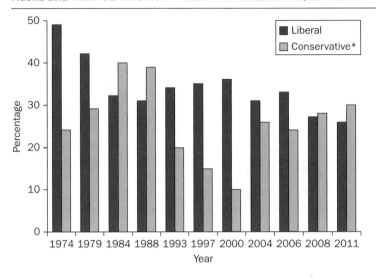

SOURCE: 1974–2011 Canadian Election Studies (*n* = 33 361).

that they, like the Liberals before them, would have to do so, in typical brokerage fashion, by appealing to at least some voters who identify with other parties or who claim to be independent of partisan feelings.

The data also show that, despite their losses in recent elections, Liberal support has not disappeared. Even in 2011, their weakest point electorally for many decades, nearly a quarter of Canadians continue to identify in some way with the Liberal party. This number, although now 8 percent lower than the number of Conservative identifiers, is nevertheless greater than the percentage of votes that the Liberals received in the 2011 election. The NDP, despite its vote surge in 2011, is the party of choice of only about 15 percent of the respondents to the 2011 Canadian Election Study—far fewer than the percentage of votes that it received in the 2011 election (31 percent). Clearly, many Canadians crossed party lines in 2011 to vote for the NDP. Taken together, partisan supporters of all three parties (Conservatives, Liberals, NDP) compose about two-thirds of the electorate. Many of these are weak or only moderately strong supporters of the party with which they identify.[16] Only about 18 percent considered themselves "very strong" supporters of *any* party, and about 20 percent of the electorate declare no partisan attachment. If we are searching for a solid base of partisan support within the Canadian electorate for any party, it is increasingly difficult to find one.

The ideological underpinnings of the Canadian party system are also extraordinarily weak in comparison to party systems in many other western democracies. While the terms "left" and "right" are widely used by political commentators and other elites in Canada, voters tend to cluster nearer the centre. Figure 19.3 shows the ideological self-identification of respondents to the 2011 Canadian Election Study. One-third of respondents to this question placed themselves exactly at the centre of an 11-point left–right scale. Other large groupings (21 percent and 24 percent, respectively) placed themselves in positions defined here as "centre-right" and "centre-left."[17] Fewer than a quarter of the survey respondents chose to describe themselves in more strongly ideological terms, with 10 percent of those in Figure 19.3 locating clearly on the left and 12 percent on the right. When we examine the ideological positioning of various groups of party identifiers (Table 19.1), we again find clustering toward the centre of the scale. The mean positions of NDP and Conservative identifiers (3.4 and 6.5, respectively) are clearly different, but both fall within the bands previously described as "centre-left" and "centre-right." Liberals, at 4.5, are close to the centre, as are those having no party identity (5.1). The observation that Canadian voters are not particularly ideological in their orientation to politics is not new.[18] The relative lack of ideological fervour does not appear to favour the prospects of those who believe that the future of the

FIGURE 19.3 IDEOLOGICAL SELF-PLACEMENT IN THE CANADIAN ELECTORATE

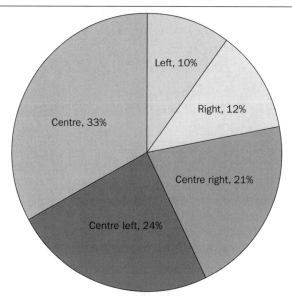

*Progressive Conservative to 2000; Conservative Party of Canada, 2004–11.

SOURCE: 2011 Canadian Election Study (*n* = 1487).

TABLE 19.1 MEAN IDEOLOGICAL SELF-PLACEMENT SCORES FOR PARTY IDENTIFIERS (0 = EXTREME LEFT, 10 = EXTREME RIGHT)

NDP	3.4
Green	3.6
Bloc Québécois	4.3
Other	4.5
Liberal	4.6
No party ID	5.1
Conservative	6.5

SOURCE: 2011 Canadian Election Study (*n* = 1487).

Canadian party system lies in "uniting the right," or in presenting voters with more ideologically polarized choices. Neither a united right nor a more radical left would appear to be well placed to win the allegiance of a very large cross-section of Canadian voters on a continuing basis.

Given the weakness of ideology in the Canadian party system, along with the relative fluidity of issue and policy agendas, political leaders have assumed great importance in explanations of voting behaviour in Canada throughout much of its modern political history.[19] Parties have been most electorally successful when they have found a leader able to capture the public imagination and reflect the mood of a particular time. Diefenbaker did this in breaking the Liberal hold on national politics in 1957–58, and Trudeau represents perhaps the clearest example of a leadership-driven politics in recent years. During the Trudeau years, the leader came to define the party. It is thus not surprising that there are fewer Liberal partisans in the electorate now than during the Trudeau era. In the present political environment, no political leader has been able to capture the public imagination in this way. However, Harper was more successful in the 2006 election in neutralizing some of the negative qualities of his image as a leader, and as prime minister, he has been able to cultivate an image of competence. He has also benefited from the weaknesses of opposition leaders.

In this political setting, voters do not make choices easily. It is not simply a matter of reaffirming support for a party or voting our ideological identity. Surveys of the electorate consistently show that only about half of the voters are able to decide how they are going to vote before the campaign actually begins. As the campaign progresses, more voters are able to come to a decision, based on their assessment of the leaders, issues, and the context of a particular election. Increasingly, high profile events, such as the televised leaders' debates, play a crucial role in this process. The 2011 Canadian Election Study shows that about a third of the electorate made their voting decision during the campaign and slightly more than 1 in 10 voters waited until the day of the election itself to decide. Thus, the campaign is vital to the election outcome. In a typical election, a significant number of voters remain undecided sometimes right until the final days leading up to the election.

THE CONSEQUENCES OF BROKERAGE POLITICS

The features of Canadian politics that I have described make for exciting election campaigns but not necessarily a healthy democracy. Parties and their leaders become cynical and manipulative. Voters become distrustful over time if they come to believe that the choices presented to them in elections are not meaningful ones. As my associates and I wrote in the mid-90s:

> Voters are profoundly and almost universally dissatisfied with brokerage politics. [Many] believe that the parties do not offer real choices and think that the parties fail to tell the voters about the really important problems facing the country. Moreover, there is virtual consensus that political parties pay too much attention to winning elections and not enough to governing afterwards, and to gaining partisan advantage rather than to solving important problems ... 91 percent of respondents agreed that there was a big difference between what a party says it will do and what it actually does if it wins an election.[20]

As Figure 19.4 shows, data from recent and older surveys confirm the impression of voter cynicism. In Canadian Election Study surveys over the past 20 years, nearly three-quarters of respondents have consistently agreed that "Members of Parliament lose touch with the people soon after they are elected." The data also show that a substantial number of respondents agree that "the people have little or no say in what the government does." This item, however, *has* improved somewhat in the most recent surveys, as Canadian politics has become more competitive since 2004. During the decade of the 1990s, it was easy for voters to feel that

FIGURE 19.4 ATTITUDES TOWARD POLITICS AND GOVERNMENT, 1988–2011

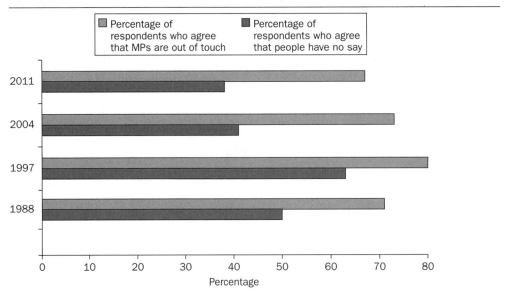

SOURCE: 1988–2011 Canadian Election Studies (*n* = 6395).

their vote was of little consequence, given the dominance of the Liberals and the weakness of the opposition parties. Nevertheless, in the more recent surveys, approximately 40 percent of respondents continued to feel that their vote in elections had little effect on government.

Declining voter turnout in federal elections over the past two decades also reflects malaise in contemporary Canadian federal politics (see Figure 19.5). While part of this decline is due to generational change and other demographic factors, there is little doubt that voter cynicism and the characteristics of the current party system have also contributed to the withdrawal of voters from the electoral process.[21] Dealigned voters with weak partisan attachments are more difficult to mobilize in elections. The strong regional patterns that have been evident in recent years have also contributed to the withdrawal of many Canadians from electoral participation because it has made elections less competitive in many areas of the country, and the choices presented in them less meaningful.[22] Turnout in the 2006 election rose slightly, in part because of the greater uncertainty regarding the outcome of that election. However, in 2008 and 2011, it again dropped to historic lows. It is easy to see why voters in many parts of the country could readily surmise that their vote would have little influence on the outcome of the election, either nationally

FIGURE 19.5 TURNOUT IN CANADIAN FEDERAL ELECTIONS, 1958–2011

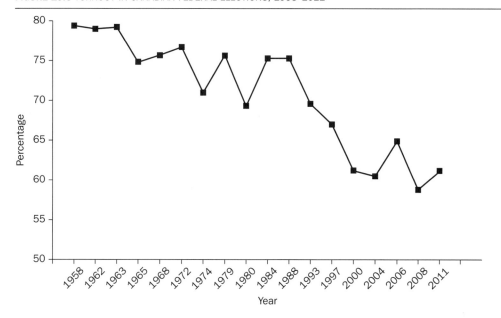

SOURCE: Elections Canada. (2012). "Voter Turnout at Federal Elections and Referendums." On the World Wide Web at http://www.elections.ca/content.aspx?section=ele&dir=turn&document=index&lang=e (retrieved 17 March 2012).

or in their own constituencies. If they also believe that little real choice is presented to them in elections or that politicians cannot be trusted to keep their promises, the motivation to participate is further diminished.

Given the dealigned electorate, the political future in Canada could be much like the past, despite the substantial changes that have occurred since 2006. The Harper dynasty is similar to some other dynasties, particularly that of Chrétien, in that it depended in part for its creation on a divided and relatively weak opposition. The Conservatives owed their majority outcome in 2011 largely to the party's substantial gains in the Toronto region. Even if the Conservatives are able to extend the length of their dynasty, they remain vulnerable to a sudden and unpredictable reversal. Any governing party is particularly vulnerable to economic adversity. The durability of the NDP surge in 2011 also remains to be demonstrated, particularly given the vulnerability of its position in Quebec. Neither should a revival of the Liberals be discounted in the present political environment, despite the tendency to proclaim the death of this once-dominant party. Given the fragility of past party configurations, there is no reason to invest more belief in the staying power of the present one, particularly given the modest size and strength of the 2011 Conservative majority.

The interpretation that I have advanced is that the Canadian electorate continues to be highly dealigned, in part because of the nature of brokerage politics. In this setting, elections are unpredictable and tend to be dominated by short-term issues, personalities, and events. With a dealigned electorate, the potential for sudden and unpredictable change is always high. Parties will continue to search for electorally successful formulae and to position themselves for short-term political advantage, even if it involves repudiation of past issues or ideological commitments. In a polity dominated by brokerage parties, a new leader or a compelling issue could easily ignite a process of sudden change. However, a party or leader in power that is able to manage these unpredictable forces skillfully can also enjoy continued political success.

NOTES

1. Cameron D. Anderson and Laura B. Stephenson. (2010). "The Puzzle of Elections and Voting in Canada." In Cameron D. Anderson and Laura B. Stephenson, eds. *Voting Behaviour in Canada* (pp. 1–39). Vancouver: University of British Columbia Press.
2. On the subject of successful leaders and coalitions of previous political eras, see Lawrence LeDuc, Jon H. Pammett, Judith I. McKenzie, and André Turcotte. (2010). *Dynasties and Interludes: Past and Present in Canadian Electoral Politics.* Toronto: Dundurn Press. For a more direct comparison of the emerging "Harper dynasty" to those of previous eras, see LeDuc, Lawrence and Jon H. Pammett. (2011). "The Evolution of the Harper Dynasty." In Jon H. Pammett and Christopher Dornan, eds. *The Canadian Federal Election of 2011* (pp. 303–29). Toronto: Dundurn Press.
3. The Liberals under Jean Chrétien won a majority of seats in the 1997 election with 38.4 percent of the vote.
4. See Harold D. Clarke, Jane Jenson, Lawrence LeDuc, and Jon H. Pammett. (1996). *Absent Mandate: Canadian Electoral Politics in an Era of Restructuring.* Toronto: Gage.
5. For a current example of this thinking, see Peter C. Newman (2011). *When the Gods Changed: The Death of Liberal Canada.* Toronto: Random House.

6. Clarke et al., *Absent Mandate*. See also Janine Brodie and Jane Jenson. (1988). *Crisis, Challenge and Change: Party and Class in Canada Revisited.* Ottawa: Carleton University Press.

7. On the subject of valence politics, see Harold D.Clarke, Allan Kornberg, and Thomas J. Scotto. (2009). *Making Political Choices: Canada and the United States.* Toronto: University of Toronto Press.

8. See Robert Alford. (1963). *Party and Society.* Chicago: Rand McNally; and John Porter. (1965). *The Vertical Mosaic.* Toronto: University of Toronto Press, for some of the classic academic statements of these themes. On the weakness of class politics in Canada, see also Jon H. Pammett. (1987). "Class Voting and Class Consciousness in Canada." *Canadian Review of Sociology and Anthropology,* 24, 269–90.

9. LeDuc et al., *Dynasties and Interludes.*

10. Clarke et al., *Absent Mandate.*

11. For a more detailed account of these elections, see Jon H. Pammett and Christopher Dornan, eds. (2006). *The Canadian Federal Election of 2006.* Toronto: Dundurn Press; and Jon H. Pammett and Christopher Dornan, eds. (2009). *The Canadian Federal Election of 2008.* Toronto: Dundurn Press.

12. R. Kenneth Carty, William Cross, and Lisa Young. (2000). *Rebuilding Canadian Party Politics.* University of British Columbia Press.

13. See Fred Engelman and Mildred A. Schwartz. (1967). *Political Parties and the Canadian Social Structure.* Toronto: Prentice-Hall; and John Meisel. (1975). *Working Papers on Canadian Politics.* Montreal: McGill-Queen's Press.

14. Harold D. Clarke, Jane Jenson, Lawrence LeDuc, and Jon H. Pammett. (1979). *Political Choice in Canada.* Toronto: McGraw-Hill Ryerson (pp. 301–19).

15. These data are from the 2011 Canadian Election Study. The 2011 study was conducted by Patrick Fournier, Fred Cutler, Stuart Soroka, and Deitland Stolle. The 2004, 2006 and 2008 Canadian Election Studies were conducted by Elisabeth Gidengil, Joanna Everitt, Patrick Fournier, and Neil Nevitte. The 1997 and 2000 studies were conducted by André Blais, Elisabeth Gidengil, Richard Nadeau, and Neil Nevitte. The fieldwork for all of these studies was carried out by the York University Institute for Social Research, and the studies were funded by the Social Sciences and Humanities Research Council of Canada. Neither the funding agencies nor the principal investigators are responsible for the analyses or interpretations presented here.

Some of the findings of the 1997–2000 studies are reported in Nevitte et al. (2000). *Unsteady State.* Toronto: Oxford University Press; and in Blais et al. (2002). *Anatomy of a Liberal Victory.* Toronto: Broadview. For an analysis using data from the more recent studies, see Elisabeth Gidengil et al. (2012). *Dominance and Decline.* Toronto: University of Toronto Press. Further technical information on the election studies is available at www.ces-eec.org.

16. There are different methods of measuring party identification in surveys. In the findings reported here, we construct the measures to maximize comparability across the surveys. Respondents reporting any party "leanings" are counted as identifiers, even though they may have rejected identification with a party in their first response. This produces a somewhat more conservative estimate of nonidentification than might be obtained by other methods of classification. The standard sequence of questions employed in the CES surveys is, "Generally speaking, do you think of yourself as a Liberal, Conservative, NDP, etc.?" [IF PARTY] "How strongly ___ do you feel: very strong, fairly strong, or not very strong?" [IF NO PARTY] "Do you feel a bit closer to any of the federal parties?" [IF YES] "Which party is that?" On some of the issues involved in employing different measures and methods of classification, see Richard Johnston. (1992). "Party Identification Measures in the Anglo American Democracies: a National Survey Experiment." *American Journal of Political Science, 36*, 542–59.

17. For this purpose, we define the two positions nearest the centre point (5) of the scale as "centre right" (6–7) and "centre left" (3–4).

18. Ronald D. Lambert, James Curtis, Steven Brown, and Barry Kay. (1986). "In Search of Left/Right Beliefs in the Canadian Electorate." *Canadian Journal of Political Science, 19*, 542–63.

19. Clarke et al., *Absent Mandate.*

20. Clarke et al., *Absent Mandate*, pp. 180–81. See also André Blais and Elisabeth Gidengil. (1991). *Making Representative Democracy Work* (Vol. 17, Research Studies of the Royal Commission on Electoral Reform and Party Financing). Toronto: Dundurn.

21. For a discussion of the effects on turnout, see Lawrence LeDuc and Jon H. Pammett. (2010). "Voter Turnout." In Heather MacIvor, ed., *Election* (pp. 251–67). Toronto: Emond Montgomery.

22. This argument is developed in greater detail in Lawrence LeDuc and Jon H. Pammett. (2006). "Voter Turnout in 2006: More Than Just the Weather." In Jon H. Pammett and Christopher Dornan, eds. *The Canadian General Election of 2006* (pp. 318–42). Toronto: Dundurn.

Chapter 20

Mass Murder: What Causes It? Can It Be Stopped?

MICHAEL MANN, University of California, Los Angeles, and

JAMES RON, University of Minnesota

GLOBAL TRENDS IN CIVILIAN MASS KILLING

MICHAEL MANN

The mass killing of civilians may be part of a regime's repression of its own subjects, or it may occur through ethnic or political cleansing, or through wars, which blur the distinction between combatants and civilians and produce massive civilian casualties. The twentieth century saw a surge in all three. Hitler and Stalin represented the century's nadir in repression and cleansing, and other genocides, like the Armenian and the Rwandan, have been widely publicized. Since I recently published a book focusing on these four cases among others (*The Dark Side of Democracy: Explaining Ethnic Cleansing*), here I mainly discuss the third type, the blurring of the civilian/combatant divide in war. But, all mass killings must be seen in their historical context. I see four long-term trends:

1. The development of an unusually imperialistic form of society in Europe. From the late tenth century, "Europe" expanded outward by colonial conquest in all four directions from its Frankish core. In a second phase, from the fifteenth to the nineteenth centuries, bigger, militarily superior states swallowed up the smaller states founded in phase one. In a third overlapping phase, conventionally labeled "imperialism," Europeans conquered most of the world. For a thousand years, war was unusually profitable for the European victors, and, as comparative research shows, Europeans therefore engaged in it more frequently and more ruthlessly than most peoples elsewhere in the world. As Europeans pioneered modernity, they also pioneered terrible wars.

Source: Excerpts from "Mass Murder: What Causes It? Can It Be Stopped?" by Michael Mann and James Ron in Contexts Forum, *Contexts 6(2)*, pp. 28–34. © 2007. Reprinted by Permission of SAGE Publications.

2. European overseas imperialism (phase three), involved murderous ethnic cleansing by settlers, who wanted the land but not the labor of natives, and colonial wars that blurred civilian/combatant distinctions. Racism, especially among Northern European settlers, made it more difficult to assimilate conquered native peoples as earlier empires had done. Racism justified the mass killing of "inferior" peoples believed to be "doomed" by the onward march of civilization. Colonists often saw the spread of their diseases among the natives as revealing the hand of God "winnowing out" lesser peoples. Then, Japan and the United States joined in the imperialism.

3. Wars within Europe became less frequent but more lethal over the centuries, culminating in the bombing and shelling of entire civilian populations. The British Empire began such bombing in Iraq in the 1920s, followed elsewhere by the French, Italian, and Japanese empires. They and others have offered four main justifications: (a) modern warfare mobilizes whole economies; thus, civilian infrastructures are legitimate targets; (b) the enemy population is either a lesser race or espouses an evil creed; (c) mass bombing and shelling of cities follows only after civilians are warned to leave—leaflets preceded the fire-bombing of Tokyo and Dresden and the dropping of the atom bombs; and (d) no individual civilian is specifically targeted. The United States became the principal inheritor of this tradition; its military has specialized since 1941 in overwhelming firepower. In recent years, U.S. administrations have emphasized the last point, arguing that its military does not deliberately target any civilian. However, when bombing is bound to produce mass casualties, this seems a specious argument.

4. The European embrace of "rule by the people" carried in certain contexts the dangers of ethnic cleansing by the "true" people of "lesser" peoples (see my *Dark Side of Democracy*). This cleansing began in and around the fringes of Europe and continued where two or three rival peoples could make plausible claims to dominion over the same territory and where outsiders could aid the weaker side.

The period from 1942 to 1950 brought two major changes. It replaced European colonialism with "nation-states" supposedly embodying "rule by the people," and it made wars between the Great Powers too lethal to be rational. These changes have led to the following results:

1. Interstate and colonial wars have declined. Europeans, having been from Mars for a millennium, suddenly went on holiday to Venus, while the two superpowers fought each other only through smaller proxies. The newer "nation-states" of the world seldom make war among themselves, though a few subimperialists (Russia, Indonesia, India, and others) have waged colonial wars around their fringes. Interstate wars have almost disappeared.

2. The last imperial power, the United States, has continued bombing and shelling civilians, with the same four justifications. Its carpet-bombing of North Korea in 1950 caused more than 3 million casualties, and of Vietnam and its neighbors, more than 2 million. Though America's adversaries in these wars were probably just as ruthless, they had less firepower and could kill far fewer soldiers or civilians.

3. Civil wars and ethnic cleansing increased in new, supposed "nation-states," which lacked agreement on the "true" nation or people. In Rwanda at least 600 000 civilians were murdered in 1994. Such events have declined since the mid-1990s, with fewer new wars starting. However, some older ones continue to wreak havoc. Total casualties in the Congo have now reached somewhere between 2 million and 4 million, though the two civil wars of the Sudan, especially the one in Darfur, are receiving much more global attention.

4. Terrorism has recently grown. Terrorism is defined in terms of deliberate targeting of civilians by small groups. Terrorist groups are invariably countered by state terrorists, who bomb and shell civilian populations among whom terrorists hide. In the Muslim world, the American empire has now become one of the state terrorists. The increasing technological disjunction between the two sides generates what Martin Shaw, in *The New Western Way of War*, calls "risk-transfer militarism," whereby the United States and its main allies (Britain and Israel) can transfer the risks of war from their own soldiers to enemy civilians. U.S. bombing in Afghanistan probably produced about 3000 civilian casualties; in Iraq, U.S. bombing and overwhelming ground firepower (in Fallujah and elsewhere) has killed between 50 000 and 100 000 civilians, perhaps more—although, as in earlier colonial wars, native deaths are not counted. Nonetheless, the ratio of American-soldier-to-native-civilian casualties may be on the order of 1:50. In Iraq, this combat has morphed into an ethnic civil war among Iraqis, whose final death count may be just as high. Compared with previous cases, these numbers are not large, but they nonetheless shock us—since we have caused them.

Throughout this entire history, international legal and moral movements have sought to restrain the atrocities. The eleventh-century "Peace of God" activists tried to lessen wars (with little success), while three-quarters of the clauses in the Westphalia treaties of 1648 "guaranteed" the survival of Europe's minnow states (of course, they did not survive). More recently, a formal law code proscribing genocide, crimes against humanity, and war crimes has become internationally recognized, but it is used only against defeated or weaker parties. The ad hoc UN War Crimes Tribunals or the new International Criminal Court could be used more vigorously against perpetrators. However, American leaders, recognizing that such laws threaten their interests, have made the United States the major obstacle to implementing a tougher regime of international law. No one has been prosecuted for "disproportionate" bombing or fire-power, and this seems unlikely to happen soon. We can be glad that most trends are now downward, but not as a result of antiwar movements.

As I showed in *The Dark Side of Democracy*, most perpetrators are not evil or primitive "others," but people like us. Mass murder has been part of our own civilization. I focus here on indiscriminate firepower not because it kills the most—in fact, the casualties in today's ethnic and civil wars are much greater. But, it is today our form of mass killing— what we in the United States (and in Britain and in Israel) perpetrate. Indiscriminate firepower is certain to cause mass civilian deaths; thus, it is the practical and moral equivalent of the butchery perpetrated by gangs of Kalashnikov-wielding kids in the Congo. It is also incapable, in an age dominated by anti-imperialism, of achieving the desired results. It only enrages the targeted civilian population, renews the ranks of the terrorists, and generates more killing by both sides.

The great delusion of modern history is that militaristic empires bring order. Actually, they have brought mass murder. Only when the last empire abdicates or is destroyed will it be possible to create an international order with greater chances of reducing mass killing.

CAN THE GLOBAL HUMAN RIGHTS MOVEMENT PREVENT SERIOUS VIOLATIONS?

JAMES RON

The international human-rights movement has grown tremendously over the past 20 years. The number of nongovernmental groups devoted to the cause has increased exponentially, the human-rights budgets of donor agencies have grown, and media usage of the term has skyrocketed. But, what effect has all this had on the incidence of actual violations? I focus on abuses of "personal integrity rights," namely, the rights not to be tortured, arbitrarily imprisoned, or murdered.

For those familiar with mass killings in Bosnia (1992–93), Rwanda (1994), Burundi (1993), Democratic Republic of Congo (1998–2005), and Darfur since 2003, the news looks bad. Widespread killings have occurred in these and other countries, often in full view of global audiences sympathetic to human rights. Hundreds of thousands died, some in circumstances of mass murder. Do events in these and other recent conflicts demonstrate the futility of human-rights activism and policymaking?

Before rushing to judgment, recall that focusing on a handful of highly visible cases may be misleading. No matter how disturbing the Darfur genocide, for example, rigorous assessments of global human-rights efforts should examine trends in multiple countries across many years. There are more than 190 nation-states in existence today. What do we know about the average impact of global efforts to ensure human rights in all of these?

Systematic evaluation is still in its infancy. Until the early 1990s, only a handful of legal scholars, moral philosophers, and activists seriously promoted human rights. Now, however, there is enough policy debate and action to suggest that promoting human rights is significant and meaningful. As a result, a growing number of social scientists are asking what works, when, and how.

Efforts to protect human rights come in three broad packages. The first is the most muscular, involving armed troops seeking to prevent killings before they begin or to stop them once they are underway. These troops include peacekeeping and peacemaking forces of all kinds, often operating under the auspices of the United Nations, NATO, the African Union, or other regional bodies. These soldiers may be deployed before hostilities begin, as in Macedonia during the 1990s, or in the midst of a shooting war, as we saw in southern Lebanon in 2006.

Research suggests that such efforts can help to end ongoing wars, reducing the potential for further abuse, but uninvolved countries rarely deploy troops effectively and quickly while gross violations are ongoing. A capable, standing UN army with a broad "right to protect" mandate would be a great step forward, but this is still a distant dream. The Darfur genocide is a case in point, as was Rwanda more than a decade ago.

The second broad package includes the web of treaties, activists, and policy incentives that make up the international human-rights network. Evidence of this web is widespread, and as a result of activist pressure, policymakers in rich donor countries are increasingly jumping on the bandwagon. Much of the European Union's foreign policy, for example, is focused on tools for promoting human rights in individual states, including targeted incentives for political leaders, legal-training programs for governments, and sanctions on individual economic sectors. As donors speak more frequently about the importance of human rights, moreover, social-justice activists in the global south are responding in kind, drawing more and more on human-rights discourse in their work. In some cases, experienced activists are reframing ongoing social-reform efforts in human-rights terms; in other cases, new types of activists are devising an entirely different set of strategies and tactics to ensure justice.

All of these new efforts are encouraging, but they are slow and incremental, working only in combination with other factors. For example, scholars find that human-rights treaties are effective, on average, when the target country has higher levels of democracy, a larger civil society, and more links to international activists. Sadly, this leaves large regions of the world beyond the pale.

Interestingly, qualitative and quantitative evaluations of human-rights activism and policies differ in tone and substance. In-depth, single-country studies often report uplifting instances of positive change, drawing upbeat conclusions about the broader potential for human-rights protection. Quantitative studies, by contrast, study the average effects of policies across several countries, finding greater grounds for pessimism.

Some of this difference may stem from a regional selection bias; some of the most detailed and convincing qualitative work has focused on Latin America, where positive change seems more possible. When the entire world is taken into account, the statistical picture is far less encouraging. Unlike many qualitative studies, moreover, quantitative studies take into account the effects of other factors, including democratization, state capacity, and international linkages.

The third protection package is more structural and includes broad processes of historical change, such as economic growth, globalization, trends in the development of nation-states, and urbanization. Activists, policymakers, and international lawyers, of course, have little control over these trends, which are so deep and complex as to defy manipulation by even the most dedicated policymaker.

Here we find several opposing trends. On the one hand, the era of massive, government-driven social engineering is largely over, and this is probably good news for human-rights promotion. In years past, the Soviet Union, China, Tanzania, and Cambodia all sought rapid growth and/or equity through massive coercion, often with horrendous results. On the other hand, many nation-states in the global south remain poor and weak, and this undercuts their governments' respect for human rights. Massive governmental "catch-up" efforts are dangerous for human rights, but so are current rates of global poverty, incapacity, and inequality.

Wealth and growth are complex affairs. Per capita gross domestic product is a predictor of government respect for human rights, but growth patterns are notoriously uneven. China and India have grown enormously, for example, but this growth has been accompanied by equally profound inequalities, which are also a source of potential tension, violence, and abuse. Global structural trends, in other words, are a very mixed bag.

In the final analysis, the human-rights era may have two lasting legacies. First, it may have blunted the sharpest edges of Western violence in the global south, even in this era of renewed imperialism. Forty years ago, American troops in Vietnam slaughtered tens of thousands in a series of devastating and indiscriminate bombardments. U.S. troops in Iraq have been comparatively restrained, despite the awful consequences of their invasion. Coalition troops have engaged in torture and murder, but there have been no reports of Vietnam-style depravity. Although this may provide little consolation to Iraq's victims, it is still important to note.

Human-rights activists may have successfully entrenched "rights" as the dominant global idiom of protest for years to come. Social-movement activists increasingly use human-rights language in their work, and this has focused greater attention on legal forms of resistance, displacing time-honored tactics, such as mass mobilization and armed insurgency.

What should policymakers and activists do? There are no clear answers. Economic growth and the processes of building nation-states have proved resistant to tinkering, foreign aid does not regularly increase growth, and externally supported efforts to strengthen governments often deteriorate into corruption. Promoting human rights is a moral imperative, and we must continue to do it whenever we can. We should not, however, delude ourselves into thinking we have discovered effective, globally applicable mechanisms for preventing gross abuses.

PART 5 | DEVIANCE AND CRIME

Deviance is behaviour that departs from a norm. It ranges from harmless fads to the most violent crimes. **Crime** is deviance that law defines as illegal. In a sense, all deviance is anti-institutional since it seeks to achieve acceptable goals, such as getting rich or happy, by generally disapproved, and often illegal, means. However, deviance is also institutionalized behaviour because it is socially learned, organized, and persistent. Thus, a person is more likely to become a deviant if he or she is exposed to more deviant than nondeviant role models. Moreover, the person learns the deviant role through socialization; just as medical students are socialized into the role of doctor, so professional robbers must learn the techniques and the moral code of thieves. Finally, deviants, including criminals, establish counter-institutions—cliques, gangs, mafias, and so forth—with their own rules of behaviour and their own subcultural norms.

Sports violence represents a grey area between deviant and non–deviant behaviour. A few high-profile cases of egregious violence beyond the rules have resulted in suspensions and criminal convictions. However, in contact sports, such as football, hockey, and boxing, much violence is allowed and even encouraged. Violence is part of the game.

Concussions and other injuries are occurring more frequently in these sports. Thus, in 2005, the National Hockey League (NHL) eliminated the red line to speed up the game and reduce offside calls. Because of this rule change, long passes into the offensive zone are now possible, causing attacking players to rush in with increased velocity for a shot on goal. More injuries result. In Chapter 21, Steve Dumas identifies the main reasons for increasing violence in hockey: competition by sports organizations for audiences and **hegemonic masculinity**, the culturally normative ideal of what it means to be a man, which causes audiences to demand more violence. Dumas also asks whether increased participation on the part of women in hockey is lowering the level of violence in the sport. He answers in the negative; women's hockey is governed by different rules allowing for less violence, while men's hockey continues on its own, violent course.

Criminal behaviour worries the Canadian public more today than it used to. There is much talk about crime waves and mounting random violence, particularly among youth. Many people are afraid to walk alone outside at night. In large cities, many people equip their homes with burglar alarms and install steel bars on their basement windows.

Yet actual crime rates are at their lowest point in more than three decades. There exists a disconnect between the average Canadian's perception of crime and actual crime rates because most people rely on the mass media for information about crime trends. The mass media often exaggerate the extent of criminal behaviour because doing so increases audience size and therefore the amount of money that businesses are willing to pay for advertising.

When people claim that crime is on the rise, they usually mean **street crime**, such as robbery, assault, homicide, and the like, which is committed mainly by lower- and working-class people. One large category of criminal behaviour scarcely enters the public consciousness: **white-collar or corporate crime**, in which middle- and upper-class people, in the course of their work, break laws intended to ensure worker safety and accurate advertising, and to prevent fraudulent financial manipulation, price fixing, market splitting, and environmental pollution. Governments do not direct the country's police forces to systematically collect and publish statistics on white-collar or corporate crime. Surveillance of such crime is relatively lax, as is apprehension, prosecution, and conviction of white-collar or corporate criminals. Yet, according to some estimates, while-collar or corporate crime costs the Canadian public more than street crime in terms of dollars and lives.

An especially sickening case of corporate malfeasance resulting in no convictions occurred in Nova Scotia in 1992, when 26 miners died in the Westray coalmine disaster. Four government commissions of inquiry found evidence of poor roof support, drilling in geologically unstable areas, insufficient cleaning of dangerous coal dust, and the hiring of inexperienced supervisors. Yet there were no convictions for these violations and oversights. As John McMullan shows in Chapter 22, the mass media were partly complicit in this legal outcome because few of the thousands of news stories about the disaster and its aftermath framed it as a case of corporate crime. Arguably, in the minds of many Canadians, individuals and even government officials can commit crimes but corporations are largely immune from criminality—and the mass media help to perpetuate this myth.

GLOSSARY

Crime is deviance that a law defines as illegal.

Deviance is behaviour that departs from a norm.

Hegemonic masculinity is the culturally normative ideal of what it means to be a man.

Street crime, including robbery, assault, homicide, and the like, is committed mainly by lower- and working-class people.

White-collar or corporate crime involves middle- and upper-class people, in the course of their work, breaking laws that are intended to ensure worker safety and accurate advertising, and to prevent fraudulent financial manipulation, price fixing, market splitting, and environmental pollution.

CRITICAL THINKING QUESTIONS

1. Is violence in hockey deviant or just part of the game—or are some types of hockey violence deviant while other types are part of the game? If the latter, which types of violence fall into each category? Should the NHL change the rules to decrease the level of hockey violence, or is the game acceptable just as it is?

2. Do official crime statistics reflect actual crime rates? What factors other than the incidence of crime influence official crime statistics?

3. Are some classes more crime-prone than others are? Or is it more accurate to say that specific types of crime are more frequent in some classes than in others?

ANNOTATED BIBLIOGRAPHY

Ian Gomme, *The Shadow Line: Deviance and Crime in Canada,* 4th ed. (Toronto: Nelson, 2007). A popular and comprehensive overview of Canadian criminological research.

Erich Goode and Nachman Ben-Yehudah, *Moral Panics: The Social Construction of Deviance*, 2nd ed. (New York: Wiley, 2009). Drug panics, witch crazes, school shootings, and terrorism illustrate the ways in which deviance and crime are created by social reactions.

Chapter 21

Are Sports Becoming Less Masculine?

STEVE DUMAS, University of Calgary

SID THE KID

Sidney Crosby is arguably the most talented professional ice hockey player of the twenty-first century. He was selected first overall by the Pittsburgh Penguins in the 2005 National Hockey League (NHL) entry draft, won a gold medal for Canada at the 2010 Winter Olympics, and, at 22, was the youngest captain to have won a Stanley Cup. Tragically, several traumatic hits to the head knocked Crosby out of the game in 2011–12 (Kelly, 2011). Now back on the ice, symptoms continue to plague him. Of course, Crosby is not the only player who has had to deal with the effects of concussion ("Crosby to Miss," 2011). To name just two other recent examples: Marc Savard of the Boston Bruins suffered a career-ending concussion in March 2010 (Mirtle, 2011) and Chris Pronger of the Philadelphia Flyers is still recovering from the effects of a concussion sustained in December 2010. In addition, the summer of 2011 ended with the suicides of three well-known NHL players—Derek Boogaard, Rick Rypien, and Wade Belak. All three were "enforcers" who had been involved in numerous fights, and speculation has swirled about the possibility that the concussions they sustained led to a degenerative disease known as chronic traumatic encephalopathy (CTE). Doctors identified this disease in Detroit Red Wings enforcer Bob Probert, who died in 2010 from heart failure at just 45 (Probert, 2010). CTE produces symptoms that include impeded speech, tremors, vertigo, social instability, memory loss, and erratic behaviour (McKee et al., 2009).

These tragic cases raise several obvious questions about ice hockey. Why does so much violence occur and why is it tolerated? Does violence simply attract fans and generate profit? Can we explain violence by characteristics unique to sports settings? Will the increased participation of women in sport reduce the number of violent incidents or will women conform to masculine practices?

This chapter examines these questions by considering how subcultural values and norms intersect with cultural standards of masculinity and femininity in our society.

GAME MISCONDUCT: DEFINITIONS OF VIOLENCE

Violence refers to the use of excessive force that causes, or has the potential to cause, harm or destruction (Coakley and Donnelly, 2009: 187–88). By contrast, *aggression* refers to verbal or physical actions intended to dominate, control, or do harm to another person. Although behaviour can be violent and aggressive, some violence occurs without the intent to do harm to another.

Michael Smith (1987) constructed a typology of violence for sports settings. He distinguished legitimate and illegitimate sports violence. Violence is legitimate if actions are deemed to be within the confines of the normative order of the sport. Illegitimate violence is behaviour that is beyond the sport's norms. Legitimate violence includes brutal body contact and borderline violence. Brutal body contact consists of permissible actions, such as tackles in football or body checks in ice hockey. By contrast, borderline violence includes fighting in ice hockey or the brushback in baseball (which occurs when pitchers throw balls close to batters to push them back and thus reduce the likelihood of their successfully hitting the ball). Illegitimate violence includes quasi-criminal violence and criminal violence. Quasi-criminal violence violates the formal and informal rules of the sport. For instance, in hockey, a sucker punch (an unexpected punch) or a late hit (a body check occurring a second or more after a player has passed or shot the puck) are examples of this behaviour. Criminal violence—for instance, an assault after a game—is the most extreme form of violence.

FROM SUBCULTURE TO CULTURAL STUDIES

Smith's typology assumes that sports settings possess their own unique norms, that they are *subcultures*—cultures associated with groups that differ from the larger culture in terms of language, values, style of life, and so on (Crosset and Beal, 1997: 74).

According to some analysts, sports subcultures involve dedication to the game above all else, striving for distinction, tolerance for pain and risk, and an attitude that refuses to accept obstacles in the pursuit of excellence. Deviance results from underconformity or overconformity to such ideals (Coakley and Donnelly, 2009; Hughes and Coakley, 1991: 308). Athletes who underconform to the sports ethic include those who, for example, refuse to endure considerable pain and injury for their teams, while those who overconform may use anabolic steroids or other performance enhancing drugs to excel.

While the subcultural interpretation of sports violence offers a useful *description* of types of sports deviance, it hardly explains why such violence occurs. For a plausible explanation, we must turn to *cultural studies*. The field of cultural studies examines the development of dominant modes of thinking and behaviour in societies characterized by high levels of inequality. Through persuasion and force, dominant groups seek to impose on subordinate groups certain modes of thinking and behaviour from which they benefit. Over time, subordinate groups tend to accept these modes of thinking and behaviour as normal. When this occurs, dominant modes of thinking are said to become *hegemonic* (Crosset and Beal, 1997: 75–76; Pfohl, 1994: 416). Under identifiable circumstances, however, subordinate groups may resist hegemonic ideas and action.

Applying these ideas to the study of sports, cultural studies analysts examine how dominant groups exercise power to achieve hegemony and how subordinate groups, including classes, ethnic and racial groups, and genders, come to accept or resist such attempts (Hiller, 2006: 96). For instance, some analysts emphasize that sports organizations are businesses seeking to maximize profits. Violence attracts big audiences and is therefore highly profitable. It is therefore tolerated and even tacitly encouraged by many owners, managers, coaches, and even players (Young, 1993, 2000). The mass media benefit from sports violence, too—paradoxically, even when they condemn it. Sports violence attracts big media audiences, and the bigger the audience, the more media outlets can charge businesses for ads.

As compelling as the argument about the profit motive may be, some analysts argue that it is not the whole story (Coakley and Donnelly, 2009: 193). After all, sports violence preceded the mass commercialization of sports. Moreover, some sports, such as tennis, are profitable without violence. Finally, the violence-for-profit thesis does not explain why so many members of the public are eager to pay for displays of sports violence in the first place. These criticisms suggest that factors in addition to the profit motive cause sports violence, the most important of which is *hegemonic masculinity*, the culturally normative ideal of what it means to be a man. The argument here is that steep inequalities between women and men in the economy, politics, education, religion, and other institutions reinforce traditional gender norms. To be sure, such norms have become more egalitarian in recent decades in Canada and elsewhere. However, they are still very much a part of life in our society, as the sociological analysis of sports demonstrates.

GENDER CONFORMITY AND RESISTANCE: FEMINIST APPROACHES

Feminists have drawn attention to women's struggles to participate in sports and the ways they reconcile general cultural pressures to behave in conventionally feminine ways with the hegemonic masculine culture of so many sports (Adams, 2006; Theberge, 2000).

Sociological research suggests that we do not identify some people as athletes just because they participate in sports regularly. We identify some people as athletes only insofar as we acknowledge and support their sporting activities. This process occurs in four stages. We (1) learn how a sport is played, (2) become familiar with people in the sport, (3) gain an understanding of the expectations of athletes in the sport, and (4) recognize certain individuals as conforming to those expectations. Athletes, in turn, establish their athletic identities by managing the impressions they make on others, self-consciously acting in ways that conform to the expectations of how athletes are supposed to behave (Donnelly and Young, 1988; Stevenson, 1991).

When women enter sports, they feel pressure to become accepted as full-fledged athletes, but acceptance is difficult because many sports are male domains (Adams, 2006; Morrow and Wamsley, 2010; Stevens, 2006; Theberge, 2000). Women were largely excluded from sports competition until the 1960s. In the late nineteenth and early twentieth century, sport in Canada was "a public forum for physical manhood, tempered by Christian values yet sometimes rationalizing the pleasures of perceived violence and aggression" (Morrow and Wamsley, 2010: 170). At the same time, considerable cultural pressure was placed on women to appear physically weak and dependent. Women who expressed interest in sports were typically informed that they were deviating from their appropriate gender role and that participation was harmful to their health. When women did become active in sports, they were highly regulated by male authorities (Hall, 1999).

In the second half of the twentieth century, women organized and lobbied to participate in sports. Consequently, in 1970, the Government of Canada struck a Royal Commission to examine gender disparities in sports participation (Coakley and Donnelly, 2009: 222). It resulted in the allocation of more resources for female participation in sports, particularly in high schools. It also led to more research on the causes of participation in sports and the relative lack of participation of women. Since the 1970s, more resources have been made available to support equal opportunity for men and women to participate in sports at all levels.

Although participation in sports declined for all Canadian children between 1992 and 2005, girls are much more involved than they used to be. Figure 21.1 displays data from the 2005 Canadian *General Social Survey*. It shows that 45 percent of girls between the ages of 5 and 14 were involved in organized sports, compared with 56 percent of boys. The gap between the sexes has been declining since the 1960s. Soccer, swimming, hockey, basketball, and baseball are the most popular sports for children in terms of participation rates (Table 21.1).

FIGURE 21.1 PERCENTAGE OF CANADIANS IN ORGANIZED SPORTS, 2005, BY SPORT, SEX, AND AGE COHORT

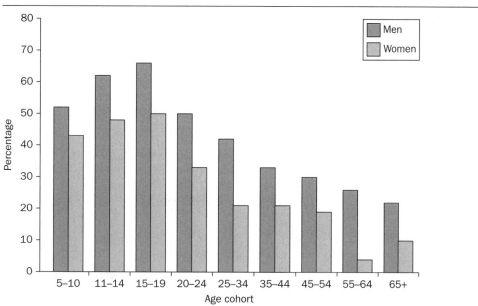

SOURCE: Chart 3: Children and adolescents are most likely to participate in organized sports. Statistics Canada, General Social Survey, http://www.statcan.gc.ca/pub/11-008-x/2008001/c-g/10573/5214736-eng.htm. Reproduced and distributed on an "as is" basis with the permission of Statistics Canada.

TABLE 21.1 PARTICIPATION RATES IN TOP SPORTS, 5–14-YEAR-OLDS, CANADA, 1992 AND 2005 (IN PERCENT)

	1992	2005
Soccer	12	20
Swimming	17	12
Hockey	12	11
Basketball	6	8
Baseball	13	5
Volleyball	5	3
Gymnastics	4	2
Karate	2	2
Skiing, downhill	6	2
Track and field	2	2
All sports	57	51

SOURCE: Statistics Canada, *General Social Survey,* 1992 and 2005.

ICE TIME FOR WOMEN

Canadian women played their first recorded ice hockey game in Ottawa in 1891 (Theberge, 2000: 1). Before World War II, women's involvement in hockey grew steadily. However, during the war (when many women were mobilized to work in factories while men went off to battle) and in the 1950s (the golden era of the nuclear family, when many women turned to domesticity and child rearing in the suburbs), a reversal began.

The modern era of Canadian women's hockey began in the 1960s. Since then, interest in the sport has grown steadily. One of the most influential developments was the formation of the Ontario Women's Hockey Association (OWHA) in 1975 and the establishment of international tournaments sanctioned by the International Ice Hockey Federation. Women's Olympic hockey competitions began in 1998.

These developments generated more interest in and involvement of women in hockey. Between 1998–99 and 2008–09, women as a proportion of all players in Canadian hockey leagues more than doubled. Nonetheless, men still dominate the sport. In 2008–09, more than 85 percent of Canadian league players were men (see Figure 21.2).

FIGURE 21.2 HOCKEY CANADA PARTICIPATION RATE BY SEX AND YEAR (IN PERCENT)

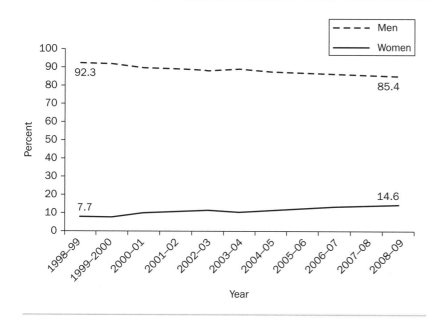

UNSPORTS*MAN*LIKE CONDUCT: GENDER AND VIOLENCE IN ICE HOCKEY

I noted earlier that people do not recognize individuals as athletes merely by virtue of their participation in sports. As is particularly evident for women in contact sports, recognition takes time, knowledge, hard work, and success. Having to reconcile gender expectations with the demands of the sport makes the task all the more difficult.

For example, boxing is an especially aggressive and violent sport, constituting just about as stark a contrast as imaginable with traditional notions of femininity. Women boxers challenge dominant ideas of gender. Consequently, unlike men, they have had to explain their motivations for participating in the sport, prove themselves to be serious athletes, ward off suspicions that they are victims of domestic violence when they are hurt boxing, cover up injuries with makeup and clothes, and deal with widespread perceptions that they are lesbians. Significantly, however, while female boxing challenges gender norms, it poses minimal threat to the male version of the sport. The female and male versions have unique rules and regulations (Cove, 2006).

Generally, experiences in many sports are different for men and women because the games are regulated differently for the two sexes. For instance, in women's hockey, players have never been allowed to body check in the same way that men do (Dumas, 2009). Women are allowed to "rub out" and bump opponents, but punishing hits are penalized. In men's hockey, violence and aggression are the norm. Most injuries occur within the rules, yet men are allowed and even encouraged to check in ways that contravene the rules of the sport.

CONCLUSION

The foregoing considerations suggest four conclusions. First, violence in sports is so widespread because it is highly profitable for sports organizations and the mass media, and because it reinforces still-dominant cultural standards of male behaviour. Second, although sports have traditionally been a male domain, female participation has increased significantly, especially since the 1960s. Third, although increased female participation in sports has challenged gender norms, it has not resulted in a reduction of violence among male athletes. That is because women have become involved in female versions of male sports—versions with different norms and regulations relating to violence. Fourth, it follows that only a decline in gender inequality in the larger society can significantly reduce sports violence. Greater equality between women and men in all institutional spheres would erode hegemonic masculinity, leading to demands for the reform of sports culture in a less violent direction. Sports organizations, the mass media, and athletes themselves would have to accede to these demands to retain fan loyalty and encourage growing participation in sports by both women and men.

REFERENCES

Adams, M. (2006). "The Game of Whose Lives? Gender, Race and Entitlement in Canada's "National" Game. In D. Whitson and R. Gruneau, eds., *Artificial Ice: Hockey, Culture, and Commerce* (pp. 71–84). Toronto: Broadview Press.

Coakley, J. and P. Donnelly. (2004). *Sports in Society: Issues and Contradictions,* 1st Cdn. ed. Toronto: McGraw-Hill Ryerson.

Coakley, J. and P. Donnelly. (2009). *Sports in Society: Issues and Contradictions,* 2nd Cdn. ed. Toronto: McGraw-Hill Ryerson.

Cove, Leslie Jean. (2006). *Negotiating the Ring: Reconciling Gender in Women's Boxing.* M.A. dissertation, University of Calgary. Retrieved 10 March 2012 from Dissertations and Theses at University of Calgary (Publication No. AAT MR19040).

"Crosby to Miss Third Straight Game; No Timetable for Return." (2011). *TSN.ca* 12 December. On the World Wide Web at http://www.tsn.ca /nhl/story/?id=382548 (retrieved 14 February 2012).

Crosset, T. and B. Beal. (1997). "The Use of 'Subculture' and 'Subworld' in Ethnographic Works on Sport: A Discussion of Definition Distinctions." *Sociology of Sport Journal, 14*, 73–85.

Donnelly, P. and K. Young. (1988). "The Construction and Confirmation of Identity in Sports Subcultures." *Sociology of Sport Journal, 5* (3), 223–40.

Dumas, S. (2009). *Reading the Play: Interpreting Violence in Canadian Ice Hockey.* Ph.D. dissertation, University of Calgary. Retrieved 10 March 2012, from Dissertations and Theses at University of Calgary. (Publication No. AAT NR64099).

Hall, M. (1999). "Creators of the Lost and Perfect Game? Gender, History, and Canadian Sport." In P. White and K. Young, eds., *Sport and Gender in Canada* (pp. 5–23). Toronto: Oxford University Press.

Hiller, H. (2006). *Canadian Society,* 5th ed. Toronto: Pearson Prentice-Hall.

Hughes, R. and J. Coakley. (1991). "Positive Deviance among Athletes: The Implications of Positive Deviance." *Sociology of Sport Journal, 8* (4), 307–25.

Kelly, C. (2011). "Kelly: Why Sidney Crosby Should Retire Now." *Toronto Star* 23 August. On the World Wide Web at http://www.thestar.com /article/1043394–sidney-s-return-a-risk-not-worth-taking (retrieved 30 January 2012).

McKee, A., R. Cantu, A. Nowinski, T. Hedley-Whyte, B. Gavett, A. Budson, V. Santini, H. Lee, C. Kubilus, and R. Stern. (2009). "Chronic Traumatic Encephalopathy in Athletes: Progressive Tauopathy Following Repetitive Head Injury." *Journal of Neuropathy and Experimental Neurology, 68* (7), 709–35.

Mirtle, J. (2011). "Savard's Career Likely Over." *Globe and Mail* 31 August. On the World Wide Web at http://www.theglobeandmail .com/sports/hockey/globe-on-hockey/savards-career-likely-over /article2148917/ (retrieved 22 February 2012).

Morrow, D., and K. Wamsley. (2010). *Sport in Canada: A History*, 2nd ed. Toronto: Oxford University Press.

Pfohl, S. (1994). *Images of Deviance and Social Control: A Sociological History.* New York: McGraw-Hill.

Probert, B. (2010). *Tough Guy: My Life on the Edge.* Toronto: Harper-Collins.

Smith, M. (1987). *Violence in Canadian Amateur Sport: A Review of Literature: Report for Commission for Fair Play.* Ottawa: Government of Canada.

Stevens, J. (2006). "Women's Hockey in Canada: After the 'Gold Rush.'" In D. Whitson and R. Gruneau, eds., *Artificial Ice: Hockey, Culture, and Commerce* (pp. 85–101). Toronto: Broadview Press.

Stevenson, C. (1991). "The Christian-Athlete: An Interactionist-Developmental Analysis." *Sociology of Sport Journal, 14* (3), 241–62.

Theberge, N. (2000). *Higher Goals: Women's Ice Hockey and the Politics of Gender.* Albany, NY: State University of New York Press.

Young, K. (1993). "Violence, Risk and Liability in Male Sports Culture." *Sociology of Sport Journal, 10,* 373–96.

Young, K. (2000). "Sports and Violence." In J. Coakley and E. Dunning, eds., *Handbook of Sports Studies* (pp. 382–408). London: Sage.

Chapter 22

News, Truth and the Problem of Corporate Crime:

THE CASE OF WESTRAY

JOHN L. MCMULLAN, St. Mary's University

INTRODUCTION

At 5:20 a.m. on May 9, 1992, an explosion ripped through a coalmine in Plymouth, Nova Scotia. It killed 26 miners. According to the report of the Westray Mine Public Inquiry, sparks from a mining machine ignited methane gas, causing a fire that created an explosion so strong that it blew the top off the mine entrance more than a mile above the blast centre (Richard, 1997). Nearly two decades after the explosion, the Westray mine disaster remains mired in controversy. Regulatory agencies filed 52 violations of the *Occupational Health and Safety Act* against the mine owner, Curragh Resources, and its managers, but dropped them in favour of criminal prosecution for manslaughter and criminal negligence (Jobb, 1994). The criminal trial, which cost an estimated $4.5 million, ended in a mistrial and the staying of all charges against the accused. The public inquiry, which cost an additional $4.8 million, concluded that the disaster "was a complex mosaic of actions, omissions, mistakes, incompetence, apathy, cynicism, stupidity, and neglect" (Richard, 1997, viii). However, criminal blame was never assigned. The Supreme Court of Canada concluded that the Nova Scotia Government could not be held accountable in civil court for the Westray deaths even if it did license and oversee an unsafe mine. To this day, the surviving miners and the families of the bereaved remain convinced that they lack answers to basic questions about the causes of the disaster and who was responsible for it. They believe that the medical examiner's office, the criminal justice system, the public inquiry, and the mass media have not adequately dug out the truth that lies buried deep beneath the mine disaster (Comish, 1993; Dodd, 1999; McMullan, 2005).

Source: From the *Canadian Journal of Criminology and Criminal Justice*, http://www.ccja-acjp .ca/en/, published by University of Toronto Press Incorporated. Reprinted by permission of University of Toronto Press Incorporated (www.utpjournals.com).

In this chapter, I examine how, between 1992 and 2002, the print media created news as a form of truth about the explosion. I analyze shifting media stories about Westray and study how the mass media produced and reproduced different "regimes of truth" about the disaster. I start by discussing the relationship between truth, power, and storytelling in the newsmaking process. I then outline the study's methodology. Next, I describe the findings of the research. Finally, I analyze the transformation of truth and story-telling in the news, highlighting the limitations of media reports of the disaster and their implication for the way Canadians understand corporate crime.

POWER, TRUTH, AND NEWS

The press produces and circulates what the public takes to be the truth. However, a variety of economic, social, and cultural factors influence the way it accomplishes this task. Advertising, business budgets, cultural priorities, and dominant beliefs enable, guide, and sustain the coverage of events, as do editorial politics, the subculture of journalism, and assumptions about audience interest (Barak, 1994; Reiner, 2002; Surette, 1998). Research shows that, when it comes to deviance and crime, these factors operate in such a way that newspapers over-represent the poor and those most vulnerable to labelling by authorities (Ericson et al., 1991; Kappeler et al., 2000). At the same time, they operate to underrepresent the misconduct of the powerful. For example, newspapers often protect corporate reputations by failing to provide frequent, prominent, and criminally oriented coverage of death, injury, and wrongdoing caused by corporations (Burns and Orrick, 2002; Evans and Lundman, 1983; Lynch et al., 2000; Wright et al., 1995). They do so by tending to place stories about business crime in the business section rather than on the front pages, where one is more likely to find stories about "street crime" (arson, homicide, burglary, and the like). They also tend to use the language of accidents, mistakes, and tragedies to talk about business crime, reserving the language of purposeful wrongdoing and evil to talk about "real" crime (Barak, 1994; Tombs and Whyte, 2001).

By helping to define what the public accepts as truthful, the operation of the mass media raises four important questions: "Who is able to tell the truth, about what, with what consequences, and with what relation to power?" (Foucault, 2001: 151). The press is typically involved in the production and circulation of *official* narratives and entire "regimes of truth" that define the limits and forms of what may be said (Foucault, 1980, 1991a, 1991b). Newspapers emphasize importance (public knowledge), immediacy (the present), interest (audience support), personalities (individuals), credibility (authoritative sources), sensationalism (good vs. evil), and recollection and retelling to frame the truth of events that journalists report and circulate as news (Fleras and Lock Kunz, 2001: 70).

Newspapers typically cite accredited experts whom journalists deem qualified to espouse truthful information about disasters, health, crime, the economy, and the like (Brown, 2004; Scraton et al., 1995). Experts create ways of seeing and thinking that act as "grids for the perception and evaluation of things" (Foucault, 1991b: 81): technical investigations, scientific studies, trial transcripts, public inquiry documents, and so on. By reporting expert claims, newspapers often render "views from above" credible, at the same time disputing and disqualifying "views from below." They deny views from below literally, by interpretation, by implication, and passively. *Literal denial* involves arranging damaging information into inaccurate or innocuous forms of story telling. *Interpretive denial* involves admitting the raw facts but developing a narrative framework that contests them. *Implicatory denial* involves recontextualizing events and excusing them as normal, justified, or necessary. *Passive denial* involves claiming that no problem really exists (Arendt, 1971; Cohen, 2001: 103–05).

Taken together, these four vocabularies of denial are manifestations of the exercise of power and the production of official truth. Significantly, however, official viewpoints do not always predominate. People may challenge official truth telling, and they sometimes do. For example, public inquiries and truth commissions—and their media accounts—can validate victims' experiences of harm and suffering, forcing powerful people to confront their misuse of power and their claim to be able to know and reproduce the truth (Gilligan and Pratt, 2004; Rotberg and Thompson, 2000). Accordingly, the news may be both an instrument of power and a starting point for opposition to power. It is possible to present news that confronts official truths in a language that promotes criticism and the need to know, and not in a conventional way that titillates and terrifies.

How, then, was the truth concerning the Westray mine disaster composed? What did the news report? What was written outside the ambit of official control? I now turn to these questions.

STUDYING WESTRAY THROUGH THE PRESS

I conducted a content analysis of newspaper accounts of the Westray mine disaster. Content analysis first involves identifying variables of interest and establishing explicit criteria for assigning values for each variable to texts, such as newspaper articles. Variables may include date of publication, source of information reported, type of narrative style used, and so on. Values for "source of information reported," for example, may be the police, the courts, corporate spokespersons, miners, and so on. I counted the frequency with which I found the values of each variable in each newspaper article. Finally, I evaluated these counts. That is, I explained their meaning in the context of larger events and social processes (Maxfield and Babbie, 2001; Neuman 2003).

I analyzed stories in the Halifax *Chronicle-Herald* because it is the most widely circulated and respected newspaper in Nova Scotia, it covered the Westray mine disaster systematically over a ten-year period, and it was easy to access electronically. Using "Westray" as a search term, I obtained a sample of 1972 news stories published between February 9, 1992 (six months before the explosion), and August 9, 2002 (six months after the explosion's tenth anniversary). These stories captured rescue efforts at the Westray mine, judicial actions following the disaster, the ten-year anniversary commemorating the explosion, and the final legal decision on civil compensation. I determined whether each story took the form of a report on a human tragedy, a tale of moral outrage and the need for social reform, an account of law and order, a description of political and regulatory failure, a testimony to legal disaster, a commentary on political economy, or some other form. This procedure allowed me to count the frequency with which each type of narrative or discourse occurred in three periods: February 1992 to December 1994, January 1995 to December 1997, and January 1998 to August 2002. Finally, for each story, I assessed whether journalists assigned cause, harm, blame, responsibility, intent, and morality in their coverage in the same way they typically do when reporting street crime—by connecting the event to organizational or interpersonal conditions and using a vocabulary of moral concern and accountability (Chermak, 1995; Cavender and Mulcahy, 1998; Tombs and Whyte, 2001; Wright et al., 1995).

NEWS, DISCOURSE, AND THE PRODUCTION OF THE WESTRAY MINE DISASTER STORY

Over the ten years covered by my analysis, almost half the stories about Westray appearing in the *Chronicle-Herald* appeared between 1992 and 1994. More than half the stories were in Section A and more than a fifth were front-page news. Seven of ten news stories were ordinary reports, followed in frequency by court reports (11 percent), editorials

(9 percent), feature stories (3 percent), cartoons (3 percent), other (2 percent), and entertainment (1 percent). Westray news was produced mainly by journalists (86 percent), followed by editors (6 percent), news wire services (4 percent), and the public in opinion pieces (4 percent).

The public inquiry into the Westray mine disaster concluded in late 1997. As the inquiry unfolded, the newsworthiness of the Westray story increased. Primary stories—stories that were lengthy and focused squarely on the explosion and its aftermath—increased from 73 percent to 83 percent of the total, even though the total number of stories declined from 939 to 671. Furthermore, the proportion of Section A stories increased from 49 percent to 54 percent while the proportion of front-page stories remained constant at about 24 percent. In contrast, from 1998 to 2002, primary focus and front-page coverage declined while the percentage of short stories increased. Thus, the end of the public inquiry in late 1997 precipitated a downturn in the newsworthiness of Westray, but as we will see, it also introduced a qualitative change in truth telling about the explosion and its aftermath, resulting in more critical, investigative journalism (McMullan and McClung, 2005).

The most prominent discourse in the overall news coverage was that of a legal disaster (31 percent). Reporters consistently covered the regulatory process, the criminal justice proceedings, and the constitutional conflicts over the trial and the public inquiry, and saw the Westray disaster primarily as a juridical fiasco. They used technical language to highlight the legal logic of the inquiry, thereby suppressing the violent effects of the explosion and distancing the corporation from the causes and sociolegal consequences of the event.

The next most common discourse was that of a human tragedy (17 percent). Here the press conveyed the message that death, grief, and suffering were the result of capricious causes: Westray was a "natural accident" in this news discourse. Coal was "in the blood" of the miners, and dying underground was a brave but necessary risk that miners knew and their families accepted. Westray was about "brave men toiling in the face of unseen dangers in the dark," where men went knowingly to meet their fate (*Chronicle-Herald*, May 11, 1992, C1).

Journalists also presented discourses of political economy and regulatory failure. About 13 percent of the news stories reported that the disaster was the result of wider economic conditions and government policy decisions that had foreseeable, harmful consequences. Another 13 percent of the coverage identified bureaucratic bungling and inspectorate incompetence for failure to prevent the disaster.

A discourse of moral judgment, condemning the loss of life and expressing incredulity over the sociolegal aftermath appeared in only 6 percent of the coverage, and only 10 percent of all news stories cast Westray within a law and order discourse signifying criminal conduct, offender/victim relationships, and criminal culpability.

As Table 22.1 shows, between 1992 and 1994, the political-economic, human-tragedy, and legal-regulatory discourses received the most coverage. However, this coverage drowned out the voices of the workers, magnified the voices of politicians and experts, and drew attention to inanimate natural forces rather than human organizational decisions as causing loss of life. Between 1995 and 1997, legal narratives more than doubled to 45 percent of the coverage, and the law-and-order discourse increased to 18 percent of the news. Hesitantly and with a narrow focus, the press started to define Westray as a crime story. Rather than investigating the culture of business and the mine operations, journalists conveyed the message that inept individuals functioning poorly in an otherwise responsible system of coal extraction and production caused the disaster. Even this nascent discourse of law and order declined to 7 percent of the coverage between 1998 and 2002, while the human tragedy and legal-regulatory discourses increased to 22 percent and 13 percent of the coverage, respectively. Despite the revelations of the criminal trial and the public inquiry, the press did not highlight safety and regulatory failure or develop a sustained crime narrative about the explosion and the loss of life.

TABLE 22.1 TYPE OF NEWS DISCOURSE BY TIME PERIOD (IN PERCENT)

TYPE OF NEWS DISCOURSE	FEB 92–DEC 94	JAN 95–DEC 97	JAN 98–AUG 02
Human tragedy	21.8	8.7	21.8
Moral outrage and social reform	4.1	4.3	14.6
Law and order	5.1	17.6	6.6
Political and regulatory failure	13.7	12.4	13
Legal disaster	20.7	45.4	33.2
Political economy	24.6	2.4	4.7
Other	10.0	9.2	6.1
Total	100.0	100.0	100.0
Frequency	939	671	362

SOURCE: Reprinted with permission from University of Toronto Press (www.utpjournals.com).

When we consider how the mass media typically create a "news crime frame" to report murder, manslaughter, and aggravated assault, we discover that they behaved differently in reporting the Westray deaths. Fully 70 percent of news stories between 1992 and 1994 did not even mention causes, increasing to 85 percent in the period 1998–2002. However, a minority of stories continued framing the explosion in the idiom of individual responsibility. Almost entirely absent in the reportage was any mention of organizational causes related to the goals, operating procedures, and environment of the company. The press told the story of the harm caused by the explosion and its aftermath. Several stories focused on death and emphasized the sacrifice and suffering that bereaved families endured with grace and dignity. Others documented the effects of the explosion on family and friends. However, the most striking finding is the degree to which news stories failed to mention harm at all—a tendency that increased over time. Even when harm was discussed, it was usually framed in an emotional vocabulary of sudden shocking death—"a history of hope and fortitude and heartbreak in the face of unbearable tragedies" (*Chronicle-Herald*, May 11, 1992, C1). Only later can one detect the language of preventable harm—"no accountability," "bureaucratic errors," "the frustration of the bereaved with the Nova Scotia justice system," and the like (*Chronicle-Herald*, May 8, 1997, C1).

Any attribution of blame and responsibility was absent in 75 percent of the news coverage, and mention of business culpability was even rarer. When journalists brought up blame and responsibility, they were usually ambiguous about who was accountable for the disaster. Between 1992 and 1994, reporters tended to blame senior politicians or a combination of sources, such as mine managers and politicians, but not corporate executives. Between 1995 and 1997, attributions of responsibility shifted to middle-level mine managers and regulatory officials. Between 1998 and 2002, 85 percent of news reports did not assign responsibility for the explosion at all. A relatively small number of news stories expressed the need for criminal resolution (increasing from 4 percent to 7 percent of all stories between 1992 and 2002), regulatory improvement (increasing from 1 percent to 3 percent over the ten-year period), and public reform (increasing from 0 percent to 9 percent). However, unlike the reporting of street crime, which highlights and dramatizes harm, blame, cause, intent, and moral messages, the reporting of the Westray disaster did not involve the construction of a new crime frame (Cavender and Mulcahy, 1998).

The sources of information that reporters tapped influenced what they emphasized in their stories, as Table 22.2 suggests. Between 1992 and 1994, political and government representatives were most frequently cited in the news (in 32 percent of stories), followed by citizens (16 percent), legal sources (14 percent), corporate sources (13 percent), and regulatory sources (9 percent). Legal sources were cited more frequently between 1995 and 1998 (in 39 percent of stories), and the frequency with which other sources were consulted declined proportionately. Between 1998 and 2002, political sources (18 percent of stories) and government sources (15 percent) returned to prominence, sharing importance with already dominant legal sources (22 percent). In short, journalists valued legal experts as the primary definers of truth. As a result, stories tended to criticize judicial proceedings, debate the disclosure of trial documents, argue the constitutionality of criminal prosecution and public inquiry proceedings, and discuss civil compensation entitlements. They tended *not* to consult engineers, mining consultants, academics, medical experts, miners, spouses of the deceased, and spokespersons for the Westray Families Group. The latter were relegated to the status of minor claims-makers in the truth telling process.

How can one account for this production of Westray's truth? Why was the Westray disaster framed largely in a discourse of legality? What limits were placed on the press's ability to tell the truth? I address these questions next.

TABLE 22.2 NEWS SOURCE BY TIME PERIOD (IN PERCENT)

NEWS SOURCE	FEB 92–DEC 94	JAN 95–DEC 97	JAN 98–AUG 02
Company	10.6	6.9	2.1
Regulatory	8.9	8.0	9.0
Police	3.1	3.1	0.8
Legal	13.7	38.7	21.5
Expert	3.6	6.6	2.9
Citizen	15.7	13.7	12.8
Politician	18.4	5.5	17.6
Government	13.4	8.7	15.1
Labour	6.0	2.3	8.2
Private industry	2.6	3.5	7.7
Other	2.9	1.6	2.1
Unknown	1.1	1.4	0.2
Total	100.0	100.0	100.0
Frequency	1462	866	522

SOURCE: Reprinted with permission from University of Toronto Press (www.utpjournals.com).

REGIMES OF TRUTH, STATES OF DENIAL, AND CORPORATE VIOLENCE

What was said about the Westray disaster, by whom, and in what words, changed over time. In the immediate aftermath of the explosion, corporate spokespersons were the main claims-makers. They tied reporters to their version of events by managing the release of information and circulating their version of the truth. Although corporate language was caring and compassionate, it disguised reality through euphemism and misdirection. By the corporation's account, the victims were "courageous workers" employed at a mine where "everything physically and humanly possible to guard against dangerous conditions" was in place and where the explosion occurred without "warnings of any kind." Corporate spokespersons thus portrayed the explosion as unforeseeable and claimed they did not understand how it happened. Ample evidence pointed to Westray's questionable mining practices, its troubled safety record, its political involvement in licensing the mine and receiving government loans, market incentives, and tax breaks, and government reluctance to take action against health and safety violations well before the explosion. However, the press downplayed this evidence, creating a story about an "accidental tragedy" and maintaining it for a decade (Glasbeek and Tucker, 1999; Hynes and Prasad, 1999; Wilde, 1999).

The press did develop a more critical, political-economy discourse of the explosion in the early years, drawing connections between regional development, high unemployment rates, and risky capital investments. However, corporate and state officials nimbly contained this radical approach. They contested and deflected attention from economic and business factors by deploying literal denial strategies, emphasizing that Westray was a natural, not a corporate, tragedy. By 1995, human-tragedy narratives faced criticism. Revelations of regulatory problems and talk of criminal prosecution realigned relations between journalists and their sources. The validity of the "natural accident" frame was undercut by inconsistencies and contradictions in the information provided by official news sources. Reporters then reworked the truth, using a vocabulary of legal suspicion and political disgrace. Still, the media rarely acknowledged the larger problem of corporate violence in the workplace. Both before and after the criminal trial and the public inquiry, reporters routinely disqualified discussions of criminal culpability. The press "refused to call the explosion a 'homicide' and rarely if ever followed up on this issue with any investigative reports" (Goff, 2001: 210).

Another discursive shift occurred when journalists started talking to family members of the bereaved, miners, union representatives, and scientific experts. These sources opened up new points of contention with the official story, challenging the "accident" and "legal disaster" narratives. A subversive tone in news reports during and after the public inquiry emphasized state arrogance, bureaucratic mistakes, regulatory wrongdoings, and official cover-ups (*Chronicle-Herald*, May 3, 1996, A3; May 16, 1996, A1). Unable to sustain literal denials, corporate and state officials now switched to legalistic and political rationalizations. They admitted the raw facts of the disaster—"it was man made"—but denied that they precipitated it. Such interpretive denial allowed powerful elites to refuse to take any blame for the tragedy (*Chronicle-Herald*, May 31, 1996, C1).

Some corporate officials, politicians, and regulators attempted to exonerate themselves by deploying implicatory denial tactics. They attacked the credibility of victims and the bereaved ("The mine blew up because of what happened that morning and not because of negligence or malfeasance"). They condemned the inquiry for bias ("They just want to blame someone so they are blaming us"). And they excused their actions through appeals to a higher morality ("We had to cut corners in order to meet production quotas") (*Chronicle-Herald*, May 29, 1996, C1; May 31, 1996, C1). Other corporate officials resorted to "passive denial." They avoided their critics and evaded the press as best they could. They signalled the absence of a problem when their version of truth was met with disbelief. They saw no need for dialogue with the rest of society and condemned the public inquiry as a "railroad job and a farce" (*Chronicle-Herald*, April 18, 1996, A1). The CEO of Curragh Resources explained his refusal to appear before the inquiry with the following assertion: "They just want to label me.... They are probably not even interested in what I have to say" (*Chronicle-Herald*, September 6, 1997, A2).

The press developed an increasingly skeptical take on official accounts of the Westray disaster. A new cluster of assertions on the theme of state and corporate moral bankruptcy emerged. Now the press spoke of "abuse of authority," "mismanagement," "government incompetence," "refusal to acknowledge mistakes," "blaming underlings," "hiding behind the skirts of its lawyers' gowns," and "covering up their actions" (*Chronicle-Herald*, January 1, 1998, B1). This new regime of truth—"Westray as a political scandal"—validated the miners' experience, disclosed anomalous acts of the powerful, criticized government for deceit and dishonesty, and enabled the perception that the Westray disaster was above all else an "abuse of trust" insofar as state overseers concealed recklessness and negligence, neutralized corporate malfeasance, and failed to deliver fairness and justice to victims.

Still, these new representations of the truth failed to acknowledge corporate crime. The media produced its own version of interpretive denial: What happened at Westray was not a calculated crime waiting to happen but a natural tragedy and a legal disaster. The *corporate* origins of death in the workplace were defined not as the result of a questionable business plan but of the actions of poorly trained managers and overseers. The causes of the explosion were not *structural* but a case of individuals playing politics or not doing their jobs properly in the context of a risky capitalist venture. The loss of life at Westray was not *crime*, but "a disgrace," "an abuse of office," and "business wrongdoing." The press eventually developed a critical "view from below" but did not see the corporation as capable of homicide (Slapper and Tombs, 1999). "What crime?" asked the press, thus helping to reinforce corporate crime as a blind spot in popular culture.

REFERENCES

Arendt, H. (1971). Between Past and Future: Eight Exercises in Political Thought. New York: Viking Press.

Barak, G. (1994). "Media, Society and Criminology." In G. Barak, ed., *Media, Process, and the Social Construction of Crime: Studies in Newsmaking Criminology* (pp. 3–45). New York: Garland Publishing.

Brown, D. (2004). "Royal Commissions and Criminal Justice: Behind the Ideal." In George Gilligan and John Pratt, eds., *Crime, Truth and Justice: Official Inquiry, Discourse, Knowledge* (pp. 26–45). Cullompton, UK: Willan Publishing.

Burns, R.G., and L. Orrick. (2002). "Assessing Newspaper Coverage of Corporate Violence: The Dance Hall Fire in Goteborg, Sweden." *Critical Criminology, 11,* 137–50.

Cavender, G., and A. Mulcahy. (1998). "Trial by Fire: Media Constructions of Corporate Deviance." *Justice Quarterly, 15,* 697–717.

Chermak, S. (1995). "Crime in the News Media: A Refined Understanding of How Crimes Become News." In G. Barak, ed., *Media, Process, and the Social Construction of Crime: Studies in Newsmaking Criminology* (pp. 95–129). New York: Garland Publishing.

Cohen, S. (2001). States of Denial: Knowing About Atrocities and Suffering. Cambridge, UK: Polity Press.

Comish, S. (1993). *The Westray Tragedy: A Miner's Story.* Halifax, NS: Fernwood Publishing.

Dodd, S. (1999). "Unsettled Accounts after Westray." In C. McCormick, ed., *The Westray Chronicles: A Case Study in Corporate Crime* (pp. 218–49). Halifax, NS: Fernwood Publishing.

Ericson, R., P. Baranek, and J. Chan. (1991). *Representing Order: Crime, Law and Justice in the News Media.* Toronto: University of Toronto Press.

Evans, S.S. and R.J. Lundman. (1983). "Newspaper Coverage of Corporate Price-Fixing." *Criminology, 21* (4), 529–41.

Fleras, A., and J. Lock Kunz. (2001). *Media and Minorities: Representing Diversity in a Multicultural Canada.* Toronto: Thompson Educational Publishing.

Foucault, M. (1980). "Two Lectures." In C. Gordon, ed., *Power/Knowledge: Selected Interviews and Other Writings (1972–1977)* (pp. 79–107). New York: Pantheon Books.

Foucault, M. (1991a). "Politics and the Study of Discourse." In G. Burchell, C. Gordon, and P. Miller, eds., *The Foucault Effect: Studies in Governmentality* (pp. 53–71). Chicago: University of Chicago Press.

Foucault, M. (1991b). "Questions of Method." In G. Burchell, C. Gordon, and P. Miller, eds., *The Foucault Effect: Studies in Governmentality* (pp. 73–86). Chicago: University of Chicago Press.

Foucault, M. (2001). *Fearless Speech.* Los Angeles: Semiotexte.

Gilligan, G. and J. Pratt, eds. (2004). *Crime, Truth and Justice Official Inquiry, Discourse, Knowledge.* Cullompton, UK: Willan Publishing.

Glasbeek, H. and E. Tucker. (1999). "Death by Consensus at Westray?" In C. McCormick, ed., *The Westray Chronicles: A Case Study in Corporate Crime* (pp. 71–96). Halifax, NS: Fernwood Publishing.

Goff, C. (2001). "The Westray Mine Disaster: Media Coverage of a Corporate Crime in Canada." In H.N. Pontell and D. Shichor, eds., *Contemporary Issues in Crime and Criminal Justice: Essays in Honor of Gilbert Geis* (pp. 195–212). Saddlewood Creek, NJ: Prentice-Hall.

Hynes, T. and P. Prasad. (1999). "The Normal Violation of Safety Rules." In C. McCormick, ed., *The Westray Chronicles: A Case Study in Corporate Crime* (pp. 117–34). Halifax, NS: Fernwood Publishers.

Jobb, D. (1994). *Calculated Risk: Greed, Politics and the Westray Tragedy.* Halifax, NS: Nimbus Publishing.

Kappeler, V.E., M. Blumberg, and G. Potter, eds. (2000). *The Mythology of Crime and Criminal Justice*, 3rd ed. Prospect Heights, IL: Waveland.

Lynch, M.J., P. Stretesky, and P. Hammond. (2000). "Media Coverage of Chemical Crimes, Hillsborough County, Florida, 1987–1997." *British Journal of Criminology, 27,* 16–29.

Maxfield, M.G. and E. Babbie. (2001). *Research Methods for Criminal Justice and Criminology.* Belmont, CA: Wadsworth.

McMullan, J. and M. McClung. (2005). "The Media, the Politics of Truth and the Coverage of Corporate Violence: The Westray Disaster and the Public Inquiry." *Critical Criminology: An International Journal, 14,* 67–86.

McMullan, J. (2005). *News, Truth and Crime: The Westray Disaster and Its Aftermath.* Halifax, NS: Fernwood.

Neuman, L.W. (2003). *Social Research Methods: Qualitative and Quantitative Approaches,* 5th ed. New York: Allyn and Bacon.

Reiner, R. (2002). "Media Made Criminology: The Representation of Crime in the Mass Media." In M. Maguire, R. Morgan, and R. Reiner, eds., *The Oxford Handbook of Criminology* (pp. 376–415). London: Oxford Press.

Richard, P. (1997). *The Westray Story: A Predictable Path to Disaster: Report of the Westray Mine Public Inquiry.* Halifax, NS: Westray Mine Public Inquiry.

Rotberg, R.I. and D. Thompson, eds. (2000). *Truth Vs Justice: The Morality of Truth Commissions.* New Jersey: Princeton University Press.

Scraton, P., A. Jemphrey, and S. Coleman. (1995). *No Last Rights: The Denial of Justice and the Promotion of Myth in the Aftermath of the Hillsborough Disaster.* Liverpool, Ireland: CC Alden Press.

Slapper, G. and S. Tombs. (1999). *Corporate Crime.* Harlow: Longman.

Surette, R. (1998). *Media, Crime and Criminal Justice: Images and Realities.* Belmont, CA: West/Wadsworth.

Tombs, S., and D. Whyte. (2001). "Reporting Corporate Crime Out of Existence." *Criminal Justice Matters, 43,* 22–23.

Wilde, G.J.S. (1999). "The Awareness and Acceptance of Risk at Westray." In C. McCormick, ed., *The Westray Chronicles: A Case Study in Corporate Crime* (pp. 97–116). Halifax, NS: Fernwood Publishing.

Wright, J.P., F.T. Cullen, and M.B. Blankenship. (1995). "The Social Construction of Corporate Violence: Media Coverage of the Imperial Food Products Fire." *Crime and Delinquency, 41,* 20–36.

PART 6

GLOBAL DEVELOPMENT AND THE ENVIRONMENT

The two main social problems facing the world today concern global development and the environment.

Some parts of the world, notably China, have undergone development over the past few decades—**development** is defined here as an increase in people's standard of living, opportunities for cultural and spiritual growth, and control over their own lives. However, as William I. Robinson argues in Chapter 23, if we examine the world as a whole, the picture is less rosy. In fact, Robinson considers development on a global scale to be largely a fantasy.

From 1945 (the end of World War II) to 1973 (when oil prices tripled because of war in the Middle East), different development models existed in different parts of the world, but all were based on national governments redistributing wealth to their citizens. At one extreme were communist governments, which controlled and redistributed nearly all wealth in the countries where they ruled. At the other extreme were capitalist democracies, which developed social welfare services and, when recession hit, borrowed and spent money to stimulate the economy. (British economist John Maynard Keynes first proposed such government economic intervention, so these policies are often termed "Keynesian.")

However, since the 1970s, economic policies have moved in the direction of **neoliberalism**, a set of economic policies that seeks to create a worldwide market for capital and trade flows free of government interference. For example, the elimination of restrictions on investment now allows corporations to invest where labour is cheapest, resulting in the deindustrialization of high-wage regions. To compete for investment, high-wage regions limit state benefits, keep wages in check, and turn full-time jobs into part-time and seasonal jobs, resulting in a deteriorating standard of living for many people. Some people in the world's less developed countries benefit from increased investment, but most do not. In many less developed countries, per capita income is declining, inequality is growing, and undemocratic governments follow neoliberal dogma by ending subsidies for water, health care, transportation, and other necessities. Robinson argues that only a more redistributive approach can reverse the course of global development, and finds hope in the popular revolt underway in some parts of the world for global justice.

The second major social problem confronting the world today concerns the sorry state of the natural environment.

The Industrial Revolution began in Great Britain about 240 years ago. Nature seemed exploitable without limit, a thing to be subdued and dominated in the name of economic progress and human development. In the last few decades, however, circumstances have forced a growing number of people to recognize that industrial-era attitudes toward nature are not just naive, but arrogant and dangerous. For example, since the Industrial Revolution, humans have been using increasing quantities of fossil fuels (coal, oil, gasoline, etc.). When burned, they release carbon dioxide into the atmosphere. The accumulation of carbon dioxide allows more solar radiation to enter the atmosphere and less solar radiation to escape. The result of this "greenhouse effect" is global warming and potentially catastrophic climactic change, including the partial melting of the polar ice caps, the release of methane from melting permafrost (methane is a more efficient heat-trapping gas than carbon dioxide), and the flooding of heavily populated coastal regions.

Some scientists dispute that global warming is taking place. Others insist that global warming is not "anthropogenic," that is, caused at least partly by human activity. Coal and oil producing companies fund many global warming sceptics. (Decades ago, a big tobacco company funded at least one of the leading skeptics to deny that smoking causes cancer.) In any case, the skeptics constitute only a small minority of the world's climate scientists. Chapter 24 explains the consensus view. It is a summary of the findings of the 2007 report of the Intergovernmental Panel on Climate Change (IPCC). The IPCC is an organization set up by the World Meteorological Organization and the United Nations Environment Programme (UNEP). It organizes hundreds of leading climate scientists all over the world to review research and write periodic reports summarizing the state of knowledge about climate change. The 2007 report finds strong evidence for a warming world climate (especially in the North), the contribution of human activity to climate change, and the devastating consequences of climate change for life on the planet. It also makes sound recommendations for adapting to climate change and mitigating it. It seems that humanity has time to avoid the worst consequences of global climate change if it is prepared to step up international cooperation, but acting won't come cheap, requiring much sacrifice and money, especially from the world's rich countries.

It is unclear whether we are willing to pay. However, one thing is clear. To the degree that people continue to think of themselves as members of a particular nation, class, or race, and not as part of humanity as a whole, the IPCC recommendations will have little consequence. In that event, many citizens of the privileged countries will believe that it is in their self-interest to limit aid to the less industrialized countries, use just as many scarce resources as they want to and can afford, and object to the imposition of high taxes on fossil fuels. They will be blind to the fact that such a narrow definition of self-interest may devastate humanity.

Much now depends on whether we will be able to think and act as members of a single human group whose members share a common interest in survival. If we fail to take such a global view, if we insist instead on fighting to protect our narrow group privileges rather than humanity's general interest, we may not go the way of the dinosaurs. However, future generations will likely suffer an existence that is nastier, more brutish, and shorter than that which we now enjoy. In Chapter 25, Michael Burawoy, president of the International Sociological Association, explains how sociology can help to prevent that outcome.

GLOSSARY

Development takes place when most people's standard of living, opportunities for cultural and spiritual growth, and control over their own lives increase.

Neoliberalism is a set of policies that seeks to create a worldwide market for capital and trade flows free of government interference.

CRITICAL THINKING QUESTIONS

1. How does the industrialization of less developed countries make it more difficult to protect the global environment?

2. Is it possible to reconcile the industrialization of the less developed countries with the protection of the global environment? If so, how? If not, why not?

3. What role can public sociology play in preventing the catastrophic scenario outlined in this unit's Introduction?

ANNOTATED BIBLIOGRAPHY

Benjamin R. Barber, *Jihad vs. McWorld: How Globalism and Tribalism Are Reshaping the World* (New York: Ballantine, 1996). This work incisively analyzes the central conflict of our times.

Lester R. Brown, *World on the Edge: How to Prevent Environmental and Economic Collapse* (New York: Norton, 2011). This book outlines the policies needed to counteract environmental decline and economic collapse.

Eric Hobsbawm, *Age of Extremes: The Short Twentieth Century, 1914–1991* (London: Abacus, 1994). It's long, it's opinionated, and it's a masterpiece by one of the world's greatest historians. Magnificently expands our understanding of global twentieth-century development and thereby provides a foundation for understanding our century.

Chapter 23

The Chimera of Democracy and Development

WILLIAM I. ROBINSON,
University of California, Santa Barbara

Globalization is the next phase in the evolution of world capitalism. It is characterized by the rise of a new system of production and finances that transcends nation-states, a truly transnational capitalist class, and new supranational legal and political institutions.

This new global capitalism can be distinguished from the nation-based capitalism that took the form of Keynesian "New Deals" and social democracies in the First World, state ("socialist") redistributive models in the Second World, and diverse developmental models in the Third World. Each of these earlier national, corporate models involved state intervention in the economy and some degree of social redistribution.

All three experienced breakdowns in the wake of the world economic crisis of the 1970s. By "going global" at this moment, capital managed to break free of state regulation and the need to redistribute the surplus it had previously appropriated through progressive tax structures and the social wage, labor laws, and stable employment and benefits for workers.

The policies that compose this new global model include fiscal austerity, privatization, deregulation, and trade liberalization. Often labeled "neoliberalism," this new model seeks to create the conditions for the free operation of capital within and across state borders and to harmonize the macroeconomic environment everywhere—in short, to create a single unified field for global capitalism.

As this globalized, market-driven order took hold in the 1980s and 1990s, the logic of global accumulation supplanted that of national accumulation. Insurgent transnational elites captured state power in many countries and implemented sweeping policy changes. They also

Source: From "Democracy and Development in the Global South," Contexts Forum, "The chimera of democracy and development" by William I. Robinson, *Contexts 7(2)*, 2008, pp. 74–77. © 2008 by the American Sociological Association. Reprinted by Permission of SAGE Publications.

helped create an international legal regulatory structure for the new global, capitalist economy.

These transformations restored the prospects for global accumulation so significantly that many economists and some social scientists claimed neoliberalism launched a new era of "development" processes after the crisis of the 1970s. However, this renewed global accumulation was made possible by the cheapening and manipulability of labor worldwide—including a decline in income and downward mobility for most and a stunning contraction in consumption for the poorest.

The shift in worldwide production from local and national to global markets meant domestic markets were no longer strategic or even necessary for the reproduction (or self-expansion) of capital. Indeed, in the new systems of global production and exchange, capital no longer needs to pay for the reproduction of labor power in order to reproduce itself. Under these conditions, development is a fantasy.

In the sociological view, development refers to a process in which masses of people experience an improvement in their living standards, opportunities for cultural and spiritual growth, and the ability to exercise a modicum of control over their lives. It means access to decent housing, health care, education, running water, adequate nutrition, an environment that is not degraded, community security, and time for poetry and for love. What little development took place earlier in the twentieth century has been largely undone by neoliberalism.

British economist Alan Freeman reports that in 1980, 118 million people lived in nine countries where income per capita was declining, whereas in 1998 there were 60 such countries and 1.3 billion such people. Annual United Nations reports inform us that just 20 percent of the world's population now monopolizes 85 percent of the world's wealth, while the remaining 80 percent of the world's population must make do with 15 percent of the wealth and the poorest 20 percent with just 1 percent.

Most work is now contingent—casualized, informalized, and flexibilized. Un- and underemployment have swollen the ranks of a new global underclass locked out of the global economy—nearly one-third of the world's economically active population, according to the International Labour Organization. Health care, education, water, electricity, transportation, housing, and other necessities of life are being commodified—privatized and turned into for-profit activities out of reach for many.

North and south are no longer geographic coordinates. Now they are power relations between the global rich and the global poor. The north-south divide has grown and so, too, have new transnational inequalities and social hierarchies. Social polarization cuts across national lines as well. New elites, middle classes, and high-consumption sectors are uplifted from their national contexts as they become incorporated into the global cornucopia. Their affluence and visibility gives the misleading impression that "development" is actually taking place.

Sociologists have long noted the inverse relation between democracy and inequality: as inequality rises, democracy deteriorates and society experiences social decay, political violence, authoritarian systems of social control, and militarization. The social fabric is unraveling in many countries and the world, and many are experiencing a breakdown of order. More to the point, the concentration of economic power leads to the concentration of political influence and is the antithesis of democracy. Democracy and development are about power relations, about who controls society's material and cultural resources, how wealth and power are distributed locally and globally.

In this age of globalization, development isn't possible without a democratization of social life—and democracy isn't possible without a model of development that broadly redistributes wealth and power in global society. Development, moreover, requires the intervention of a political authority in the accumulation process in order to renew, redistribute, and reorient productive resources toward poor majorities. For democracy and development, in other words, there must be mechanisms to rein in transnational capital, assert social and political controls over unfettered market forces, and redistribute wealth globally.

The replacement of neoliberal, global capitalism with a new, more redistributive approach won't come about by the generosity or good sense of ruling groups but by the global revolt from below that is already underway. Popular forces from the global justice movement are demanding the substantive democratization of global society.

Chapter 24

Climate Change: Causes Impact, Solution:

INTERGOVERNMENTAL PANEL O CLIMATE CHANG

In 1988, the World Meteorological Organization and the United Nations Environment Programme created the Intergovernmental Panel on Climate Change (IPCC) to assess what we know about climate change, its impact, and options for dealing with it. In 2007, the IPCC published its fourth assessment. Leading climate scientists— about 500 lead authors and 2000 expert reviewers—contributed to the four-volume report. This article outlines its main findings. The IPCC report focused on projections with a high probability of occurrence and conclusions in which researchers expressed a high level of confidence.

CAUSES OF CHANGE

It is unequivocal that global warming, as measured by global average air and ocean temperatures, widespread melting of snow and ice, and rising global average sea level, has been occurring since the mid-20th century. Global warming is very likely due to the observed increase in greenhouse gas emissions resulting from the burning of fossil fuels by humans. The emission of such gasses—especially carbon dioxide, methane, and nitrous oxide—has grown since pre-industrial times, with an increase of 70 percent between 1970 and 2004. During the past 50 years, solar and volcanic forces would likely have produced cooling were it not for greenhouse gas emissions caused by humans.

PROJECTED CLIMATE CHANGE AND ITS IMPACT

Continued greenhouse gas emissions at or above current rates will cause further warming and induce many changes in the global climate system during the 21st century. For the next two decades, a warming

Source: This summary, prepared by Robert Brym, is based on Intergovernmental Panel on Climate Change (2007), "Synthesis Report Summary for Policymakers," *Climate Change 2007: Synthesis Report,* http://www.ipcc.ch/publications_and_data/ar4/syr/en/spm.html (retrieved July 13, 2011).

of about 0.2°C per decade is likely to occur. By 2095, global average surface temperature is likely to be 1.8 to 4.0°C warmer than in 1990, while the sea level is likely to be 18 to 59 cm higher.

Warming will be greatest over land and at most high northern latitudes and least over southern oceans and parts of the North Atlantic. Snow cover area will continue contracting. Thaw depth will increase over most permafrost regions and the extent of sea ice will decrease. In some projections, Arctic late-summer sea ice disappears almost entirely by the latter part of the 21st century. It is very likely that hot extremes, heat waves, and heavy precipitation will increase. It is likely that tropical cyclones will increase in intensity, but not necessarily in frequency. Extra-tropical storms will likely shift towards the poles, and it is very likely that precipitation will increase in high latitudes while decreasing in most subtropical land regions.

High confidence exists that by mid-century, annual river runoff and water availability will increase at high latitudes and in some tropical wet areas, and decrease in some dry regions in the mid-latitudes and tropics. There is also high confidence that many semi-arid areas (the Mediterranean basin, western United States, southern Africa, and northeast Brazil) will suffer a decrease in water resources.

Climate change is likely to strongly affect tundra, boreal forest, and mountain regions because of sensitivity to warming; Mediterranean-type ecosystems because of reduction in rainfall; tropical rainforests where precipitation declines; mangroves, salt marshes, and coral reefs due to multiple stresses; the sea ice biome because of sensitivity to warming; water resources in some dry regions at mid-latitudes and in the dry tropics, due to changes in rainfall and the water cycle, and in areas that depend on snow and ice melt; agriculture in low latitudes, due to reduced water availability; low-lying coastal systems, due to threat of sea level rise and increased risk from extreme weather events; human health in populations with low adaptive capacity; the Arctic, because of the impacts of high rates of projected warming on natural systems and human communities; Africa, because of low adaptive capacity and projected climate change impacts; small islands, where population and infrastructure are exposed to projected climate change impacts; and Asian and African mega-deltas, due to large populations and high exposure to sea level rise, storm surges, and river flooding.

Since 1750, oceans have become more acidic because of the uptake of carbon. Projections suggest a reduction in average global surface ocean pH of between 0.14 and 0.35 units over the 21st century.

While the effects of observed ocean acidification on the marine biosphere are undocumented, progressive acidification is expected to have negative impacts on marine shell-forming organisms and their dependent species.

Human-caused warming could lead to some abrupt or irreversible impacts, including partial loss of ice sheets on polar land, resulting in meters of sea level rise; and major changes in coastlines and inundation of low-lying areas, with greatest effects in river deltas and low-lying islands. Such changes are projected to occur over millennial time scales, but more rapid sea level rise on century time scales cannot be excluded.

Medium confidence exists that approximately 20–30 percent of species assessed so far are likely to be at increased risk of extinction if increases in global average warming exceed 1.5–2.5°C relative to 1980–99. As global average temperature increase exceeds about 3.5°C, model projections suggest significant extinctions (40–70 percent of species assessed).

Low latitude and less developed areas generally face greater risk from the consequences of climate change than do high latitude and more developed areas. In high latitude and more developed areas, the poor and the elderly face greater risk from the consequences of climate change than other people do.

ADAPTATION AND MITIGATION

We must simultaneously mitigate global warming and adapt to the warming that is bound to occur. Given current policies aimed at mitigating climate change and encouraging sustainable development, global greenhouse gas emissions will continue to grow over the next few decades. Even if greenhouse gases concentration stabilizes, human-caused warming and sea level rise would continue for centuries.

A wide array of adaptation options is available, but more extensive adaptation than is currently occurring is required to reduce vulnerability to climate change. These adaptations include changes in lifestyle, behaviour patterns, and management practices. Recommended mitigation actions include trillions of dollars of investment in low-carbon energy infrastructure, the implementation of carbon emission targets, and an effective tax on carbon emissions. Such actions would have near-term benefits, such as improved health due to reduced air pollution, that may offset a substantial fraction of costs. Mitigating global greenhouse gas emissions in coming decades could offset the projected growth of global emissions or reduce emissions below current levels.

There exists high confidence that neither adaptation nor mitigation alone can avoid all climate change impacts. However, the two strategies can complement each other and together can significantly reduce the risks of climate change. In the long term, unmitigated climate change would likely exceed the capacity of natural, managed, and human systems to adapt. Early mitigation actions would avoid further locking in carbon intensive infrastructure and reduce climate change and associated adaptation needs. Many impacts can be reduced, delayed, or avoided by mitigation. Delayed emission reductions significantly constrain the opportunities to achieve lower stabilization levels and increase the risk of more severe climate change impacts. Experts estimate that the cost of achieving minimally acceptable stabilization of carbon concentrations would lower annual global GDP growth by 0.12 percent.

Chapter 25

The Future of Sociology

MICHAEL BURAWOY

University of California, Berkeley

A wave of marketization is sweeping the world. Entities that used to be embedded in human bodies, communities, and nature are being ripped out of their habitats, appropriated by new classes of merchants, and sold in chains of markets that stretch across the globe. This is not the first wave of marketization; it is not the first time markets have expanded their reach by turning common goods and public services into new commodities. The Industrial Revolution of the nineteenth century worked through a similar global expansion in the marketization of labour and its products. The financial revolution of the twentieth century turned money into a full-blown commodity, eventually threatening the very viability of markets. The ecological transformation that now besets us digs even deeper, making land, water, air, and genes the subject of market exchange, thereby threatening human existence.

So far, each wave of marketization has set in motion a countermovement, erecting institutions to regulate, channel, and contain commodification. Yet each wave also swept away the ramparts erected against the previous wave. Under demolition today are rights won by Western labour movements against the marketization of the nineteenth century (such as the right to form unions) and the social rights guaranteed by states against the marketization of the twentieth century (the provision of minimum standards of economic security). In the end, nothing seems immune to the third wave of marketization. Will there be a countermovement strong enough to contain its destructive powers?

Behind the third wave are predatory classes colluding with nation-states and sometimes also with multilateral agencies, such as the World Bank and the International Monetary Fund, imposing their will on the desperate and the destitute, on workers, students, farmers, and the middle class. The last holdout against this economic storm is society itself, or more precisely civil society, composed of *associations* with a measure of collective self-regulation, *movements* forged out of a collective will, and *publics* of mutual recognition and communication. Will society measure up to the challenge? What role can sociology play in meeting it?

SOCIOLOGY VERSUS THE MARKET

If there is a common thread to sociology's diverse traditions, it is opposition to the reduction of society to a market. Whether it is Marx's critique of capitalism, Durkheim's critique of the abnormal forms of the division of labour, Weber's critique of rationalism, or Parsons's critique of utilitarianism, each tradition opposes market reductionism, albeit from different viewpoints. Today, it is even more important for sociology to continue its tradition of opposing market reductionism as commodification actually threatens to destroy society and with it human existence. In meeting this challenge, sociologists can join one of four groups of practitioners:

1. *Policy sociologists* help to formulate policies that side with the state against the market, using what remains of state autonomy to help regulate market forces. In Northern European countries with a continuing legacy of social democratic politics or welfare provision, this approach might make sense.

2. *Professional sociologists* argue that their discipline must be based on firm scientific foundations before it can be of any practical use. From this point of view, by wading into stormy seas prematurely, we will discover only that we cannot swim. Professional sociologists may understand the dangers of rampant marketization, but they sit tight waiting for the storm to pass, hoping that it will not sweep them up with the rest of society.

3. *Critical sociologists* agitate against the first two groups, writing tracts against their moral bankruptcy, complaining about those who collude with state and market, and about those who busy themselves writing scientific papers. Critical sociologists are a shrinking band. Like the professionals, they live in insulated communities, seeking to preserve the power of critique, acting as if their words have the power to hold the storm at bay. Yet their message is often incomprehensible and few are listening.

4. *Public sociologists* refuse to collaborate with the market and the state. They say that science without politics is blind and that critique without intervention is empty. They engage directly with

communities, institutions, and social movements, listening and speaking, observing and participating, learning and writing in order to defend society against rampant marketization. Third-wave marketization calls forth the age of public sociology.

There may be a need for public sociology, but it can move forward only on the legs of policy, professional, and critical sociologies. Without the kind of sociological knowledge accumulated in our discipline and presented in this book, public sociology cannot exist. Public sociology also depends on critical knowledge that keeps professional science honest, steering it away from irrelevance and self-referentiality. At the same time, critical knowledge infuses public sociology with the values and direction that motivate its engagement with publics. Public sociology is nothing if it cannot help to bring about social change. It cannot, therefore, dismiss policy science. It can examine it from without, pushing it in appropriate directions, opposing the temptations of serving power. Public sociology must be the conscience of policy sociology.

Together, public, professional, critical, and policy sociologists form a discipline that takes civil society as its standpoint—as opposed to political scientists, who take the standpoint of the state, and economists, who take the standpoint of the market. Sociology's existence depends on the health of civil society, thereby declaring its commitment to the future of humanity that is currently threatened by the collusion of state and market. Here is the paradox: sociology has never been so important, yet its foundations have never been more precarious.

THE GREAT TRANSFORMATION

To appreciate the future of sociology, we must understand the context of third wave marketization, within which it is forced to operate. For that, I draw on Karl Polanyi's classic, *The Great Transformation* (1944).

Polanyi (who, incidentally, lived outside Toronto from the early 1950s until his death in 1964) devoted himself to understanding the dangers and potentialities of the market. He showed that markets that advance too far cause a social counter-movement. This was the "great transformation"—not the rise of the market, but the *reaction* to its rise.

Perhaps Polanyi's most important but least developed idea was that of "fictitious commodities"—entities that lose their value when subject to unrestricted exchange, unrestricted commodification. For Polanyi, there were three fictitious commodities: labour, money, and land.

When *labour* is overly commodified, people lose their capacity to work. For example, in a perfectly free labour market, where only supply and demand determine the cost of labour, the absence of laws governing minimum wages, child labour, safety standards, and the length of the working day allows some workers to die prematurely because of accidents, ill health, or starvation. Typically, when the New Poor Law was passed in England in 1834, revoking certain forms of labour protection and poor relief, the ensuing desperation forged a spontaneous reaction in the form of social movements, such as the factory movement to restrict the length of the working day, and associations, such as burial societies, trade unions, cooperatives, and experiments in creating utopian communities. The nineteenth-century commodification of labour led to the spontaneous self-reconstitution of society.

Similarly, when *money* is overly commodified, it loses the capacity to facilitate exchange. The full commodification of money began in the early twentieth century and continues today. Thus, before the global financial crisis that began in 2008, important American laws regulating financial institutions were scrapped, encouraging banks to invest ordinary people's money in extraordinarily risky ways. In the process, the richest 1 percent of Americans multiplied their wealth many times over. However, when mortgages and other credit vehicles began to fail, millions of ordinary Americans lost their homes. Soon, the Occupy Wall Street movement emerged to protest growing economic inequality.

Finally, when *land* is overly commodified, it loses its capacity to deliver human subsistence. When land is enclosed and sold as real estate, as is happening in so many parts of the world, the livelihood of small farmers is threatened. However, it is not just land but also other elements of nature that are being commodified. For instance, in Bolivia in the mid-1990s, the government decided to sell water supplies and delivery systems to a private company. The company soon set water prices higher than many poor Bolivians could afford. Water's availability—its human value as a source of life—fell as the cost of commodified water skyrocketed. Poor Bolivians naturally rebelled to protest the untenable conditions of their existence.

Polanyi (1944) wrote about the first two waves of marketization and the reactions to them—the nineteenth-century marketization of labour (and the ensuing rise of workers' rights) and the twentieth-century marketization of money (which led to the Great Depression of 1929–39 and the ensuing rise of the New Deal in the United States, Nazism in Germany, and Stalinism in the Soviet Union). Polanyi believed that, after the horrors of World War II, most people would come to understand the importance of regulating markets. He was wrong. In the mid-1970s, a third wave of marketization began, whose distinctive feature would be the commodification of nature as well as labour and money. How, more specifically, should we characterize the third wave of marketization? What societal reactions to it can we observe?

THIRD-WAVE MARKETIZATION

First-wave marketization generated a counter-movement against the commodification of labour. Second-wave marketization generated a counter-movement against the commodification of money. Third-wave marketization is generating a counter-movement against the commodification of land or, more broadly, of nature. Of course, land began to be commodified before the third wave. However, the commodification of nature as a whole did not yet threaten the devastation of the planet. Today it does. Squatters and shack dwellers now defend themselves against local governments trying to clear them out of cities. Middle-class city residents oppose high-rise developers. Indigenous peoples refuse to give up their land so large commercial plantations can take their place. Farmers battle against dams that threaten their existence. Activists struggle for clean air, against the dumping of toxic waste, and against privatization of water and electricity. The list goes on. The commodification of labour and of money, of course, continue to be important, generating their own counter-movements, but the reaction to the commodification of nature will define the reaction to third-wave marketization and, thus, the future of humanity.

A second way to characterize the third-wave marketization is by its scale, which is global in its causes and ramifications. The response to the commodification of labour under first-wave marketization was mainly local, although it eventually aspired to become national (through the creation of national trade unions and political parties, for instance). The response to the commodification of money under second-wave marketization was mainly at the level of the nation-state (through Central Banks) but eventually aspired to be global (through the creation of the International Monetary Fund and the World Bank, for instance). The response to the commodification of nature under third-wave marketization has to be initiated by society—first at the local level but then rising almost immediately to the global level. Because the effects of climate change, nuclear accidents, water privatization, and the spread of contagious diseases are global, so the response to third-wave marketization must ultimately assume a global scale.

A third way of characterizing successive waves of marketization is in terms of the destruction of the defences people have erected against marketization. Second-wave marketization destroyed the trenches defended by labour before it generated a counter-movement to build new trenches of state social protection (the welfare state). Third-wave marketization is rolling back labour and social rights. We see this almost everywhere as trade unions decline, the real wages of workers stagnate or fall, and budgets for social security, pensions, and welfare contract. On what foundation will the next round of defences be built—defences that will fend off the degradation of nature but also recover labour and social rights? The deeper the challenge to humanity and community, the deeper the reaction must be. In response to third-wave marketization, we will need to develop the defence of human rights—the defence of a community of mutual recognition as human beings—that will necessarily incorporate labour and social rights, too.

Of course, human rights may be appropriated and narrowed to suit particular interests. For instance, electoral democracy has become a human right that, for some people, can justify invasion, killing, and subjugation abroad. Similarly, markets have been promoted in the name of the human right to freedom of choice and the protection of private property, ignoring what this means to those who cannot choose and who lack property. Human rights that are universal, and that therefore include labour rights and social rights, must aim for the protection of the human community as a whole, which involves first recognizing and treating each other as ends rather than means. Human rights, then, is a complex terrain of struggle in which groups stake their claim on the basis of their own interests, but ultimately human rights are about the protection of humanity with the potential to galvanize struggles of global proportions against third-wave marketization. I have described the major characteristics of third-wave marketization and its counter-movement, but what is their significance for sociology?

THREE WAVES OF SOCIOLOGY

A distinctive sociology emerges with each wave of marketization. Sociology grew up in the nineteenth century together with civil society, itself a response to first-wave marketization. Thus, sociology began as a moral enterprise defending society against the market, especially the destruction of community, as newly proletarianized, destitute, and degraded populations made the city their home. It was foremost a critical enterprise, but it was also utopian. Sociology imagined life outside the market. For example, Marx and Engels postulated communism, which they expected to arise out of the ashes of capitalism. Comte imagined a familial order led by sociologists. Durkheim envisaged an organic solidarity built on corporatist organization. In English Canada, the religious principles of the social gospel movement influenced sociology in its early stages.

Comte, Marx, Durkheim, and other early sociologists would object to my characterization. They saw themselves as scientists, committed to what is and what could be by virtue of the laws of society. Still, from today's standpoint, for all the scientific breakthroughs they brought to the study of society, their science was partly speculative, especially regarding the future, and strongly imbued with moral concerns aimed at reversing the degradation brought about by nineteenth-century capitalism. At the heart of their utopianism lay the critique of the division of labour and its transformation.

Second-wave marketization, which took off following World War I, challenged the rights that labour had won through trade unions and political parties. As Polanyi (1944) argued, the ravages of international trade and exchange threatened the conditions of capital accumulation and prompted protectionist reactions by the state. In countries that reacted to second-wave marketization with authoritarian regimes, notably Germany and the Soviet Union, sociology was eclipsed, but in countries that reacted with some form of social democracy, a new type of sociology emerged. It collaborated with the state to defend society against the market. In the United Kingdom, the United States, Sweden, Canada, and elsewhere, a policy-oriented sociology developed. Even in the colonies, there was a policy science, although there it was called anthropology. This was the golden era of state-funded research into social problems.

Where sociology remained relatively divorced from the state, as in the United States, it also developed a strong professional branch, committed to the expansion of specific research programs chiefly concerned with social stability. There, stratification studies highlighted achievement-based mobility up the occupational hierarchy. Family studies emphasized the benefits of the smoothly functioning nuclear family. Studies of crime and deviance focused on regulation and control. Industrial sociology was chiefly concerned with pacifying labour and maximizing the extraction of value from it. Political sociology underscored the social bases of electoral democracy and the containment of extremism. The overarching theoretical framework was summed up by structural functionalism—the delineation of the functional pre-requisites needed to keep any social system in equilibrium and the mechanisms allowing social institutions to meet those prerequisites. During this period, sociologists gave detailed attention to empirical research, new methods of data collection and analysis, and the elaboration of "middle-range" theories that nestled in the scaffolding of structural functionalism. This approach was a reaction against the earlier, more speculative traditions that were propelled by the desire for moral reform. It wanted to expunge moral questions from sociology.

If the first wave of sociology invented utopias, the second wave of policy-oriented and professional sociology opposed utopian thinking, in effect claiming that utopia was almost within reach, or even already at hand. Indeed, in the United States and the Soviet Union, structural-functionalism and Marxism-Leninism, respectively, mistook utopia for reality. These were sociological traditions that were riveted to the present, concerned only with ironing out its small irrationalities. A critical sociology developed in reaction to these presuppositions of harmony and consensus, restoring an interest in struggle and conflict, but also in imagining a world beyond capitalism.

What sort of sociology marks the response to third-wave marketization? As we have seen, the third wave rolls back the statist defence of society, taking the offensive against labour and social rights. Unlike the second wave, which provoked an anti-market reaction from the state—variously involving protectionism, economic planning, wage guarantees, the welfare state, and public ownership of the means of production—third-wave marketization is promoted by the state. Still a regulatory state, it is nonetheless regulation *for* rather than *against* the market. It undoes all that was achieved against second-wave marketization. Society is thus under a double assault from economy and state. Unable to gain much leverage in the state or from the market, the fate of sociology rests with society. In other words, sociology's self-interest lies in the constitution of civil society where it barely exists and in its protection where it is in retreat—hence the claim we are living in the age of public sociology.

Today, sociology cannot limit its engagement to local or national publics, but must be concerned with knitting together a global civil society. Moreover, the third wave of sociology calls for a science quite different from the speculative science of the nineteenth century and the policy-oriented professional science of the mid-twentieth century—one that seeks to combine scientific rigour with the development of alternative values. We no longer strive for a single paradigmatic science but a discipline made up of multiple intersecting research programs, founded on the values of different publics, working out theoretical frameworks through engaging their anomalies and contradictions. I call this a reflexive science, a science that is not frightened of reflecting on its value foundations or of articulating them publicly, but a science nonetheless (see Table 25.1).

As sociology becomes more global, borrowings across national lines become more feasible and important. For example, after its 1974 anti-authoritarian revolution, Portugal drew on critical and professional traditions in American and French sociologies, harnessing them to a vibrant civil society. This small country is one of the leaders in public sociology, connected to policy, critical, and professional sociologies. Public sociology has flourished in other countries, such as Brazil, South Africa, and India, based on selectively imported North American or European professional sociology but reshaped in anti-authoritarian or anti-colonial struggles.

Global borrowings present dangers as well as possibilities. Notably, the domination of the United States' professional sociology can constrain the responsiveness of national sociologies to local concerns. Facing the dilemmas of the United States on its doorstep in the late 1960s and early 1970s, many Canadian sociologists led a hostile attack on the Americanization of academic life. Farther afield, the dilemmas can be even deeper. Pressures to write in English for remote professional audiences not only disadvantage peripheralized sociologists but also inevitably threaten the vitality of local public sociology. Writing of the Middle

TABLE 25.1 SOCIOLOGY VERSUS THE MARKET

	First-Wave Marketization	Second-Wave Marketization	Third-Wave Marketization
Dominant "fictitious commodity"	labour	money	land ("nature")
Dominant locus of response	local	national	global
Dominant rights protected	labour	social	human
Dominant orientation of sociology	utopian and critical	policy and professional	public
Dominant thrust of sociological science	speculative	positivist	reflexive

East, Sari Hanafi (2011) has expressed the dilemma as follows: publish globally and perish locally or publish locally and perish globally. Are there ways to transcend this chasm, to constitute a public sociology that is not isolationist but globally connected? That remains our challenge.

CONCLUSION

I have argued that sociology is taking a public turn in response to third-wave marketization. Sociology lives and dies with society. When society is threatened, so is sociology. We can no longer rely on the state to contain the market, and so sociologists have to forge their own connections to society, that is, to develop public sociologies. We have to do more than serve society passively. We must conserve and constitute society. In this, sociology has many potential allies and partners as they too come under increasing assault from state and market. That is the broader contemporaneous context within which public sociology can be a guiding spirit and directing force.

However, we cannot think of the contemporary context outside of its past. We cannot compartmentalize the three waves of marketization and the corresponding configurations of sociology as three separate periods. Each wave deposits its legacy in the next wave. The waves of commodification deepen as they move *regressively* from labour to money to nature, each wave incorporating the commodification of the previous period, just as the counter-movement leads *progressively* from labour rights to social rights (which includes labour rights) and then aspires to human rights that include all three.

The development of sociology is different. Policy and professional sociology, with their value-neutral, scientific approach, are a reaction against utopian and critical sociology, with their speculations and moral infusions. Public sociology tries to synthesize the value commitment of the first period with the scientific advances of the second. However, even here we should be careful not to think in terms of discrete sociologies, but rather reconfigurations of the four elements of sociology, in which the weight of professional, policy, critical and public sociologies shifts over time. Indeed, a public sociology cannot really take off in a sustained manner unless it is impelled by critical sociology and grounded in professional sociology.

The rhythm and spacing of the waves of sociological development vary from country to country. For the advanced capitalist world today, the waves are more clearly separated in time, whereas for such countries as Russia, India, and China, the waves are compressed, with the commodification of labour, money, and nature occurring almost simultaneously in recent decades. National variation notwithstanding, we can still identify the present era as one in which the commodification of nature concentrates within itself the cumulative impact of the commodification of labour and money. In its subsumption of all commodification, the commodification of nature becomes the planet's most pressing problem, generating social movements that are held together by the principle of human rights.

It is unclear whether these movements can reverse third wave marketization and whether the result will be to expand or narrow the confines of human freedom. It is possible that sociology itself will succumb to commodification—the commodification of the production of knowledge in the university and elsewhere, the commodification of the distribution of knowledge by the mass media, and the commodification of the consumption of knowledge as student fees continue their upward trajectory. Conversely, there may be a place for public sociology to participate in the knitting together of organizations, movements, and publics across the globe, helping to fortify a civil society beyond the control of market and state. The world needs public sociology engaging publics across the globe: one that rests on the shoulders of a dynamic professional sociology that is inspired by a vital critical sociology, while holding policy sociology to account.

REFERENCES

Hanafi, Sari. (2011). "University Systems in the Arab East: Publish Globally and Perish Locally vs. Publish Locally and Perish Globally." *Current Sociology*, *59* (3), 291–309.

Polanyi, Karl. (1944). *The Great Transformation*. New York: Farrar & Rinehart.

Index